Consumer sovereignty and human interests

Consumer sovereignty and human interests

G. PETER PENZ
York University
Toronto

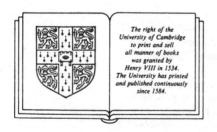

The right of the
University of Cambridge
to print and sell
all manner of books
was granted by
Henry VIII in 1534.
The University has printed
and published continuously
since 1584.

CAMBRIDGE UNIVERSITY PRESS

Cambridge
London   New York   New Rochelle
Melbourne   Sydney

CAMBRIDGE UNIVERSITY PRESS
Cambridge, New York, Melbourne, Madrid, Cape Town, Singapore, São Paulo

Cambridge University Press
The Edinburgh Building, Cambridge CB2 8RU, UK

Published in the United States of America by Cambridge University Press, New York

www.cambridge.org
Information on this title: www.cambridge.org/9780521265713

First published 1986
This digitally printed version 2008

A catalogue record for this publication is available from the British Library

Library of Congress Cataloguing in Publication data
Penz, G. Peter
Consumer sovereignty and human interests.
"Developed out of a doctoral dissertation for the
University of Oxford" — Acknowledgements.
Includes index.
1. Welfare economics. 2. Consumers' preferences.
3. Basic needs. 4. Utilitarianism. 5. Political
ethics. 6. Political sociology. I. Title.
HB846.P46   1986   330.15′5   85–22407

ISBN 978-0-521-26571-3 hardback
ISBN 978-0-521-07091-1 paperback

TO THE MEMORY OF
HORST PAUL PENZ (1912–1975) and
ERNA OLGA PENZ (1888–1981)

The acceptance of "consumer sovereignty" as a basis for judging economic systems is fundamentally perhaps as much a matter of ethics, philosophy and political theory as it is of economics. In discussions of economic theory proper, it is often taken as a postulate for which the primary justification lies outside the realm of economics.

—William S. Vickrey, *Microstatics* (New York: Harcourt, Brace & World, 1964), 217

Contents

vii

Contents

Preface

Whether consumer sovereignty is an appropriate principle for the optimization and evaluation of the design and performance of economic systems is a question that is posed *by* economics, but it can, by and large, not be answered *within* economics. Instead, the exploration undertaken in this book pursues issues raised by this question into the territories of moral and political philosophy, of sociological role theory and socialization theory, of clinical psychology and the sociology of mental illness, and of the literature on indicators of the "quality of life" and of deprivation. The areas within economics that are traversed are, apart from conceptions of consumer sovereignty, primarily welfare economics and the economics of income distribution. Writings that bridge two or more of these diverse areas have been particularly emphasized. It should be noted, however, that I refer not so much to the recent literature that has straddled specifically political philosophy and neoclassical economics as rather to writings that take cognizance of sociology's central idea of socialization.

Acknowledgments

This book has developed out of a doctoral dissertation for the University of Oxford. Thus my debts are not merely those incurred in the preparation of the book, but also those for assistance given to me over the lengthy period during which I wrote the dissertation.

First of all, there are the supervisors of the thesis at various times. I thank Paul Streeten for his interest, encouragement, and guidance in the early years. In the last stage, Anthony Heath provided intensive supervision during my second stay at Oxford and, during my nonresident period of revising, advised me on the general approach to the revisions and facilitated administrative matters. I also had help from G. B. Richardson, J. S. Flemming, and J. A. Mirrlees, who were supervisors for shorter periods.

Several other people commented on parts of earlier or later drafts. In this respect I am grateful to B. M. Barry, John Gray, I. M. D. Little, David Miller, and Mervyn Norton. I owe particular thanks to Larry Biesenthal and Michael McDonald, who read substantial portions, or all, of an earlier version and gave me very thoughtful comments. The two rounds of examiners' comments of Alan Ryan and John Broome greatly influenced the eventual shape of the book. The final reworking was also significantly guided by the supportive and stimulating comments of Michael McPherson; the basic-needs approach in Chapter 8 emerged in response to those comments. Finally, there have been conversations with various people about issues in this book that have also helped me along. In this regard I would like to mention in particular Adrian Ellis, Bill Leiss, Mark Orkin, and Don MacNiven. The perspectives of the persons who have thus influenced the book are much too diverse for me to have followed all of their advice, and their suggestions also did not always fit into my own pattern of thinking, so that there is no question where the responsibility for any errors, omissions, and unproductive lines of reasoning in this book must rest.

With respect to financial assistance, the Canada Council enabled me to get started on this work with a doctoral fellowship for over three years. More recently, the Faculty of Environmental Studies at York

University, Toronto, covered some of the costs involved in bringing the book to completion and also made its printer available to me during preparation of the final manuscript. Martin Schneider was very helpful in assisting me to set up my microcomputer files for printing. I must also mention the forbearance of two consecutive Deans of the Faculty, Gerald A. P. Carrothers and Rodger Schwass, for giving me the time to complete the dissertation at my own pace.

In bringing the book to its completion I have benefited from cooperation, assistance, and tolerance of delays from several persons at Cambridge University Press. In particular, the conscientious copyediting by Janis Bolster deserves acknowledgment.

Finally, and most important, I acknowledge the vital help provided by Victoria Heftler. At a time of particularly great difficulties, she gave me continuous encouragement and support. She also devoted several hundred hours to reading various drafts and making critical comments on the structure of the book, on problems of consistency and coherence in the argument, and on stylistic deficiencies.

To my children, Erik and Rebecca: Thank you for putting up so patiently with my "thesis quarantine" and, more recently, with the line "When the book is finished. . . ."

CHAPTER 1

Introduction

Consumer sovereignty is a central normative principle in contemporary assessments of economic policies and systems. It underlies discussions of optimization and evaluation regarding the design and performance of economies and their constituent institutions, and in particular of the coordination mechanisms in economic systems, such as markets and collective planning. It has been referred to as the "Archimedian point of reference" in economic evaluation (Worland 1967:205). There is certainly no question that it is the core value of welfare economics. In Western industrially advanced nations – of both the conservatively capitalist and the social-democratic variety – it also underlies several of the most central goals guiding actual economic policy.

Given this normative centrality of the principle of consumer sovereignty, one would expect that it would have received considerable attention in the literature. In fact, it has not. It has been explicitly analyzed only to a very limited extent. (Hutt 1936:ch. 12; Fraser 1939; and Rothenberg 1968 are noteworthy in this respect.) At the same time, however, much normative discussion in welfare economics, political theory, and social philosophy has concentrated on ideas that are part of or overlap with the notion of consumer sovereignty.

In this book I take these discussions as points of reference for what is the basic task here: to analyze the meaning and adequacy of the normative principle of consumer sovereignty. The central question is: *What is a morally reasonable version of, or alternative to, consumer sovereignty as a principle for optimizing and evaluating the design and performance of economic systems?* The tasks for such optimization and evaluation vary from those that apply to relatively short-term policies, where the affected population, their preferences, and the general pattern of opportunities and prices can be assumed to remain roughly constant, to the much more ambitious task of designing or assessing whole economic systems. The concern in this book is with the appropriateness of consumer sovereignty for these tasks *as a whole*, and in particular for the more ambitious ones.

At the outset, in Part I, a relatively simple and uncomplicated con-

1

ception of consumer sovereignty is formulated. This "interest conception" focuses on consumer preferences as an expression of the interests of individuals concerning production and distribution. This conception is then compared to a variety of other meanings of consumer sovereignty, which are shown to be less suitable to the optimization and evaluation of economic systems. The interest conception of consumer sovereignty makes it apparent that the basic question in assessing the principle of consumer sovereignty is whether consumer preferences are an adequate representation of interests and, if not, how they have to be extended, qualified, or replaced to provide such an adequate representation.

First, the range of wants to be covered by the principle needs to be considered. Are *consumer* preferences too restrictive? If so, should we include environmental amenity wants, work and leisure wants, social-interaction wants, distributive and other moral concerns? These are the questions addressed in Part II.

Second, wants are subject to distortion and to processes of formation that raise problems related to self-determination. This issue of the quality of wants is pursued in Part III. Ignorance and irrationality and the feedback effect from the processes of production, distribution, and consumption on the development of preferences are considered there. Although this book focuses on the question what constitutes the relevant interests with respect to the economic system rather than on issues of measurement, a brief treatment of the problem of comparing the different want structures of individuals, time periods, and economic systems is provided in Part IV. It helps to pinpoint the crucial source of the difficulties in evaluation and optimization based on consumer sovereignty and its extended versions. This source is an inherent feature of the latter, namely, the fundamental subjectivity and open-endedness of consumer sovereignty and the want-satisfaction principle it represents.

This critique then leads to the search for an alternative, objective conception of human interests appropriate for economic evaluation and optimization. After an exploration of alternative versions, a basic-needs conception is proposed in Part V. Finally, some of the implications of this conception for the evaluation of economic systems are brought out by an illustrative application to a comparison of a set of pure forms of economic coordination.

PART I

Consumer sovereignty

CHAPTER 2

The interest conception of consumer sovereignty

2.1   Consumer sovereignty and interests

The interest conception of consumer sovereignty

As a starting point for the discussion of various conceptions of consumer sovereignty, let us consider a particular conception that both constitutes a widely held interpretation of consumer sovereignty and offers at least initial promise of being suitable to economic evaluation and optimization. This conception is the principle that what is produced, how it is produced, and how it is distributed are to be determined by consumer preferences expressed through individual choices in a free market. A free market is one where there is no collective control over what is produced or over how the output is distributed. (This is intended merely as a definition of what is *conventionally* meant by "free market," not as a justifiable conception of economic freedom nor even as the only possible meaning of "free market," since the latter could conceivably also refer to the market's freedom from monopoly power, from control by the capitalist class, etc.)

The basic reason for treating this conception as potentially more suitable than others is that consumer preferences expressed through free-market choices can be taken to be an initially plausible representation of the interests of individuals in relation to production and distribution. This interpretation implies that interests are taken to be the supreme determinant of production and distribution. The latter is a morally reasonable starting point and parallels the widely held notion in political philosophy that the fulfillment of the interests of individuals is "a (. . . perhaps the) fundamental objective of the political order" (Flathman 1975:277–8). Because of the exclusive focus of this conception of consumer sovereignty on a representation of interests, it will be referred to as an "interest conception of consumer sovereignty."

The term "interests," which is current in political theory, can be considered a synonym for "welfare" as it is used in economics. I have chosen to refer to "interests" rather than "welfare" for three reasons. (1) The term is conventionally used in political theory, where the notion has been submitted to much more of the kind of conceptual analysis relevant to the discussion in the following chapters than it has been in economics. (2) It sounds awkward to add to "welfare" the qualifying adjectives that it later becomes important to use, for example, "consumer," "private," and "developmental." (3) Outside economics, "welfare" can have much more restricted meanings, such as that which refers to the material necessities to maintain health (Barry 1965:187–8); the notion of "interests," on the other hand, is generally accepted to be a comprehensive one – at least when qualified by "of individuals."

Before exploring the whole range of conceptions of consumer sovereignty and contrasting them with the initially adopted conception, it will be useful to consider two difficulties with the claim that market-revealed consumer preferences are a plausible representation of the interests of individuals in production and distribution. The first is that market-revealed consumer preferences and individuals' interests are not quite the same; the second (to be addressed in the next subsection) is that the meaning of "interests" is not beyond dispute.

Concerning the representation of interests by consumer preferences revealed in market choices, it has to be remembered that it is not interests in general but only *relevant* interests, specifically interests with respect to production and distribution, that are at stake. Thus the claim that is treated as initially plausible is not that interests in general are appropriately represented by market-revealed consumer preferences, but only that the latter represent those interests that are relevant to production and distribution. That market-revealed consumer preferences are the only type of interest that has this relevance is an argument that has been made (by Hutt 1936:ch. 16 and Seldon and Pennance 1965/1976:74,[1] for example); it can therefore serve as a starting point for the analysis of the adequacy of this representation. (The argument will be considered in Section 3.2.)

Relevance is a criterion that can be used to limit the range of interests that need to be considered. Another criterion works in the opposite direction: the criterion of comprehensiveness. It requires that *all* relevant interests be included in the evaluation principle. It raises the question: Are market-revealed consumer preferences a sufficiently comprehensive representation of interests relevant to pro-

---

[1] Where more than one date is given, page references are always to the most recent edition listed in the text citation.

duction and distribution? This question provides the agenda for Part II.

Interests and consumer preferences

The second difficulty that I raised in the previous subsection was that of the meaning of "interests." A review of the literature on interests, even when restricted to contemporary writings, reveals an extremely diverse range of conceptions. Instead of committing myself to one of these conceptions at this stage in the analysis, I will adopt an approach according to which a conception of interests can *evolve* with the analysis. The approach involves an initial statement of a broad "framework definition" and a specific "starting definition," with the latter being amended in response to the shortcomings that are brought to light by its analysis, but within the limits set by the framework definition. This process ultimately leads to a "final definition," which is offered in Part V. The *framework* definition of interests to be used equates them with states, conditions, events, and actions that are subject to some form of human control and that are of benefit (or, on the negative side, are detrimental) to individuals. The *starting* definition of interests is the conception of interests contained in the interest conception of consumer sovereignty, namely, that in the framework definition "benefit" is to be interpreted in terms of consumer preferences revealed through market choices. The central question for the analysis thus becomes: Is this conception of "benefit" adequate?

The reason for this approach, in which the definition evolves in the course of the analysis rather than being presented in a final form at the outset, is twofold. (1) A useful definition is contextually contingent, and the requirements of the context emerge only in the course of the extensive analysis that follows. By referring to contextual contingency I mean to say that with elastic concepts such as "interests" it normally does not make sense to search for a unique meaning of the term; instead, it is necessary to recognize that a variety of meanings are in use and that to some extent the particular meaning will depend on the particular context in which the concept is used. The concept of "interests" so far has not been systematically analyzed in the context of the evaluation of economic systems. The following analysis is to make apparent the requirements of this particular context. (2) "Interests" can be regarded as a concept which serves a similar role to that served by want satisfaction in welfare economics and in certain liberal conceptions of democracy, but which has been freed of objectionable features that want satisfaction has when cast in this role. A careful analysis of the shortcomings of want satisfaction as an evaluation criterion can therefore serve to produce a conception of interests that meets this expectation.[2]

To put this approach to articulating the conception of "interests" into the context of recent discussions of the concept, and to justify the choice of the framework and starting definitions, a very brief review of this literature is needed. First, a basic dichotomy is conventionally made between "subjective" and "objective" conceptions of "interests." The distinction between "subjective" and "objective" that is most appropriate in this context is that provided by Grenville Wall (1975:502):

a judgment is subjective if the individual whose judgment it is is necessarily the only authority on its correctness; a judgment is objective insofar as its correctness is something which it is possible to determine publicly. The objectivity of judgments therefore depends on the existence of *public* criteria of correctness.

Subjective conceptions of interests, then, are conceptions relying on first-person judgments, whereas objective conceptions rely on public third-person judgments. However, instead of a dichotomy, Richard E. Flathman (1975:283) has suggested that there is a "continuum of uses of 'interest'" with subjective and objective ends, allowing for conceptions that involve a mix of subjective and objective elements. In terms of such a continuum, the various conceptions of the interests of *individuals* can be approximately arrayed as presented in Table 2.1, beginning with the subjective end of the continuum. This classification is not to be taken as a serious attempt to rank the different conceptions according to degrees of objectivity. Objectivity here is not a one-dimensional variable; there are differences in the *kinds* of objective elements in conceptions of "interests." Third-person judgments may take the forms of interpersonally *common* requirements, of *prudential* judgments, or of *moral* judgments, based either on conventional morality or on justifiable morality. There are thus various kinds of "objective" criteria that have been introduced by different authors into the conception of "interests."[3]

---

[2] Wants and preferences are nearly synonymous, but not quite. Wants refer to desires in general, whereas preferences are sets of desires or wants weighted relative to each other in terms of conative intensity.

[3] Conceptions of the *public* interest or of *group* interests are omitted since these refer, on the one hand, either to particular kinds of interests of individuals (e.g., collective-good wants, discussed in the next chapter, or politically articulated demands) or to particular ways of aggregating the interests of individuals, or, on the other hand, to socially "organismic" conceptions that I am not concerned with here. Also omitted, because of its lack of relevance here, is the purely psychological conception of "interests" as objects of an individual's interest or attention.

Table 2.1. *An overview of alternative conceptions of interests*

(1)	Wants	Referred to in Benditt 1975:245 and criticized in Barry 1965:175; Peters 1966:169–70; and Connolly 1974:53–9
(2)	"Goals, aspirations, values and achievements"	Proposed in McCloskey 1976:8–9
(3)	Choices or revealed preferences	Used in behavioristically oriented political science and economics and criticized in Benn 1960:124–31; Wolff 1968:27–8; Balbus 1971:154–66; and Connolly 1974:48–52
(4)	Hypothetical wants based on requisite experiences	Proposed in Connolly 1974:62–72 and criticized in Wall 1975:496–505
(5)	Rational wants	Advocated in Oppenheim 1975 as the descriptive meaning of interests and discussed in Flathman 1975; cf. Rawls 1971:93 and Brandt 1979:126–9
(6)	Happiness, or factors contributing to it	The classical utilitarian position, which has been considered in Wolff 1968:28–9, advocated in Benditt 1975:254–7 and McDonald 1978:110–12, and criticized in Barry 1965:175–6 and Flathman 1975:281–5
(7)	Generalized opportunities for want satisfaction	Proposed in Barry 1964/1967:115–17 and 1965:176–86 and criticized in Benditt 1975:246–54
(8)	"Central concerns" of the community	Advocated in Scanlon 1975 and criticized in Griffin 1982:343–5
(9)	Impacts on life chances	Proposed in Balbus 1971:152 and criticized in Wall 1975:491–6
(10)	States or conditions meeting reasonable desires and expectations or potentialities of normal persons	Proposed in Benn 1960:138; Peters 1966:168–9; and Wall 1975:506
(11)	Justified claims	Advocated in Plamenatz 1954:7 and, with a moral conception of "justified," in Benn 1960:127–8 and criticized in Barry 1965:175
(12)	"Primary goods"	A transcultural version of [7], proposed in Rawls 1971:90–5 and criticized in Teitelman 1972; Barry 1973; and Wolff 1977:133–42
(13)	Needs	Proposed in Bay 1968 and discussed in Connolly 1974:59–62; Flathman 1975:283; Miller 1976:ch. 4; McCloskey 1976:7–10; and Griffin 1982:340–3

The framework definition of interests that I am using can be seen to encompass these various conceptions of interests. That is to say, these conceptions can be regarded as particular interpretations of what is of benefit to individuals. There is, however, one restricting feature that I intend to apply to the framework definition, and that is that benefits be interpreted in a wholly prudential sense. The argument for ruling out distributive-justice and other moral wants is presented in Chapter 4, Section 4.4.

None of the conceptions of interests surveyed in Table 2.1 fits exactly the starting definition that is being adopted here, namely, that of interests as the fulfillment of consumer preferences revealed through market choices. The one that comes closest is "choices or revealed preferences," but it includes no reference to *consumer* preferences or *market* choices. The basic reason is that the concept of "interests" has been discussed in the context of political evaluation, and not in the context of the evaluation of economic systems. In the latter context, however, much discussion can be interpreted to imply that the interests of individuals consist of having their preferences, as revealed through consumer choices, satisfied.

2.2   The normative centrality of consumer sovereignty

At the beginning of Chapter 1 I presented consumer sovereignty as being central not only to welfare economics, but also to economic policy making in industrially developed market economies. Having clarified the concept at least to the point where we have a starting definition – the principle that what is to be produced, how it is to be produced, and how it is to be distributed are to be determined by consumer preferences as revealed through consumer choices in free markets – I can now elaborate on that assertion.

It might be argued that the aim of having a high *level* of consumption is distinct from the goal of providing for a pattern of consumption that accords with consumer preferences. And it is true that the notion of prosperity could be used to refer to life-styles involving consumption not really valued by the consumers but envied by observers. However, that is not the idea underlying policies concerned with promoting a high level of consumption; what is pursued is a high level of *wanted* consumption. Thus the goal is the maximization of consumption in accordance with consumer preferences, that is, consumer sovereignty.

Another important goal for economic policy is economic growth. The accumulation of capital as such clearly is only instrumental –

instrumental to the growth in living standards. But such growth, like consumer sovereignty, is incomplete as a goal, since it can be either maximized or optimized in some particular sense, and this sense has to be specified. Maximizing the growth of consumption or of living standards in the strong sense is not appealing, as it requires maximally sacrificing consumption *now* for the sake of increased investment and thus consumable output in the future. There is a trade-off between current consumption and future consumption, so that it makes much more sense to think of growth as something to be optimized. And that is also probably the best way to interpret policy decisions regarding growth in Western industrialized countries.

But what is the optimization criterion for economic growth? Consumer sovereignty provides the most plausible criterion here. It makes optimal growth dependent on the preferences of individuals concerning the trade-off between their own consumption now and their own consumption in the future. The criterion of efficiency, as well as the criteria of intra- and intergenerational equity, has to be introduced to make this dependency determinate, but, as will be shown, these criteria are naturally complementary to consumer sovereignty. In this way, the goal of economic growth depends on intertemporal consumer sovereignty. Economic growth can, of course, also be optimized according to other criteria, such as military strength or the expansion of corporate empires, but these are certainly not part of the ostensible goals in Western, industrially advanced, democratic countries.

Perhaps the politically most visible goals in these countries are high employment and low price inflation. These are somewhat less closely related to consumer sovereignty, and yet there is a definite connection. High employment is a goal because individuals *want* employment and because unemployment represents waste with respect to the production of *wanted* goods and services. The second of these reasons represents an inefficiency with respect to consumer sovereignty. The first reason, though it does not fit into *consumer* sovereignty in the strict sense, since preferences concerning work, leisure, and income, rather than merely consumption, are involved, is part of an extended notion of consumer sovereignty that can accommodate work and leisure preferences (to be dealt with in the next chapter). In this way the goal of high employment, too, can be traced to consumer sovereignty.

Different reasons are given to explain why price inflation is bad. By and large, however, they boil down to its alleged detrimental effects on production and thus on the capacity of the economy to satisfy consumer wants or, alternatively, to its equity effects on savings and income entitlements, that is, on the distribution of the ability of individuals to satisfy their consumer wants. Thus the goal of price stability also hinges on efficiency or equity in consumer sovereignty.

Consumer sovereignty, then, is not a goal that competes with other primary goals of economic policy, but rather is a core value that underlies the most important economic policy goals in liberal or social democracies.

2.3   Alternative definitions of consumer sovereignty

Overview

Although the term "consumer sovereignty" was not coined until 1936 (by W. H. Hutt), it is, as Jerome Rothenberg (1968:326–7) has pointed out,

one of those influential concepts that flourish and are widely influential long before they are explicitly recognized and named. (Their belated recognition is often concomitant with their decline.) Much of the substance of consumer sovereignty is implied in Adam Smith. The focus of subsequent classical economics on cost of production as the basic determinant of market decisions temporarily sidetracked this emphasis. It returned more strongly with the Austrian school of Wieser and Menger, and in the work of Jevons, Pareto, Marshall, Pigou and Wicksell.

However, at the time of the explicit formulation of the concept, L. M. Fraser (1939:548), after pointing to a number of difficulties in it, made the following plea: "Might we not agree: (1) to refrain from introducing 'sovereignty' into the vocabulary of economic theory, or failing this, (2) to define it with complete precision, and (3) to dissociate it from 'consumers'?" Fraser's first suggestion has not been heeded, since the term has certainly been accepted into economic terminology as well as popular language.[4] Concerning the second part of Fraser's plea, although there are definitions of consumer sovereignty that are reasonably precise, there is considerable divergence in the definitions. The third of Fraser's proposals has been accepted by some, who treat consumer sovereignty as the sovereignty of indi-

---

[4] In 1979 I looked at general textbooks on economics and books on microeconomics, as well as welfare economics, shelved in the Economics and Statistics Library at the University of Oxford under the library code HB 171; the survey revealed that about one-quarter of the nearly one hundred books had "consumer sovereignty" in their indexes. Moreover, every post–World War II dictionary of economics kept in that library (Horton et al. 1948; Seldon and Pennance 1965/1976; Hanson 1965/1977; Taylor 1966/1969; Gilpin 1966/1977; Bannock, Baxter, and Rees 1972) contained an entry for consumer sovereignty. The *International Encyclopedia of the Social Sciences* also has an article on consumer sovereignty (Rothenberg 1968).

viduals with all their wants (or at least those revealed in the market), including their preferences concerning work; but there are others who see consumer sovereignty as the opposite of "producer sovereignty," interpreting the former to refer to "consumers" in the conventional sense of that word, which excludes the producer preferences of individuals.

The variety of meanings of consumer sovereignty is indicated by the following sample of definitions, which were selected to reflect the different features that have been attributed to the notion. They are being considered in order to show why the interest conception of consumer sovereignty that has been adopted as the starting definition is to be preferred for the task of this book:

1. *consumer sovereignty*[:] The theory that consumers' preferences, as shown by the way in which they spend their money, determine what should be produced. This implies that production is undertaken in anticipation of demand [Horton et al. 1948:67]

2. Consumer sovereignty . . . simply means that all economic processes are ultimately focused toward satisfying the wants of the final consumer. Production, exchange, and distribution are all means; consumption is the end. [Rothenberg 1968:327]

3. In a market economy, consumers, by registering their dollar votes, determine which goods and services shall be provided and in what quantities. Items that are not wanted, or that are overproduced, will suffer a fall in price, while items that are in short supply rise in price. These price movements act as *signals* to profit-seeking firms, which then produce larger amounts of the goods whose prices rise and less of the goods whose prices fall. This mechanism is what we call consumer sovereignty. [Baumol and Blinder 1979:790]

4. . . . it is useful to break the [Pareto] criterion into four more specific components: efficiency in distribution, efficiency in production, consumer sovereignty, and aggregative efficiency. [Dorfman 1967/1972:175]
   . . . in competitive equilibrium every productive resource is being used in such a way that if it were shifted to a different commodity it would not produce goods that consumers valued more highly than the ones it currently produces; every resource is being used as consumers want it to be. An economic system that allocates resources in this way is said to obey consumers' sovereignty. [Dorfman 1967/1972:142]

5. Who ultimately decides what will be produced by the economy? If it is consumers − say, by exercising effective demand in the market − and if production is closely attuned to consumer preferences, then the economist says that *consumers' sovereignty* prevails. In fact, because the preferences of households as resource owners (especially as suppliers of labor) also affect production, it is better to speak of *household sovereignty*. [Grossman 1967/1974:11. Abram Bergson (1948/1966:

200 and 1966a:52–3) has simply included the producer preferences
of households under consumer sovereignty.]

6.   . . . the consumer is . . . viewed as possessing the full initiative in buy-
ing goods and services. He is assumed to respond only to wants that
he originates or needs which are given to him by his environment.
He is, above all, independent, and his purchasing behavior in the
market place instructs producers as to what he wants to buy; ultimately, all power is held to lie with the consumer – that is what is
meant by *consumer sovereignty*. [Thompson 1973/1977:90–1. Cf. Scitovsky 1976:7.]

Only definition (1) precisely represents the interest conception of
consumer sovereignty proposed herein. Definition (2), Rothenberg's,
comes close, but omits the requirement that consumer preferences
are to be revealed through choices in a free market. (I will, however,
return to Rothenberg's conception at a later point.) Definition (3)
does require a free market for the sphere in the economy in which
consumer sovereignty is deemed to prevail, but not merely or primarily for the purpose of *articulating* interests. Rather, definition (3)
requires the free market as the particular mechanism by which consumer preferences *control* producer decisions. In that sense, this definition goes beyond the articulation of a conception of interests relevant to production and distribution and specifies the instrumental
mode of production and distribution by which these interests are to
be fulfilled. (Incidentally, the reference in some definitions [Hanson
1965/1977:93; Hailstones and Brennan 1970/1975:54] to consumers'
"deciding" what is to be produced is misleading. Consumers do not
decide what is to be produced; what they decide is what they will buy
and if consumer sovereignty prevails, this will *determine* what the producers decide to produce. What is meant by the reference to "deciding" is that consumer choices are the deciding factor.) Definition (4)
requires overall microeconomic efficiency. Definition (5) includes the
producer preferences of individuals or households. Definition (4) can
be interpreted as making such an inclusion as well. Definition (5) has
been presented in a manner suggesting that it is otherwise the same as
definition (2), which does not specify an optimization formula, but
Grossman's subsequent discussion makes it clear that, instead, he accepts the formulation that requires efficiency, that is, definition (4).
Definition (6) requires that consumer choices be autonomous, that is,
free from producer influence.

S. K. Nath's (1969:9) interpretation of consumer sovereignty as a
"value judgment," that "an individual should be considered the best
judge of his economic welfare," has been omitted from this list because it is idiosyncratic and, more important, because it curiously

treats an essentially empirical proposition as a value judgment. In fact, Nath was not consistent on this point, because he later in the same work allowed that ignorance can be treated as a case for setting aside "consumer sovereignty" in the sense of free choice (p. 87). Nath also presented an "alternative version" of that value judgment, which asserts that "even if [the individual] is not the best judge, he should have the right to decide" (p. 9). This is a plausible position to take, but it makes more sense to treat it as a value judgment on which the principle of consumer sovereignty rests, rather than to identify it as the principle of consumer sovereignty itself, since no reference is made to the determination of production and distribution.

In the light of this diversity of definitions, the following questions need to be asked: (1) Is the market mechanism an essential aspect of consumer sovereignty? (2) Does consumer sovereignty require efficiency in want satisfaction? (3) What does the presumably opposite notion of "producer sovereignty" mean? (4) Should consumer autonomy be a definitional requirement of consumer sovereignty? These questions will now be addressed in turn. Other questions, relating to the representation of interests, will be left for subsequent chapters.

The market

Some definitions require some kind of market mechanism for satisfying consumer preferences (definitions [1], [3] and [6], whereas others do not specify it as an explicit definitional requirement (definitions [2], [4] and [5], with definition [5] not wholly clear on this point). Rothenberg (1968:327–8) explicitly argued against the inclusion of this requirement. His claim was that the market represents a *means* to the end of satisfying consumer wants and that it is not part of this end. Although it "can become valued as an end in itself, this is not the same end as envisaged under consumer sovereignty."

However, market *choice* by consumers is an at least plausible condition for the *articulation*, or "revelation," of the preferences that are to be treated as interests. In other words, the market may be required, not as a unique instrument by which producer and distributor decisions can be controlled, but as a setting necessary for a satisfactory articulation of consumer preferences. In this way, the market may be a requirement in a pure interest conception of consumer sovereignty. One reason for stipulating market choice as the setting for the articulation of consumer preferences is the conviction held by some that this is the only setting in which the articulation will be comprehensive, undistorted, and sufficiently concrete to make preferences both representative of interests and relevant to production and distribution.

Accepting this as a plausible position for the time being, the question now becomes whether the market choice of consumers requires the market mechanism or something more limited. If market choice requires merely Grossman's (1967/1974:9–11) conception of "freedom of consumer choice," it is clearly a much more limited requirement. The conception of freedom of consumer choice requires only that consumers be "free [i.e., unhindered] to buy any goods *available for purchase*" (p. 9, emphasis added). This means that even when production decisions are not in accordance with consumer preferences, freedom of consumer choice is still possible, because whatever is produced can be distributed through a retail market that is free of collective restraints (p. 11). However, this is a quite impoverished notion of freedom of consumer choice and seems insufficient to meet the concern that gave rise to treating market choice as a condition for the articulation of preferences. The reason is that it refers only to the absence of constraints on the act of choosing and not to inadequacies in the range of choice. It is possible that production generates such a limited range of choice that "free" consumer choice (in Grossman's sense) reveals very little about consumers' preferences. To establish a worthwhile condition for the articulation of preferences it is necessary to extend the condition to include the range of choice.

There is, unfortunately, no obvious standard for the range of choice necessary for a satisfactory revelation of preferences. The range of choice cannot be maximized in any straightforward way. For one thing, it is not clear how one compares situation I, in which there is great variety in good type A but little variety in good type B, with the situation where the reverse is the case. Moreover, there is a trade-off between variety and quantity, since standardization in production is at the expense of variety but provides a greater quantity of output for the same resource input. Increasing variety at the expense of quantity is not necessarily an enhancement of the range of choice, because consumers reveal preferences not merely about kinds of goods but also about the desired quantities of each of them. One possible answer to the question of a standard for the range of choice is that of free-market choice, where "free" refers not merely to absence of collective restraints on the distribution of goods, but also to production, so that it can be said that consumers are free to induce the production of certain goods by offering a sufficiently high price for them. This condition combines the conventional emphasis on markets in definitions of consumer sovereignty with an interest conception of consumer sovereignty. For this reason, this "market version" of consumer sovereignty will serve as the definition with which to begin the analysis of consumer sovereignty in terms of the adequacy of its representation of interests.

Efficiency

Another connection that has been emphasized is that between consumer sovereignty and efficiency in the satisfaction of consumer wants. The argument is that consumer sovereignty requires overall microeconomic efficiency. What I intend to argue is that equating consumer sovereignty with social efficiency confuses the former with optimization, or at least with a part of optimization. To make this argument, however, it is necessary to present briefly the conceptual structure of optimization.

Maximization is the simplest form of optimization, and the basic questions for optimization are presented most easily in relation to maximization. The first is: What is to be maximized? The answer to this question represents what I will call the *constitutive principle* of optimization. The second question is: How do we conduct the maximization? The answer here is given by the *optimization calculus*. It consists, at the very least, of a method of measurement. Thus, if social optimization takes the form of maximizing national production, then the constitutive principle of national production has to be supplemented by a method of measuring it, such as the Gross National Product method.

However, in the case of optimization of an individualistic kind, as is involved in the optimization of the want satisfaction or interest fulfillment *of individuals*, we also need an interpersonal weighting principle to make it possible to aggregate across individuals, or at least some distributive principle that allows us to identify optimality. Such a principle will be referred to as a *calculus principle*. Whereas happiness, freedom, and want satisfaction are conceivable constitutive principles of individualistic optimization, alternative examples of calculus principles are equality, the maximization of the sum-total, and the maximin principle of distribution. Any of these calculus principles can, at least theoretically, be applied to any of the constitutive principles mentioned. (Interpersonal weighting is not required in collective optimization, such as the maximization of power or glory of the state or the maximization of freedom somehow defined as a characteristic of the general state of affairs, rather than as a characteristic of the different conditions of individuals.)

One approach to the conceptualization of the optimization calculus in economics has been in terms of a social welfare function. This is a comprehensive formulation of the optimization calculus representing both the conception of distributive justice and, to the extent that it is applicable, the trade-off between distributive justice and aggregation that is to be embodied in the conception of optimality.

However, such a comprehensive conception of optimality introduces controversy about distributive justice. Welfare economists in the twentieth century have tried to sidestep this issue by isolating the facet of the optimization calculus that avoids the question of the optimal distribution, namely, efficiency. (In the past it has been conventional in economics to use the term "optimum" for "efficient," but that usage is misleading because it claims too much. The consequent need to introduce the absurd double superlative of "optimum optimorum," the "best of bests," makes this problem evident.)

This separation of efficiency from the optimal distribution is accomplished by defining efficiency in such a way that the question of the interpersonal distribution of want satisfaction is left open. Such want-satisfaction efficiency is the absence of inefficiency, where the latter consists of the existence of unexploited opportunities to satisfy additional wants of some persons without reducing want satisfaction for others. This concept of efficiency, "Pareto efficiency," is represented by what is conventionally referred to as the welfare (or utility possibility) frontier, which indicates for any individual the level of welfare or want satisfaction that is possible for him, given the levels that are being provided to all others and the limits imposed by productive resources and the state of technology. Assuming that there are no difficulties in moving along this frontier, an infinite set of alternative interpersonal distributions of want satisfaction is possible, including complete equality (assuming that levels of want satisfaction can be measured). These alternative distributions can then be evaluated for equity. Conceived in this way, efficiency and equity are *complementary* facets of optimality, or, more precisely, of the calculus principle of optimality. Efficiency is a necessary but not sufficient condition for optimality; by itself it represents merely a *possibility* frontier, not optimality as such.

Returning now to the definition of consumer sovereignty, what I am proposing within this conceptual structure is that consumer sovereignty should be regarded as identifying a particular constitutive principle of optimization, not a particular calculus principle. The alternative of defining consumer sovereignty as efficiency is subject to two objections. The first is that such a definition implies that in the assessment of consumer sovereignty, of how well consumer preferences are fulfilled, efficiency counts but equity or distributive justice does not. Contrary to this position, it seems reasonable to insist that in assessing how well consumer preferences are fulfilled, it is just as important to consider the relative degree to which the preferences of different individuals are fulfilled as it is to consider the degree of general waste. These are all judgments regarding the calculus of optimization. They are best regarded as criteria that complement the constitutive principle, with the latter being what is really basic to the notion of consumer sovereignty, that is, fulfilling consumer preferences. In other words, it is best to treat calculus principles as complementing the principle of consumer sovereignty rather than as being part of it.[5]

The second objection to the efficiency conception of consumer sovereignty is that it makes it impossible to distinguish between inefficiently exercised sovereignty and sovereignty constrained by other centers of sovereignty or power. The fact that an absolute monarchy is inefficiently administered does not mean that the monarch's sovereignty is abridged, as would be the case if a foreign power, the aristocracy, or popular democracy limited the monarch's scope for action. Similarly, there is a critical difference between inefficiency in the exercise of consumer sovereignty and the restriction of consumer sovereignty by other goals or interests, for example, those of a military state or of business organizations. Consider the case of inept producers. Their ineptitude will create inefficiencies in the satisfaction of consumer wants. To refer to this creation of inefficiency as a negation or diminution of consumer sovereignty suggests that power is being used to subvert the pursuit of consumer-want satisfaction and to displace it by the pursuit of other interests. But this is not the case here; it is rather that the supremacy of consumer wants is exercised in an inept way because the functionaries of consumer sovereignty, the producers, lack knowledge, rationality, or imagination. If, on the other hand, there are interests in the economy that supersede consumer wants in certain respects, then an actual violation or restriction of consumer sovereignty is involved.

One final point that needs to be made concerns the possibility of using efficiency, not as a criterion of the extent to which the *fulfillment* of consumer preferences governs the system of production and distribution, but as one of the required conditions for the adequate

---

[5] Rothenberg (1968:328–9) has also explicitly rejected the insertion of the efficiency criterion in the definition of consumer sovereignty.

expression of consumer preferences. In the discussion of the market requirement the issue of the appropriate range of choice came up, and the market mechanism was admitted as a definitional requirement because it is one view of how an adequate range of choice for the expression of preferences can be assured. Instead of the market mechanism, however, efficiency could be used as a criterion for the best range of choice. The reason it is not so used here is twofold. First, what is really required is not an efficient range of choice, but an optimal range of choice that includes the criterion of equity. However, no proposal of any widespread currency has been made for a particular version of equity and optimality. Secondly, since it would merely change the requirement from *free*-market choice to *optimal* market choice, it would not remove the need for the requirement for some kind of market in the definition of consumer sovereignty. For the starting definition for the ensuing analysis, the former is simpler than the latter.

"Producer sovereignty"

Producer sovereignty is sometimes considered to be the opposite to and the negation of consumer sovereignty. (See, e.g., Galbraith 1970:476–7.) On the other hand, some authors have argued that the preferences of people as producers need to be considered together with their preferences as consumers and have alternatively suggested that this meaning be given to consumer sovereignty (Bergson 1966a:52–3) or that the expressions "complete consumer and producer sovereignty" (Nath 1969:9) or "household sovereignty" (Grossman 1967/1974:11) be used instead. Producer power of the latter kind is obviously different from the power referred to in the first instance. In the second case we are dealing with the producer preferences that are directly related to the welfare of *individuals,* whereas in the first case it is the power of producer *organizations,* that is, businesses, that is at issue. Since Hutt's original argument for the concept of consumer sovereignty was phrased in terms of the opposition of consumer interests and producer interests and since *consumer* sovereignty is an odd and misleading term for a principle that covers both types of interests, it is probably best to restrict "consumer sovereignty" to consumer preferences, and to use a different term to encompass the producer preferences of individuals. The concern of the following discussion, however, will be with producer sovereignty of the first kind, namely, market power.

Consider first the power of a profit-maximizing monopoly. Does it violate consumer sovereignty? Contradictory answers have been given to this question. On the one hand, there is Hanson's (1965/1977:93):

Since consumers' demand determines the quantity of a commodity that can be sold at a price, it is said that even a monopolist is subject to the sovereignty of the consumer since, though he can either fix the price of his product or decide how much he will produce, he cannot do both of these things at the same time.

On the other hand, there are others who see monopoly power as an infringement of consumer sovereignty. J. Harvey (1969/1974:122) has argued that it is an infringement because consumers do not have the power to switch to another seller. This would apply only to the case of a pure monopoly and not to other forms of market power, such as collusion in price setting. (A variety of prices cannot be a requirement of consumer sovereignty, since the ideal of perfect competition is characterized by uniform prices.) More important, what is significant for consumer sovereignty is that the output structure (that is, the kinds and quantities of goods) of the production sector is determined by consumer preferences. If we think of homogeneous categories of goods, for example, refined sugar or paper of a certain specification, then a monopoly for each of them will not reduce the range of choice between different kinds of goods for consumers to spend their money on. What will happen is that higher prices will be demanded than under perfect competition. The first impact of such imposition of monopoly power is to reduce consumer demand for each category of good. But if the monopoly profits are ultimately used to increase the consumption of the monopolistic owners of capital, this increase will become part of consumer demand, and the net effect will be a redistribution of purchasing power and a reallocation of production efforts in accordance with the new pattern of effective demand, and in accordance with consumer sovereignty. It is true that it will normally involve certain losses in efficiency with respect to the satisfaction of consumer wants. But if it is accepted that consumer sovereignty and efficiency are concepts distinct from each other, then it can be said that the market power of a profit maximizer does not displace consumer sovereignty by some other social goal, but does affect the efficiency with which consumer sovereignty is pursued, just as it affects the equity with which it is pursued.

The point that John Kenneth Galbraith (1967:chs. 11–15) has made about the market power of corporations is, however, somewhat different. He has regarded them not as purely profit-maximizing organizations but as organizations that have the freedom and power to pursue an additional set of goals. The basic goals that he has interpreted them as having are the survival, growth, and autonomy of the organization as well as "technological virtuosity." These goals emerge from the partial, but significant, autonomy of the corporation's managerial and technical experts, or "technostructure," vis-à-vis both the corporation's stockholders and market competition. Whether this situation is to be interpreted as a displacement of consumer sovereignty or an infringement of the efficiency and equity with which it is to be pursued depends on whether one treats these corporate aims as goals of the economic system that compete with the goal of consumer-want satisfaction or as motives that parallel the profit motive. From society's point of view it makes more sense to treat such organizational aims as instrumental motives, as the profit motive in a market system is also treated, so long as these aims are merely the goals of organizations and do not become societal goals. If, on the other hand, organizational longevity and technological progress become legitimated societal goals that do not wholly serve the satisfaction of consumer wants, then we have not merely an inefficiency or inequity in consumer sovereignty, but a fundamental restriction of consumer sovereignty as such.

Consumer autonomy

What makes technostructure autonomy possible is demand creation through advertising, which Galbraith also raised as a major issue for consumer sovereignty. The absence of producer power to influence consumer preferences is a requirement of definition (6) of consumer sovereignty given earlier. The autonomy version makes such producer influence a violation of consumer sovereignty *by definition*. There are other authors who have expressed concern about or have referred to this process, but have not made it clear whether it is to be regarded as a violation of consumer sovereignty or as a condition that makes the desirability of consumer sovereignty doubtful (e.g., Horton 1948:67 and Taylor 1966/1969:46). Still others have explicitly denied that it calls consumer sovereignty into question. Thus Hailstones and Brennan (1970/1975:55) have argued that even though the consumer, when responding to advertising, "may not always exercise his prerogatives and powers [as 'king in our economy'], his acceptance is necessary if particular goods and services are going to continue to be produced and consumed."[6]

---

[6] Cf. Fraser's (1939:546) earlier summary of this perspective: "a monarch [the author of a contemporaneous standard textbook says] is still sovereign even if he allows

The major implication of including the autonomy requirement in the definition of consumer sovereignty is that it makes advertising a problem for the *implementation* rather than the *desirability* of consumer sovereignty. My argument for the exclusion of this requirement as a component of the definition is based on convention and on analytical convenience. The first is simply that this requirement is not typical in the literature as a whole. The second is that the problem of preference patterning is a fairly complex one and that in order to be able to deal with it at length in analyzing the desirability of the principle of consumer sovereignty, it is necessary to exclude the autonomy requirement at least from the starting definition.

---

himself to be advised and cajoled by his subjects. And Professor Hutt (though he does not deal with the point explicitly) might add that while in such cases the actual power is wielded by the propagandist, yet the 'ultimate' power continues to rest with the consumer."

PART II

The range of wants

CHAPTER 3

Consumer sovereignty and private-want satisfaction

3.1 Private wants

The first challenge to be considered here to the starting definition of consumer sovereignty, that is, the market version of the interest conception, is the question how well it covers individuals' *private* wants that are relevant to production and distribution. "Private wants" here refer to those wants whose satisfaction the individual enjoys privately, as opposed to collectively. They exclude wants concerned with social interaction for its own sake, which are left for the following chapter. (To avoid confusion, it is important not to regard private wants as synonymous with wants for "private goods," as that term has come to be used in welfare economics. Private wants include wants for many kinds of "collective goods." To the extent that the latter involve the collective *use* of such goods for private *enjoyment*, we are dealing with private wants for collective goods. An example is a highway, which is used jointly, but for private ends.)

This challenge involves, in particular, the questions whether, first, wants regarding personal producer interests, such as the amount and kind of work to be performed, and, secondly, wants regarding environmental amenities and conditions should be included in the conception of consumer sovereignty or not. The latter raises a more general question, which is whether the free-market-choice requirement is to be retained, given the existence of market failures and alternative modes of preference expression.

3.2 Work wants

Arguments against the inclusion of producer interests

One argument in support of a version of consumer sovereignty that excludes the preferences of individuals as producers is the original argument by Hutt (1936), which he presented when he first coined the term "consumer sovereignty." It was an attempt to identify power relations that prevail in a market system and was more descriptive than prescriptive. The core of it went as follows: "as a producer [the individual] is the servant of the community. He must apply himself and the property and equipment he possesses to producing what the community wants or he will obtain nothing in the form of claims on others in return. As a consumer, he commands other producers" (pp. 257–8).

This is a misleading description because it neglects the fact that production decisions are influenced not only by consumer demand but also by the producer preferences of individuals, which determine the availability of labor services and other inputs. Complete consumer sovereignty would imply that productive inputs be given and that the owners of these inputs be *required* to make them available regardless of preference. This would require that the structure of jobs be determined not by the interaction of labor supply and demand, but by an authority representing consumer interests, presumably on the basis of workers' capabilities and not of their preferences. The allocation of people to the jobs could be left to market choice, but this process would merely be analogous to consumer market choice without consumer sovereignty (i.e., using the market to distribute goods but not to determine production priorities). The labor market would in effect auction off jobs but would not determine the jobs. However, this is not how the labor market is supposed to work.

Hutt made two further points that can be taken to be responses to this objection. The first is that "the notion of consumers' sovereignty covers all the individual's strivings to the extent to which those strivings influence the environment and hence the choices of other individuals. All the 'ultimate motives and interests' . . . are understood in the word 'preferences'" (p. 265). In this context, however, Hutt did not refer to the preferences that an individual may have concerning the nature and conditions of his work. If he had, the oddness of referring to them as *consumer* preferences would have been immediately apparent.

In the context in which he did discuss the preferences of producers (pp. 262–3) he made a second point, which Fraser (1939:547) more clearly paraphrased as follows:

In so far as individual labourers (or property-owners) decide not to produce, preferring leisure and/or the enjoyment of their own resources to receiving money income, they are to be regarded as contracting out of the productive process. *Qua individuals,* then, they admittedly escape from the sovereignty of the consumer – the words "consumer" and "producer" cease to be applicable to the case. Nevertheless *qua producers* – *i.e.* in so far as they do in fact decide to produce – they remain the subjects of the consumer. [Emphasis in original]

Apart from the fact that it seems odd that a system of sovereignty allows the subjects to opt in and out of the system at will, there is a more basic objection. It is that producers have preferences not just concerning *whether* to make their labor services and productive assets available for production but also concerning *how*, that is, under what conditions, to make them available. Hutt (1936:263) gave the example of the artist who can choose between commercial art and self-realizing art; the implication was that the latter involves opting out. But, in fact, the individual would have a great number of choices. One option might be to maximize his purchasing power by pursuing an occupation that does not make use of his artistic talents at all. Offering his services as a commercial artist may thus represent a compromise between his consumer interests, that is, income or purchasing power, and his distinct producer interests, that is, the exercise of his artistic talents. Moreover, different jobs may allow different combinations of income and opportunities for artistic self-expression. As long as there is a labor market where the individual can choose among careers and jobs, his work preferences will marginally affect what comes to be available to consumers, just as his consumption preferences marginally affect what will be produced and what jobs will be available. The process of determination in a market system is a two-way process.

Having rejected Hutt's *description* of the market system as one of the sovereignty of consumers over producers, let us consider the argument by Seldon and Pennance (1965:86–7) that producer interests *should* be subordinated to consumer interests:

Man is both consumer and producer; but his interest as producer is immediate and obvious, his interest as consumer distant and diffuse. The two conflict sharply: the interest of consumers is to replace uneconomic coal pits by profitable pits or by other sources of power; the interest of miners is to keep all mines working whatever their cost or efficiency. The case for consumers' (rather than producers') sovereignty is that, to safeguard his interest as producer, man would be tempted to stultify change by suppressing invention, new methods and ideas; the result would be stagnation and ultimately impoverishment. Consumers' sovereignty is disturbing to established producer interests, but to impede it is to put sectional before general interests.[1]

This statement contains three separable arguments. They are (1) that consumer interests are general while producer interests are sectional, (2) that only public interests are relevant to economic evaluation, and (3) that the sovereignty of consumer interests induces pro-

---

[1] In the authors' 1976 revision, the last sentence has been replaced by an observation concerning developments in the 1960s and 1970s (p. 74), but this amendment reduces rather than enhances the comprehensibility of their argument. Consequently, the original version is dealt with here.

gress while the assertion of producer interests results in impoverishment.

(1) What Seldon and Pennance seem to mean by sectional interests presumably are interests that are well organized; the latter thus contrast with public interests that are, in the absence of government intervention, poorly organized. (This is the meaning that Brian Barry 1964/1967 has proposed for the distinction between public and special interests.) It is, however, incorrect to claim that all producer interests are well organized. Before miners were unionized, they did not represent a sectional power. Moreover, even nowadays there are important producer interests that are poorly organized. For example, unions may be unable to protect workers against unemployment resulting from depressed business conditions, and so a level of economic activity conducive to low unemployment can be said to be in the public interest.

(2) Even if it were true that producer interests are sectional and consumer interests general, this would not justify subordinating sectional interests to general interests. If producer interests are intensely affected while consumer interests are involved only to a limited extent, then the intensity of the former may make them more important than the latter.

If the argument merely led to the position that general interests require special institutional protection in order to be attended to *as much as* sectional interests are, then it would be unobjectionable. (Cf. Barry 1964/1967:125 on the need for balance between special interests and the public interest.) But the notion of consumer *sovereignty* and the argument as it stands imply the *subordination* of producer interests to consumer interests. It seems that the argument is not merely that consumer interests are the only ones that need institutional protection, but also that they are the only ones to be valued.

A further objection to the public-interest argument applies to the use of consumer sovereignty as a criterion with which to assess institutions. It is not possible to make sense of the distinction between public and sectional interests without presupposing a particular institutional structure. Certainly a guild system and a monopolistic market system are characterized by considerable producer control. But it is possible to envisage an alternative system of consumer cooperatives where consumer interests are organized interests and producer interests need special protection. The distinction between public and sectional interests is relevant as a guide to the need for government intervention *within* a particular system, but not to the articulation of human interests that is necessary for the evaluation of institutional systems, such as the market system.

(3) In the argument that the sovereignty of producer interests impairs progress there seems to be an element of circularity. The terms "uneconomic," "stagnation," and "impoverishment" are used in such a way as to admit only consumer interests; they do not seem to refer to the stagnation and impoverishment of work as an activity that affects well-being and about which individuals have preferences. Thus the rationale for the sovereignty of consumption interests derives from an exclusive concern with consumption interests. Moreover, even if the sovereignty of producer interests is a threat to social progress, it is wrong to suggest that producer interests therefore have to be repressed. If "producer interests" are intended to refer to income interests and thus consumption interests at one remove, producer interests require an optimal (efficient and equitable) distribution in their fulfillment. If, on the other hand, "producer interests" refer to those interests that do not serve the consumption interests of the producers, then these are to be included in a comprehensive set of interests and not to be denied normative significance.

The inclusion of work and leisure wants

The question now is which producer interests are to be considered as parallel to consumer wants and are to be included in an expanded conception of economic sovereignty. First of all, there are those concerning work. Here it is necessary to distinguish between the earnings from work, which represent purchasing power and therefore serve to fulfill *consumption* interests, and *pure work* interests. These include occupational safety and health, a pleasant and stimulating pattern of activities, and enjoyable surroundings. (Social relations in the workplace are excluded here because the discussion is limited to private wants for the time being.)

Moreover, people also want time to spend away from socially productive work, that is, leisure time. Leisure, however, does not require a further conceptual category; instead, it can be treated as a form of consumption. This becomes apparent not only when it is seen as withheld from production and in that sense "consumed," but also when it is seen as an activity like work. It may, in fact, like work, be socially productive, but what distinguishes it from productive work, at least in a market setting, is what happens at the margin of the activity. If in increasing the level of an activity, the point of satiation, where there is no further desire to do it for the intrinsic satisfaction it provides (assuming that intrinsic satisfaction per unit of activity declines with an increasing proportion of one's time spent on it), is reached before the social productivity of the activity has declined to zero, then the activity has scarcity value, has to be remunerated to induce a consumer-desired level, and becomes productive. If, on the other hand, the activity's productivity, considered as output for which there is demand, declines to zero before its intrinsic desirability to the performers has been exhausted, then it is a free good; if, furthermore, the activity involves other costs, the activity itself becomes a form of consumption that the performer of the activity has to pay for. Thus it is possible to imagine that in one situation pottery may be a well-remunerated activity, that is, work, whereas in another it will be done as a club activity that has to be paid for by the potters. The basic point here is that if an activity is not productive at the margin, it can formally be treated as a consumption activity and no further conceptual category, such as "leisure interests," is needed.

The binary distinction between work and consumption interests applies also to the provision of productive assets, that is, land, capital, and materials. To the extent that the interest in providing them consists simply of income interests, they can be treated as consumption interests. If the interest is the desire to accumulate wealth for the attainment of social status or the exercise of economic power, we are forced beyond the limits of private wants into the realm of social wants, which will be discussed in the next chapter. If, in the absence of such social wants, an individual wants to use his capital in a certain way that does not maximize purchasing power, then it can be interpreted as being used to serve his work-activity interests; an example would be the printer who sets up his own printing press. If, finally, the person brings certain moral considerations into preferences concerning the employment of his productive assets, we are again going beyond private wants and interests. In the absence of social wants and moral considerations, producer interests can be taken to constitute, or derive from, either consumption wants or pure work wants.

Thus, at this stage, it is only work wants that need to be added to consumer wants to get an adequate representation of economically relevant interests. However, their inclusion in the principle for economic evaluation and optimization makes the term "consumer sovereignty" no longer appropriate, but suggests the term *private sovereignty* as more suitable. The market version of private sovereignty is thus the principle that production and distribution, including the structure and distribution of work activities, are to be determined by the private preferences of individuals as expressed through choice in a free market.

3.3 Environmental wants

Consumer wants, as they are normally thought of, also exclude wants that concern environmental amenities and settings. Individuals tend to have interests in such things as neighborhood shopping facilities, accessible transportation facilities, or a setting offering a rich variety of leisure opportunities. They usually want attractive surroundings, both built and natural. All these are things that are not "consumed" in the strict sense of that word. However, by and large, the wants for them are private wants, in that they are distinct from wants for social interaction for its own sake. Moreover, in the formal sense, they can be viewed as a form of consumption wants, even though the process of consumption does not destroy them. This simply means that environmental amenities and settings provide "final" benefits to individuals, that is, benefits that are not instrumental in the process of production and distribution. Moreover, they can be provided for or affected by production, as in the case of the construction of a bridge or the environmental degradation resulting from industrial pollution.

All this is merely a classification issue, and nothing fundamentally new is added, since we can simply put environmental wants into the formal category of consumption wants, together with leisure wants. What is, however, distinctive about environmental wants is that they usually involve collective goods and external effects, which are phenomena that market competition cannot deal with, or at least not efficiently or equitably.

Collective goods are goods whose use or "consumption" by one person does not reduce their availability for use by another. An example is an uncongested bridge. Collective goods are the opposite of "private goods," such as ice cream or a pair of shoes, which are unavailable to others once one person consumes or uses them. One reason collective goods create problems for market coordination is that in many cases they do not lend themselves to the price exclusion that is necessary to impose a charge. Thus the light beacon from a lighthouse cannot be withheld from ships that do not pay for it; the market therefore does not provide an incentive for the construction of lighthouses. A second reason is that even where price exclusion is possible, such as by fencing in a park and charging admission, it is socially inefficient. This is so because it excludes those persons whose access to the park would have provided positive benefits to them but less in value to them than the admission price, while such access involves no additional cost to anybody else (assuming the absence of congestion).

External effects are the unintended and untraded benefits and costs that fall on others and arise from production or consumption activities. Pollution and the neighborhood effects of improving and maintaining the exterior of one's residential property are two obvious examples. Such spillover effects clearly affect the environmental wants of others. They also represent a form of market failure: They circumvent the market, so that the price mechanism does not convey the incentives that would make the producers of external effects take into account their benefits and costs to their recipients.

Although some environmental wants operate through the market, as in the case of the housing market, where prices reflect the value not just of the residential property as such but also of its environment, market failures and inefficiencies are predominant in this sphere of interests. This raises a problem that is much more important than the question whether to classify environmental wants as consumer wants or some other category of private (or even social) wants. The problem is that the initial definition of consumer sovereignty contains a requirement for a free market, but we now have encountered wants that are not effectively mediated by the market. We need to return to this requirement, therefore, for closer scrutiny.

3.4   The free-market-choice requirement and the core version of private sovereignty

The problem and the optimization calculus

The free-market-choice requirement, in fact, involves two problems. (1) To require, as part of the definition, the market mechanism for preference revelation means that the institutional methods for controlling producer decisions are limited to the market mechanism, so that the market version of private sovereignty cannot be used to evaluate or justify the market mechanism as a system for coordinating production and distribution. (2) There are other choice conditions that are possible and have prima facie plausibility. Thus the performance of the market, both as a coordination mechanism and as a process for preference revelation, needs to be assessed, and the question arises whether it is appropriate as a definitional component in consumer sovereignty.

The free market as coordination mechanism

It is conventionally claimed that if market competition is "perfect" it will be socially efficient. This claim, however, comes close to being a tautology, since "perfect competition" either is defined so as to satisfy the requirements of efficiency or is complemented by an appropriate set of further conditions to achieve this result. It certainly does not apply to *free* markets. All that needs to be done to indicate that free markets are prone to inefficiencies is to reiterate the conventional list of static and intertemporal market inefficiencies. I have already mentioned collective goods and externalities. Other static inefficiencies result from the existence of monopolistic and quasi-monopolistic market structures and from increasing returns to scale in production. Inefficiencies involving investment for production over time include macroeconomic imbalances that leave labor and productive resources unemployed; inadequate coordination in investment planning, since market signals do not convey information to the producer about the investment plans of potential suppliers, customers, and competitors; and, as a third instance, the "moral hazard" involved in the insurance market, that is, the ability of the insured to take advantage of insurance by neglecting to minimize the risk that is partly under his control.[2] There are no inherent processes in the market mechanism to prevent these problems from arising.

The other calculus criterion for optimization is equity. Equity, however, is conceptually not standardized in the way that efficiency is. The judgment whether the market mechanism violates equity thus depends on the particular conception of equity. A marginal-productivity conception of equity, according to which purchasing power is to be distributed according to individuals' marginal contribution to production, as valued by consumers, is largely satisfied by competitive markets. It has, however, nothing to say about equity regarding externalities and collective goods. More important, as a principle of merit or desert, it can be challenged on the grounds that effort rather than contribution, which is affected by innate and therefore unearned abilities, is what ought to be rewarded. Moreover, it neglects equity concerns other than desert.

---

[2] General discussions can be found in Bator 1958/1971; Burkhead and Miner 1971:ch. 4; Millward 1971:chs. 5–6; and Winch 1971: pt. II. Unemployment as an inefficiency is discussed in Baumol 1952/1965:ch. 7. The investment coordination problem is treated in Scitovsky 1951/1971:229–37; Sen 1967/1972:270–74; Dobb 1969:148–9; Richardson 1971:436–41; and Lindbeck 1971:99. The insurance problem is covered in Nath 1969:61.

The Pareto criterion of social improvement, which can be referred to as "compensation equity," is another possible equity criterion. It requires that in any social change that represents a net improvement for society as a whole, any losers be compensated for their losses. If this equity criterion is applied to all such changes, then it is violated systematically by the market mechanism. Changes in the patterns of demand and supply and the resulting price changes and discontinuation of goods and employment opportunities will normally make some better off and others worse off.

Another important equity dimension is equality. Interpreted as equality of opportunity, and that interpreted in turn in a relatively weak manner, equality provides a criterion that open and competitive markets do not violate in a systematic way, but that, on the other hand, they cannot be counted on to ensure. Racial, religious, or sexual discrimination may be financially penalized by competition, but penalties do not prevent people from continuing to sacrifice income for discriminatory preferences. If equality of opportunities is interpreted to include background conditions such as education and familial milieu, it begins to look very much like the criterion of equality in outcomes. Although there are some equalizing processes in the market mechanism, there are distinct sources and cumulative processes of inequality on which the equalizing processes do not exert themselves. Sources of inequality are differences in inherited wealth, in talent, in family size, in education, and in luck. (For a fuller discussion, see Chapter 9, Section 9.2.)

The free-market-choice requirement was introduced as a choice condition. However, to accept it means also to accept the market mechanism as the particular institutional mode of coordinating production and distribution, with all its inefficiencies and inequities. To do so is objectionable in the formulation of a pure *interest* conception of consumer sovereignty because the requirement would make the conception partly *institutional* and unsuitable for considering which institutional systems are superior in fulfilling the interests of individuals. In particular, it has been argued by Oskar Lange (1938:95–6), Abram Bergson (1948/1966:206–7), Joan Robinson (1964/1972), and others (e.g., Whittaker 1956:125 and Tisdell 1972:410–11) that central economic planning can effectively fulfill consumer preferences and that it can be superior in this respect to the freely operating market because it can take the measures necessary to avoid the inefficiencies and inequities of the market mechanism. A definition of consumer sovereignty without the market requirement would at least make it an open question whether a market system or central planning can provide for consumer sovereignty more efficiently or equitably, rather than rule the question out by definitional fiat. Even if the requirement were changed from *free* markets to *perfectly competitive* markets, so that some of the inefficiencies of the former were ruled out, most of the points of the general argument against its inclusion in the definition would still apply. (If the existence of a market mechanism itself were the basic desideratum, then the term "market sovereignty" would be more appropriate; it would then be somewhat analogous to "the sovereignty of parliament" in that both parliament and the market mechanism are social institutions, and it is the sovereign institution that is thus identified by the particular sovereignty concept.)

The free market as a choice condition

Some of the market inefficiencies that have been identified also make the desirability of the market mechanism *as a choice condition* doubtful. If the economies of scale in newspaper production are such that because of the size of the market they result in a newspaper monopoly, there is little scope for consumer choice. When production creates externalities in the form of pollution, the market provides no opportunity for choice between highly polluting and cheap production, on the one hand, and "clean" but more expensive production, on the other. When the market fails entirely to provide something, for example, collective goods such as lighthouses or arterial roads and their maintenance, there is not even the yes-or-no choice available in a purely monopolistic market. Under conditions of general unemployment, the choice of employment opportunities that the market provides to workers is not very impressive. Nor will the market provide them with opportunities to express their preferences regarding insurance against the eventuality of personal unemployment.

Not only may market choice be too limited to be adequate for preference articulation, but it can actually be misleading. Take a Prisoners' Dilemma type of problem such as the situation where the absence of gun control combined with extensive lawlessness and violence forces individuals to be self-reliant in providing for their security. In such a situation an individual may arm himself for his self-protection, and his choice then suggests that he prefers owning a gun to not owning a gun. If all people make the same decision, then their choices seem to indicate that they prefer not to have the ownership of guns outlawed. In fact, however, there may be crucial unrevealed preferences. Each individual may prefer (1) owning a gun but having it outlawed for all others, to (2) having it outlawed for everyone, to (3) everyone owning a gun, to (4) not owning a gun while all others own one. Whether the others own guns or not, individuals prefer to own guns; they prefer (1) to (2) and also (3) to (4). The market in this case tends toward outcome (3). Yet all the individuals prefer (2), that is, a general prohibition of guns, to (3). The market not only does not reveal this preference, but suggests that (3) is preferred to (2). (The implications of the Prisoners' Dilemma for the concept of preference are discussed in a more comprehensive way in Sen 1973:249–57.)

Another category of difficulty with market choice is that it depends on what producers decide to offer. Although the market provides incentives to producers to make available goods and services that conform to consumer preferences, the market does not actually reveal to producers unfulfilled preferences. The risk of serious losses that uncertainties about unrevealed preferences create for producers in a market context can be an important deterrent to making the investments necessary to provide for suspected but unrevealed preferences. It is only through the process of producers' attempting to fulfill preferences that the market reveals the latter. It is true that a consumer-research market can reveal preferences before investment risks are incurred, but as will be elaborated shortly, such research can also be undertaken outside a market context.

Finally, even for the goods and services that are offered for purchase, the market transactions reveal only preferences within a particular price structure and a particular income distribution. Aggregatively, this means that the price–income schedule of demand as a whole is not revealed, but merely one point on it. As far as individuals are concerned, market transactions do not reveal their whole indifference surface, but only one point on it. Consequently, the preferences revealed by market choice may reflect a pattern of incomes and prices that is inefficient or inequitable or both. In other words, the free-market mechanism may not reveal the preferences appropriate to an efficient and equitable pattern of their fulfillment. For example, it may not tell us what the pattern of demand of those who currently are inequitably poor would be if they had the incomes that they are entitled to, according to equity requirements.

Alternative processes for revealing preferences

The inadequacies of the free market as a process for revealing preferences might be something that we would simply have to put up with if the free market were the only possible process. In fact, however, there are alternatives that, although they may not perfectly reveal preferences, nevertheless suggest that a conception of consumer sovereignty should be open-ended enough not to rule them out. First of all, it may be possible to improve market choices by abandoning the free market, that is, the market with no government intervention, and relying on a market partly regulated or supplemented by government action. Three examples will suffice to demonstrate this point. The first is the institution and judicial protection of environmental property rights so that those who generate environmental harm have to compensate the affected parties. The second is the governmental provision of certain collective goods, which reveals demand either at zero price or at a positive price, depending on whether access is free or involves user charges. The third is government-provided optional unemployment insurance combined with a government-operated labor exchange. Most of the problem of "moral hazard" that undermines the viability of privately operated unemployment insurance could then be overcome by requiring the beneficiaries of compensation to demonstrate a willingness to take employment through the labor exchange.

Not only can government action extend the range of choice provided by the free market, but if it is democratic it is an alternative means for individuals to pursue their interests, so that the political process represents another choice setting. Since the range of options available to voters is generally much more limited in detail, voting is in this respect an inferior mode of choice to market choices. However, the political process can make available very important options that the market cannot: for example, the provision of collective goods such as the prohibition of guns for the sake of the personal security of the community as a whole, the control of foods to prohibit health-endangering ingredients that are difficult for consumers to recognize, or the standardization of weights and measures to facilitate trade. These are instances of compulsory measures that formally restrict the range of lower-level choices but represent higher-level choice options (i.e., choices about choice settings), which either provide a better reflection of preferences, as in the first example, or improve the lower-level choice setting in quality by reducing the effort required for good choices or reducing the hazards involved in choices, as in the second and third examples.

Choices have so far been discussed as actions where the *revelation* of preferences by individuals is incidental to the pursuit of the *fulfillment* of preferences. However, there are also processes suitable merely for the communication of preferences from individuals to experts, planners, or governors. Some of those that have been mentioned by various authors are choices by representative samples of citizens in simulated settings, questionnaire and interview surveys, and even psychological projective tests (Bergson 1948/1966:206–7; Rothenberg 1968:327–8; Sen 1973:257–8). A further approach to ascertaining preferences, one that does not even require communication, is what might be called "empathetic attribution." It requires the experts, planners, or governors to imagine themselves in the situation of the group of persons whose preferences they are concerned with, to visualize fully their circumstances, and then infer from these circumstances the preferences that can be expected to characterize the group. There is no need to downplay the susceptibility of such methods to error, distortion, and manipulation (both by respondents and by governors or their functionaries). The point here is merely that these alternatives to preference-fulfillment choices are available and that under certain conditions, such as those of choices that cannot be made through the market or those prone to ignorance and irrationality (as discussed in Chapter 5), they may be superior to preference-fulfillment choices.

The core version of private sovereignty

The upshot of the discussion of the inadequacies of free-market choices – inefficient and inequitable preference fulfillment and inadequate preference revelation – and of the alternative processes for revealing preferences is that it is inappropriate to include the free-market-choice requirement in the conception of private sovereignty itself. It may in a wide range of instances be the most appropriate means for revealing preferences, but it is not the only means, and controversies about the best means are better left as such, rather than turned into definitional controversies. Removing the free-market-choice requirement brings us back to Rothenberg's definition of consumer sovereignty discussed in Section 2.3. The only difference is that work wants are now included and the term "private sovereignty" is adopted. The version of private sovereignty that we might think of as the "core version" of the interest conception of consumer sovereignty is the principle that what is to be produced, how it is to be produced, and how it is to be distributed are to be determined by the private consumption and work preferences of individuals, where "private" qualifies the nature of the enjoyment and does not exclude environmental or collective goods.

CHAPTER 4

Social wants, normative concerns, and interests

4.1 Social wants and the constitutive conception of interests

Social wants

Private wants have been conceptualized as excluding social wants, and the latter now need to be brought into the picture. Social wants do not need to be given a very precise definition. They are simply nonprivate wants, that is, wants that are not merely for some form of individually private enjoyment, but involve the behavior, feelings, or interests of others.[1] That social wants are part of the interests of individuals is self-evident. What does deserve to be emphasized, though, is that they are also interests relevant to production and distribution. Some examples of wants that have this relevance will suffice. First of all, there are social wants that individuals satisfy by using economic goods, that is, goods involving opportunity costs; such goods may be groceries for a dinner party or purchased gifts. Secondly, in a market economy entrepreneurs provide profit-making opportunities for sociability, such as dating services and facilities and programs for socializing in high-rise apartment buildings. Finally, governments and nonprofit organizations provide sociability facilities such as community centers and churches, and these clearly involve economic costs. These are social wants that have obvious economic relevance, and nothing very striking is done by the inclusion of such wants in the appropriate extension of the economic concept of normative sovereignty.

[1] The term "social wants" here has a different meaning from that given to it by R. A. Musgrave (1959:9–12), which is simply wants for collective goods. In the terminology used in the present discussion, wants for collective goods may be private, i.e., joint consumption for private enjoyment (e.g., broadcasts), or they may be social, i.e., joint consumption for social enjoyment (e.g., the use of a dance hall). Social wants as used here involve what have variously been referred to as "interdependent preferences," "interdependent utilities," and "consumption externalities." See Duesenberry 1949:93–104; Little 1950/1957:130–3; Harsanyi 1955/1969:275; Graaf 1957:51–2, 58–9; Mishan 1960/1969:74–5; Rothenberg 1961:30–6; Nath 1969:74–6; Hochman and Rodgers 1969:542–57: Burkhead and Miner 1971:129; Winch 1971:166–7; and Peacock and Rowley 1972:482–4. Such essentially mathematical conceptions, however, are not very helpful in coming to terms with their normative significance.

However, the inclusion of social wants introduces more difficult issues. It raises the question whether *all* social wants are to be treated as interests and included in the new version of normative sovereignty. Five kinds of social wants can be distinguished. (1) *Social-relation* wants are wants for particular forms of personal interaction, such as friendship, belongingness, power, and nurturing. (2) Since individuals are sensitive to interpersonal differences in resources for want satisfaction, in status, in power, and so on, they are likely to have wants concerning the nature of those differences. They will be referred to as wants for *relativities.* (3) Wants for the fulfillment of the interests of others, when combined with a willingness to sacrifice one's own interest, are *altruistic* wants. (4) An individual not only may be concerned about promoting the interests of others as they themselves see them, but may want those others to meet certain standards for reasons that have nothing to do with his own self-interest (in any ordinary sense of self-interest). I shall call such wants *norm-imposing.* (5) The latter kind of want may apply, not to individuals in particular, but to society or the environment at large. Thus a person may want whales to be preserved, not because of a concern for the whales themselves, nor because he expects to have the opportunity to see whales, but because he has a particular image of the integrity of the environment that he wants to see protected. It is, of course, a social want in a rather extended sense of that term. This category can be referred to as *collective-state* wants. The question to be posed with respect to each of these categories is whether they are to be treated as interests.

The constitutive conception of interests

My answer to the question just raised will be based on what I will call the "constitutive conception of interests." It refers to interests that it is appropriate to include in the constitutive principle of economic optimization and evaluation. This conception, in turn, will be based on the following triple criterion.

(1) The first part of this criterion is that, where both instrumental and ulterior wants are articulated, only the ulterior wants count as constitutive interests. This step is required to avoid double counting. For example, double counting would be involved if both the want for a nearby bridge over the river and the want to visit, without great inconvenience, one's relatives on the other side of the river were counted as interests in the constitutive principle.

(2) The particular want must not represent an element in the calculus principle. Here the question is: What makes a want an element

in any particular calculus principle? In the first instance, it has to be a normative concern and must not be self-interested, in the sense in which Richard B. Brandt (1979:330) has proposed that self-interest be conceived:

> I propose . . . that self-interested desires include desires for one's own hap-piness, wealth, power and status, and indeed, desires for any states of affairs which imply the existence of the person [in those states of affairs], except the desire to have benevolent desires, and the desire to act morally or to have moral qualities of character for their own sake (and not just as a mark of superiority or achievement). . . .
> Obviously not all desires are self-interested in this sense: the desire for one's daughter to be happy, or for a student to get his personal problems solved, or for the tennis underdog to win, for example. Some non–self-interested desires are impersonal, such as wanting the state of the arts to flourish in one's city, or for there to be an egalitarian society.

To be a calculus element, however, more is required than merely that the want be normative and non–self-interested. It also has to identify an aspect of the particular calculus principle that is used in the evalua-tion. A normative concern, such as the want for others to be pious, may not be part of the evaluation calculus, which might be egalitarian distribution and social efficiency. The test for whether a normative concern is also a calculus element is that as a calculus element it would be fulfilled under complete optimization, even if the concern were not held by any individual. For example, individual A may be con-cerned that individual B is unjustly poor and may want B's unjust poverty removed and may give B money to alleviate it; under op-timization that includes just distribution, the same goal would be reached even if A did not have this concern. If, however, B's poverty were just, in the light of the conception of distributive justice con-tained in the evaluation calculus, then A's concern would be nor-mative without being a calculus element.

(3) The third part of the criterion concerning the constitutive con-ception of interests is that the want must be such that the individual is prepared to trade off other interests for this particular want. Thus the normative concerns that remain outstanding after the calculus principle, applied to self-interest wants, is implemented can be treat-ed as interests insofar as they meet this criterion. These residual nor-mative concerns are included in the constitutive conception of in-terests because there is no reason for not acknowledging as a good thing the fulfillment of such concerns when they do not interfere with the pursuit of social justice and efficiency. (Parts [2] and [3] of the triple criterion represent a more elaborated version of the position

that requirements of moral principles should be kept separate from the concept of interests, or "utility" [Griffin 1982:339], and differ from the stand that the ideals of individuals are to be counted as their interests in the same way as their self-interested wants are [Hare 1976/1982:29].)

The triple criterion can now be used to determine whether it is appropriate to count the five kinds of social wants as constitutive interests (which will, from here on, be referred to simply as "interests").

4.2   Various kinds of social wants as interests

Social-relation wants

Wants for direct social relations can be categorized as follows. (a) The most obvious is the want for personal companionship, friendship, and love from others. Its pursuit may include the adoption of a position of dependence and subordination in order to elicit responsibility and nurturance from others (Zigler and Child 1969:533). (b) Communitarians from Rousseau to Elton Mayo have emphasized the human interest in and even need for a sense of belonging provided by group membership (Lukes 1973:65). (c) Some writers (e.g., Polanyi 1944:46) identify social standing or respect as the primary human concern. What appear to be private interests, such as income and consumption, can then be interpreted as deriving from this social want. (d) Another social-relation want involves control over others. Its most obvious form is the desire to be the "boss." (e) Another kind of want in social interaction takes the form of a desire for competition, which reveals itself in the popularity of competitive games. (f) A counterpart to (a) is a want for giving and nurturing. (g) The opposite to (f) is malevolence, the desire to hurt others (Boulding 1969:6). (h) Finally, there is the want for privacy or independence, for a sphere of life free from interference by others. It is the opposite of (b) or (a), depending on the kind of interference from which freedom is sought. It is a social-relation want in the sense that it is a want for noninterference. These eight kinds of social-relation wants are relatively pure forms; in fact, social wants will often be mixtures of these pure forms.

All of these social wants are to be treated as interests to be included in the constitutive principle of optimization. This is fairly obvious in the case of the wants for friendship, group membership, social status, power, competition, and privacy. If A has the same level of private-want satisfaction as B and has, beyond that, certain friendship wants satisfied that B does not, A is better off than B. The same thing applies to the other social-relation wants just mentioned. There may be measurement problems, but they are no greater than for private wants. If the marginal-value approach to the measurement of want satisfaction is used, then the benefit obtained from having social wants satisfied is reflected in the individual's willingness to trade off other kinds of benefits in order to obtain this particular one.

The two social wants whose treatment as interests requires some further comment are malevolence and the want for giving. Whether the claim that the want of one person not to be hurt must prevail over another person's malevolent want should rest on the considerations of optimality and justice or on the moral illegitimacy of the latter, which would deny it as an interest, will be considered in Section 4.4.

The want for giving poses a different problem. The question here is whether it should properly be treated as a form of self-interest or as a normative concern that is in effect an opinion concerning the appropriate calculus principle. The want for giving is a form of altruism, but it need not be a pure form of altruism. If we distinguish between justice-promoting altruism and spontaneous altruism, it is possible to claim that the former does not involve self-interest and is in that sense pure, whereas a want for giving as such does involve self-interest in the sense that the role of the person who holds that want is critical. It is not that A wants B to attain a certain state that is independent of the existence of A (see Brandt's formulation of self-interest, quoted in the preceding section); rather, A wants to be the one that does the giving. It is, of course, possible that individual A wants to give to individual B merely because A wants B to attain a certain state and realizes that no one else is sufficiently willing or able to give what is necessary; in that case, the want is simply instrumental to a purely altruistic want. The latter is to be discussed shortly. In the meantime, the implication of this discussion is that in the social-relation want for giving, only that part is to be counted as an interest which is not an instrumental justice-promoting altruistic want.

Wants for relativities

The second group of social wants identified at the beginning of this chapter consists of wants for standing in a certain comparative relationship to others in the level of want satisfaction. The latter might be concretely expressed as the standard of living, but such goods as working conditions, status, power, and sociability opportunities may be involved as well. However, since relativity wants apply to the level of satisfaction of wants, the satisfaction of relativity wants cannot be part of the level of want satisfaction to which these relativity wants apply. To distinguish want satisfaction that excludes relativity wants, the term "living conditions" will be applied. "Living conditions," then, include the satisfaction of all self-interest wants including social-relation wants, but not relativity wants, and relativity wants can thus be taken to apply to living conditions or particular elements in them. The following kinds of relativity wants are fairly typical: (a) a want for a smaller or zero discrepancy between one's own living conditions and those of others who are currently better off; (b) a want for a smaller or zero discrepancy between one's own living conditions and those of certain others who are currently worse off; and (c) a want for being better off than certain others. Purely altruistic wants are being excluded for the time being, so that (b), a want by the better-off for less inequality, must be interpreted as benefiting the better-off by making them more comfortable in the community or some such reason.

To the extent that relativity wants disappear once the optimality calculus, including the notion of distributive justice embodied in it, is implemented, or simply become wants for the maintenance of the status quo as far as distribution is concerned, they are calculus concerns and not interests to be included in the constitutive principle of optimization. The relativity wants that remain outstanding once the optimization calculus has been implemented for living conditions should be included in the constitutive principle. To show that this makes sense for the three relativity wants just identified, I will work out the implications of giving them the status of interests in this residualist fashion in the context of three different calculus principles: (1) pure equality; (2) the maximin principle of distributive justice, which states that it is the living conditions of the worst-off that are to be maximized; and (3) aggregative maximization, that is, the maximization of the sum of all interests. In the brief analysis that follows, I use the highly simplified model of two groups, the better-off and the worse-off.

In the case of the calculus criterion of pure equality, relativity wants are not relevant interests. The want for reducing or closing the gap between the better-off and the worse-off, regardless of which group holds the want, is not an interest, since it will be satisfied and thus removed with the fully egalitarian optimization of living conditions. As far as the converse want by the better-off for *increased* discrepancies is concerned, in order to treat it as an interest, the better-off must be prepared to trade off their living conditions in return for a discrepancy in their favor after optimization has provided for equality in living conditions. But they cannot both sacrifice and improve their living conditions at the same time. Thus, although this relativity want formally constitutes an interest, it is not one that it is possible to provide for.

More interesting is the case of the quasi-egalitarian maximin criterion. Here the interests of the worst-off are to be maximally fulfilled. The want of this group to have the difference between the living conditions of the better-off and their own reduced may persist even after their own living conditions have been maximized. In that case the want for further reduction in the disparity constitutes an interest, which has to be included in full maximin optimization for all constitutive interests. This interest would manifest itself in the willingness of the worse-off to sacrifice living conditions for the sake of still greater equality. For example, if in situation I living conditions of the worse-off were represented by an index level of 100 and those of the better-off by 200, and in situation II the living conditions of the worse-off were only 90 and those of the better-off 100, the worse-off might prefer situation II to situation I. To what extent the worse-off would want to make this kind of trade-off would depend in part on how much inequality maximin optimization of living conditions would leave. The relativity wants of the better-off, of course, do not enter the optimization calculus at all. Although, to the extent that such wants remain after the maximin optimization of living conditions, they are interests that meet the triple criterion, as the interests of the better-off they are not considered under the maximin principle.

When equality is not a consideration and the calculus principle consists of maximizing the aggregate of interests, all relativity wants are interests, except when they are purely altruistic. Thus disparity-reducing wants must be considered in the interests that are to be maximized. This applies also to disparity-increasing wants by the better-off, but it is unlikely to make a difference in the optimization calculus. They would have to prefer lower living conditions with greater inequality in their favor, on the one hand, over higher living conditions with less inequality, on the other. For such an interest in relative superiority to become effective would require that it be assessed as greater than both the relativity interests of those who do not want increased disparities and all the nonrelativity interests that would have to be sacrificed in the move from maximal aggregate living conditions to a situation of greater inequality than the former involves.

To sum up, under a purely egalitarian calculus principle the different relativity wants are not relevant interests, either because they are calculus elements or because, even though they may be constitutive interests (as in the case of the want to be better off than others), it is not feasible to fulfill them. Under the maximin principle, the relativity wants of the better-off, whether they are interests or not, are not relevant to optimization; the relativity wants of the worse-off will, before the achievement of optimality, usually be mostly calculus elements, but they may also contain a residual element of interest. Under a purely aggregative calculus principle, all three kinds of relativity wants are to be treated as interests, but it is unlikely that disparity-increasing wants will have enough weight to affect the optimization calculus in any way. Making the simple model of two homogeneous groups, which formed the basis of this analysis, more complicated does not seem to alter the basic thrust of these conclusions.

It is true that it is awkward to have a conception of interests that makes the treatment of relativity wants depend so greatly on the choice of the particular calculus criterion. It means that interests cannot be completely formulated until after a calculus criterion has been decided on. On the other hand, the consequences of this dependence for the outcomes of optimization are not unreasonable. Moreover, the reasons that were given to explain the triple criterion of the constitutive conception of interests have not been undermined by this analysis and continue to hold.

Altruistic wants

As in the case of the other social wants, altruistic wants that disappear once distributive justice is implemented as part of optimality are to be treated as justice concerns, not as interests. This means that it is appropriate to distinguish between justice-promoting altruism and other kinds of altruism. The latter then are to be treated as interests.

Justice-promoting altruism persists as a want only if distributive justice is not actually implemented. If, because of systemic inadequacies, there are distributive injustices in an economic system, then altruistic actions to reduce them are not to be treated as adding to the level of interest-want satisfaction of the altruists; instead, their actions can be taken to be self-sacrificing and to reduce their own level of interest-want satisfaction for the sake of increasing unjustly low levels. Thus, if there are two individuals, A and B, whose level of interest-want satisfaction is the same, but A makes altruistic sacrifices while B does not, A is not to be considered as having a higher level of interest-want satisfaction than B but rather a lower level.

Forms of altruism that are not justice promoting and are therefore to be treated as interests might be referred to as "surplus altruism." Surplus altruism might consist of a social-relation want for giving that does not depend on the recipients' being unjustly disadvantaged. Thus giving presents to one's socioeconomic peers is a form of interest, so that there is no distinction needed between purchases for one's own consumption and purchases of gifts. The one difference between gifts and self-regarding purchases is that the former fulfill two interests at the same time, that of the giver and, to the extent that the gift serves the interests of the recipient, that of the latter as well. This does not involve double counting, because two different interests are being satisfied. (To the extent that the gift unintentionally harms the recipient, the impact on the latter's interests will be negative, and this impact must be counted.)

Where such spontaneous altruism is also justice promoting, it makes sense to give priority to the justice-promoting features of such actions and therefore not to count them as interests. Such a priority rule helps to avoid difficulties such as the exploitability of the altruistic and the possible claim that counting altruistic actions as being in the interests both of the giver and of the recipient involves double counting. If altruists who help to reduce injustices have their actions interpreted as self-interested, then they will be seen as requiring a lower level of living conditions to be as well off as those who are not altruistic. This interpretation may then, for example, justify paying lower wages in occupations that attract altruists concerned with injustices, although such a policy can with good reason be described as exploitative (cf. Pattanaik 1968/1973:311). This argument suggests that when in doubt, it is better to err on the side of treating altruism as justice promoting than to treat it as self-interested.

Norm-imposing and collective-state wants

Certain social wants appear to be essentially normative concerns and yet are not part of the calculus principle. Are they then interests that are to be counted in the constitutive principle of optimization? These wants are of two kinds: norm-imposing wants, which are wants for the behavior of others, and collective-state wants, which are wants for the general conditions of society or the environment. Excluded from both are those wants that are in the person's self-interest in any obvious sense, such as the want for help from others, the want for social conditions that make the person better off as measured by private interests, and those social wants that have been accepted as interests so far. The focus here is on wants that are deemed to be for the good of other persons in ways not including advancement of their want-regarding interests, or that are for some greater, suprahuman good, or that are indirectly aesthetic in certain ways, such as the want for a social system that one finds intellectually pleasing. (Directly aesthetic wants, like those for sculpture, music, and drama, are primarily private interests, although a social-relation element may enter, as in the case of drama with audience participation.)

To show that the latter two parts of the triple criterion for the constitutive conception of interests (namely, that wants which are to be treated as interests must not qualify as elements in the optimization calculus and must be made effective by a willingness to trade off other interests for their satisfaction) apply in these instances as well, I will consider the norm-imposing examples of wants for others to behave rationally and to avoid "obscenity," and the collective-state want that marginal-cost pricing be used in publicly owned enterprises. Willingness to trade off other interests, such as purchasing power, must not be tested merely on an individual level, since even private interests can fail this test when collective goods are involved; but individuals must at least be prepared to make some contribution to a collective effort if the arrangement is such as to prevent the free-rider problem. If they will not make such a contribution, then their positions on proper behavior and good social organization are mere opinions about what is right and do not represent interest wants. If they do show such willingness but the wants disappear with the implementation of optimality, including assistance to individuals to behave rationally (see Chapter 5), the prevention of obscenity on the grounds of its illegitimacy (see Section 4.4), and the implementation of marginal-cost pricing, then these wants are optimality promoting and on that ground not part of interest wants.

The remaining case is that of the willingness to make sacrifices for the satisfaction of these wants and their persistence after the implementation of optimality for other wants. Suppose that the rationalist wants a degree of rationality in others that neglects the mental costs of such rationality and is therefore not good for them, the moralist wants a prohibition of obscenity that there are not sufficiently good reasons to include in optimization, and the welfare economist wants marginal-cost pricing even though it is not compatible with the requirements of that notion of distributive justice which is part of the applicable optimization calculus. There is no need to insist that such wants are illegitimate. They can be treated as interest wants, just as has been proposed for "surplus altruism" and certain relativity wants. As long as no one is made worse off than under optimality with respect to all other wants, there is no reason not to allow, for example, the norm-imposing individuals to make mutually advantageous deals with the individuals whose behavior they are trying to influence. If we treat such wants as interests, the resulting improvements in want satisfaction can be allowed without disrupting the requirements of optimality. Whether such wants are self-interested or not is no longer the critical issue; it simply makes sense to treat them as additional elements in the constitutive principle of optimization.

4.3 "Privately oriented" and "other-regarding" wants

"Privately oriented" and "publicly oriented" wants

In political theory some work has been done on the general issue of the distinction between interests and normative concerns. It will be useful to contrast the constitutive conception of interests presented so far with the positions to be found in that literature. Brian Barry (1965), for example, has drawn a dichotomy between "evaluations with oneself or one's family as their object [which] I shall call *privately-oriented* and evaluations with everyone or some large group such as a country as their object [which] I shall call *publicly-oriented*" (p. 65). He used this distinction to make the following argument:

Unlike a privately-oriented want, which carries a certain automatic claim to satisfaction with it, a publicly-oriented want carries a claim to satisfaction only as being a want for what ought to be done anyway. The want-regarding theory can very well be interpreted subject to a limitation on the meaning of "want" which makes it equivalent to "privately-oriented want." In my opinion at least, the theory becomes far more implausible if publicly-oriented "wants" are treated as similarly carrying with them an automatic claim to satisfaction, regardless of whether they are frivolous or serious, aimed at justice or injustice. [P. 65. Barry developed this argument at some length: See pp. 62–5, 71–2, and 295–9.]

By and large, this distinction between privately oriented and publicly oriented wants accords with the distinction developed in the previous section between interests and those normative concerns that form appropriate elements in the calculus principle. However, some qualifications to this equivalence must be made.

(1) It is not only normative concerns but also wholly instrumental political interest wants that appear to be part of publicly oriented wants. Thus the reason for excluding publicly oriented wants of this kind from the constitutive conception of interests is that they are

derivative from privately oriented wants and their inclusion would involve double counting.

(2) "Privately oriented wants" sounds like the private wants dealt with in Chapter 3 and seems not to include social wants. However, if they are interpreted as self-interest wants (including what might be called "self-centered wants," which include those elements of "self-referential altruism" [Mackie 1977:84–5] that apply to other members of one's family), then social-relation wants and those forms of altruism that are not optimality promoting are included, and "privately oriented wants" refer to the same category as interest wants.

(3) Barry does not deal with residual normative concerns. The implication is that they are not entitled to fulfillment, since they are not privately oriented wants nor are they acceptable publicly oriented wants. My argument, however, has been that to the extent that they do not impede the implementation of the calculus principle for self-interest wants, there is no reason not to provide for their fulfillment.

"Other-regarding" wants and interests

Another important concept that has been employed in the literature is "other-regarding" wants or interests. Three general interpretations of such wants can be found. (1) One is that only private wants count as interests (Oppenheim 1975). (2) An opposite position is that moral concerns are part of interests (Flathman 1966). (3) An intermediate position is that there are self-interested social wants that are distinct from moral concerns and altruism, and these are part of interests (Connolly 1974).[2]

(1) Oppenheim (1975), who represents the first position, has made his point as follows:

Only if the agent's choice of x would be rational with respect to some welfare goal is doing x in his own, or in the public, interest. In other words, actions or policies must be of a utilitarian kind. "Welfare" and "utility" are to be taken in the broad sense. . . . On the other hand, we must avoid interpreting "welfare" in an all-inclusive sense; thus, it should not be applied to the psychological

---

2 In economics, similar disagreements can be found. K. J. Arrow (1951/1963:18) and Rothenberg (1961:30–6) threw social interests and moral concerns together, Arrow under the term "values" and Rothenberg under the term "external relations in consumption." Arrow concluded that a sharp distinction had to be made between what I refer to as private wants and social-interest wants in considering their treatment in optimization, whereas Rothenberg denied the significance of that distinction and also of that between self-interest wants and moral concerns. Harsanyi (1955/1969) criticized Arrow's distinction (p. 276nll) and proposed a distinction between "subjective preferences" and "ethical preferences" (pp. 275–7) that is similar to the one I am advancing here.

satisfaction someone may derive from foregoing material well-being for the sake of doing what he happens to consider morally right. [Pp. 261–2]

Moreover, "acting in one's interest must . . . be distinguished not only from conforming to non-utilitarian principles but also from being guided by utilitarian considerations of either an altruistic or universalistic kind, i.e. from promoting the utility of others . . ." (pp. 262–3).

Oppenheim's conception is rejected here because his notion of "welfare" or "utility" is so restrictive that it excludes important forms of interests. Though he did not directly specify the limits of "welfare" or "utilitarian actions," he indicated as specific exclusions both "self-realization" and "the capacity to act as a morally responsible agent" (p. 267). This limit is too restrictive in both the private and the social sphere of an individual's interests. In the private sphere, there is no reason for excluding self-realization from a want-regarding conception of interests if self-realization is a want of the individual. Why should a person's want for a certain job or certain hobby materials not be in his interest merely because they are seen as opportunities for self-realization, when another's want for the same job or the same hobby materials wholly for the purpose of increasing his income is in his interest? In the social sphere, Oppenheim's conception does not acknowledge that having social relations can be in a person's interest; instead, in his criticism of Connolly, Oppenheim treated social interests as identical with altruistic concerns (p. 263). Oppenheim's restrictions are thus not well founded.

(2) Flathman's (1966:27) position goes to the opposite extreme by including "other-regarding interests" and defining them as follows: "If I have an other-regarding interest, it is *my* interest, but my interest *in* the profit, advantage, or welfare of *others*. . . . Contrary to egoism, my interest is satisfied by serving the other man, not by any reward, pleasure or satisfaction which I obtain as a consequence of serving that man." The problem with treating all "disinterested interests" (Flathman 1966:27) as constitutive interests is that it means that anyone who wants the interests of the members of society as a whole to be optimized would have such optimization counted as part of his interests and would be considered to have a higher level of interest fulfillment than a person who is not concerned about interests other than his own. To avoid these difficulties, only those normative concerns that are not calculus elements have been accepted for inclusion in the constitutive principle.[3]

---

[3] James Griffin (1982:338) has mentioned another objection, which is that the interests of persons who attract the benevolent concerns of others would count for more than

(3) The third position, which comes closest to the position adopted in this chapter and which distinguishes social interests from private interests as well as from altruism, is represented by Connolly (1974), who has argued that the "dichotomy between egoistic and altruistic action is too crude to capture the richness of human relationships and motivation" (p. 56).

When my interests as a social being are at stake, more than private wants are involved. Certain kinds of relationships with others are fostered – relationships involving trust, friendship, shared convictions, and the like. One who cherishes the social dimension of life may often be willing to sacrifice purely private satisfaction for the mutual benefits of social life. For instance, a person may decide to forgo certain material benefits in the interests of maintaining a relationship of trust with another. . . . He is surely acting in his own interest in this case. There is a *sacrifice* here, of course, but not in the sense that an act of altruism is a sacrifice of one's own interest. The person is simply sacrificing a lower-order interest for the higher-order interest he has as a social being. [Pp. 54–5].

It is unfortunate that Connolly identified social interests as "higher-order interests" and that he equated egoistic interests with private wants (p. 55); this position might suggest that there is something moral about social interests, and it is in this light that Oppenheim responded to Connolly's argument. What needs to be made clear is that there is a difference between wants *for oneself* (self-interest wants) and wants for something to be enjoyed *by oneself* (private wants). Wants for oneself do not have to be for something to be enjoyed exclusively by oneself but may include interaction with others, which makes them *social-interest wants*.

It is true that in certain kinds of social relations it becomes difficult to distinguish between social-interest wants and altruism (cf. MacIntyre 1967:466), but this problem applies to private wants as well. Is it

---

the interests of those who do not attract such positive other-regarding wants. The interests of orphans, for example, would thus appear to count for less than those of children with caring parents. The triple criterion certainly avoids the relative neglect of the orphans to the extent that parental concern simply reflects the notion of distributive justice contained in the calculus criterion. Under a purely aggregative approach to optimization, this proposal would clearly create a bias in interest fulfillment against the orphans. However, a certain egalitarian element in the calculus criterion would rule out this undesirable consequence. The problem lies really in the lack of distributive justice in aggregative maximization, rather than in the conception of interests. To the extent that "surplus altruism," as discussed previously, is involved, it is not that the interests of the children with caring parents are double counted, but that the child-caring interests of the parents are included. It means that it is not objectionable if parents transfer interest entitlements to their children, or anyone else for that matter, as long as doing so does not create injustice.

altruistic or self-interested to provide food to a neighbor in need, in the expectation that if one is in need oneself the neighbor will behave in a reciprocal manner? We may have elements of both in this action, and perhaps in social-relation wants as well. In this case we include only the self-interested part of the want as part of interests and exclude the altruistic part.

In terms of the constitutive conception of interests proposed in the previous section, it is not necessary to make difficult judgments concerning motivation but merely to identify which wants represent elements in the calculus principle.

4.4   Normative criteria for interests

Subjective and objective conceptions of interests

The conception of interests that has been used so far is subjective in the sense that "the individual whose judgment [concerning interests] it is is necessarily the only authority on its correctness" (Wall 1975: 502n25). An alternative conception that has considerable support is the objective one, which involves "*public* criteria of correctness" (Wall 1975:502n25) or at least some kind of third-person judgment. The question now to be considered is what kinds of criteria external to the individual whose interests are at stake it would make sense to admit.

Two kinds of criteria must be distinguished here: moral criteria and prudential criteria. Both are normative in the sense that they emanate in "ought" statements. But prudential criteria are wholly concerned with the self-interest of the individual and can include rationality, and the treatment of self-destruction as being against one's interest. Moral criteria, on the other hand, are concerned with what individuals owe to others, to the community, or to some still higher good, both in actions and in forms of abstinence. (Wall's [1975:506] treatment of all third-person interest-regarding judgments as moral judgments simply because the former are evaluative seems to me seriously misleading. There is a fundamental difference between evaluating someone's actions as imprudent and evaluating them as immoral.) I will consider possible moral criteria first.

Moral criteria

We are concerned here with moral norms that rule out certain wants as immoral and possibly elevate certain others as moral, rather than treating them as morally neutral. We have already considered norm-imposing wants, but only for their eligibility as constitutive interests, not for their eligibility as calculus elements. Thus certain kinds of enjoyment, such as reading pornography, may conceivably be designated as immoral, not as a result of individual preferences, but on the basis of an appropriate collective morality. This would mean that the calculus principle is such that it accords to wants for pornographic reading value weights of zero, a process that has the effect of denying their significance as constitutive interests. In other words, the distinction made by Robert Paul Wolff (1968:24) between legitimate and illegitimate interests would be introduced. But what would be the basis of such a distinction?

I will discuss this question by considering specifically the example of wants for pornographic reading. (1) If it is regarded as bad for the individual because it stimulates him sexually without satisfying him, it is a prudential judgment, not a moral judgment. (2) If it is regarded as socially bad because it induces violence harmful to others, it is illegitimate *as the outcome of optimization*. This point makes it important to draw a distinction between two kinds of illegitimacy. One is the illegitimacy resulting from optimization, or what I shall call *consequential illegitimacy;* the other is illegitimacy that is conceptually prior to optimization, or *prioristic illegitimacy*. Consequential illegitimacy does not require that a want be barred from the constitutive principle or be explicitly negated by the calculus principle; it simply applies to wants whose satisfaction, always or characteristically, either does more harm than good or violates distributive justice. If reading pornography induces sexual violence, then we can expect that optimization will require that this want not be satisfied on these grounds. There is no need for requiring their illegitimacy on a priori grounds. (3) If, as a third possibility, pornographic reading is regarded as bad because it is offensive to some deity, then we are not dealing with interest-regarding optimization at all, or at least not with optimization of *human* interests. (4) If it is regarded as bad because, as a result of its offensiveness to some deity, the individual will be punished in this life or in some afterlife, then assuming the existence, sensitivity, and power of the deity to be factual, the judgment is again prudential. None of these four instances constitutes a case for excluding the want for pornography from interests on moral grounds.

Similar arguments can be applied to other more obviously unpalatable wants: for snooping, harrassing, stealing, performing malevolent acts, killing, and so on. The consequences of these actions for the victims will be such that they will have to be made illegitimate on consequential grounds, so that there is no need to make them illegitimate on prioristic grounds (cf. Hare 1976/1982:30). This stricture applies also to wants whose satisfaction we would normally think ought to be encouraged, such as mutual respect, friendliness, and helpfulness.[4] The significance of limiting the illegitimacy and priority judgments concerning kinds of wants to consequentialist moral criteria is that the latter do not determine what is to *count* as interests or what calculus weights are to be attached to them, but only how society and its members are to go about *fulfilling* these interests. Prioristic morality is necessary only in the formulation of distributive justice, not in the discrimination between wants.

Prudential criteria

The previous discussion should not be taken to mean that the conception of interests does not involve any prioristic norms at all; it is only moral norms that are rejected at that level. The very judgment that interests should be interpreted to consist of wants and their satisfaction is a prioristic one, and any modifications of it are prioristic as well. But these are prudential judgments, not moral judgments. They must be universalizable, just as moral judgments have to be, but the universalizability is not in order to remove selfishness, only to avoid mistakes.

One such modification is that only wants that are rational are to be considered as representing interests. This rationality criterion will be extensively explored in the next chapter. It is certainly a prudential rather than a moral one. Subsequently presented criticisms of the want-regarding conception of interests are also based on prudential considerations. The basic point is that prioristic norms concerning interests are to be restricted to prudential ones and are to exclude moral ones, except that the latter are involved in the conception of distributive justice.

Prudential norms are as objective as moral norms. Consequently, by rejecting moral norms in the conception of interests I am not defending the subjective conception of interests. However, the subjective conception of interests has been the starting point, and objective norms – other than the basic norm that interests consist of want

---

[4] These might be referred to by Musgrave's (1959:13–14) term "merit wants." However, the discussions of this notion among economists have taken either the position that the concept involves prudential criteria, i.e., of knowledge and rationality (Head 1966; Andel 1969), and not moral norms, or the position that it involves moral norms, but ones that cannot be justified in an individualistic approach to interests (McLure 1969; Burkhead and Miner 1971:126).

satisfaction – will be introduced only to the extent that there is a demonstrated need for them.

4.5   Personal sovereignty

In this chapter the conception of interests has been extended to include those interests that represent social wants. The term "personal sovereignty" may now be used to refer to the extended range of wants that is thus to be included in the constitutive principle of optimization and evaluation. That is to say, personal sovereignty is the principle that what is to be produced, how it is to be produced, and how it is to be distributed are to be determined by the interest wants of individuals.

PART III

The quality of wants

CHAPTER 5

Limits to individual rationality

5.1 The rationalistic conception of interests

Having established in the previous chapter that the most appropriate conception of interests is essentially prudential and self-regarding but not private, it is now necessary to look at the possibility of prudential errors in this range of wants. The relevant feature in the notion of interests that identifies such errors is rationality. Most theorists who have dealt with the concept of interests and who have not adopted an objective, impersonal conception of interests, such that the distinctiveness of the individual is not relevant to the articulation of his interests, have made rationality of one form or another a critical requirement. Errors in wants are irrationalities that must be removed from the wants before they appropriately represent interests. This requirement is the core of what can be referred to as the *rationalistic conception of interests*.

The introduction of the rationality requirement is different from the previous modification in the conception of interests, as reflected in the various sovereignty conceptions. Whereas the latter, that is, "consumer sovereignty," "private sovereignty," and "personal sovereignty," as well as the market, core, and constitutive conceptions of each of these, have referred to certain *ranges* of types of wants, what rationality indicates is a certain *quality in wants*, regardless of what types of wants are involved. The issue here is one not of inclusion or exclusion, but of acceptance or correction. The qualitative requirement of rationality is at the heart of the preference-based notion of interests, since, in order for normative principles requiring the fulfillment of preferences to be persuasive, it is necessary to assume that individuals know what is best for themselves.

To facilitate the discussion it will be useful first to make some basic distinctions between conceptions of rationality. One is the conventional distinction between *epistemic* rationality, or rationality in beliefs, and *practical* rationality, or rationality in decision making or action. (The term "epistemic" is from Benn and Mortimore 1976:4.) Rationality in preferences requires both. Rational preferences have to be based on adequate information about current and future conditions and opportunities as well as on an adequate comparison of the opportunities in the light of that information.

The notion of adequacy here suggests another distinction among conceptions of rationality. This is the distinction between what I will call *ideal-observer rationality* and an individual's *constrained rationality*. Ideal-observer rationality presupposes omniscience about the range and nature of current and future opportunities available in society, about current and future general environmental conditions, and about the individual's own current and future capacities, psychological makeup, and attachments; and it presupposes also an unlimited capacity to consider choice options and to weigh them against one another.[1] Constrained rationality refers to what is rational considering the limitations on the knowledge that is available to the individual and on his capacity to use it in decision making. (Cf. the distinction between objective and subjective rationality in Rawls 1971:417 and that between "global" and "approximate" rationality in Simon 1955.) Given the costs to the individual of obtaining correct beliefs and pursuing correct reasoning, it may not be rational for him to identify his interests fully and accurately; nevertheless, what his interests are depends on completely correct beliefs and reasoning.

The requirement for ideal-observer rationality applied to interests, however, creates a serious difficulty. None of us, including experts or expert teams, has the capacities required to articulate wants, either for ourselves or on behalf of others, in such a way that these wants satisfy ideal-observer rationality. This does not mean that the criterion of ideal-observer rationality is inappropriate, only that, for practical purposes, it is an asymptotic criterion that can only be approached to a greater or lesser extent. The difficulty applies to the identification of interests. How can an evaluation of interests be undertaken if the latter are defined by an asymptotic concept? One approach to dealing with this difficulty is to give revealed preferences the benefit of the doubt and to correct them only when it is clear how to do so. In other words, revealed preferences are taken as rational unless it is explicitly shown both that they are not rational and that there is an appropriate form of correction. In the end, the difficulty

---

[1] Technological omniscience is not included. If it were, it would make it ideal-observer-irrational for many people – at least those with appropriately materialistic aspirations – not to enrich themselves with the introduction of futuristic and currently unavailable technological knowledge. Limitations to society's state of technology are not an issue relevant to what we are concerned with when we recognize wants as misrepresenting interests because of ignorance.

turns out to be more serious, but to show this, it will be useful to adopt such an approach initially.

5.2 Interests and ignorance concerning current conditions and opportunities

Ignorance as irrationality

Wants based on ignorance are epistemically irrational and thus do not appropriately coincide with and serve interests. Ignorance can apply to the range of opportunities available to the individual, to the nature of these opportunities, and to their context, that is, the conditions surrounding each of the options. If there is ignorance about the range of opportunities, the best options may be the ones that the individual is unaware of, so that he makes his choice among inferior options. Thus, if faced with a choice among treatments for an illness, he may forgo the most appropriate treatment because he is unaware of it. On the other hand, he may be aware of all the relevant treatments available but may not properly understand their primary effects and side effects. Finally, he may be mistaken about the nature of his illness, so that even if he chooses the best treatment for the illness he thinks he has, it is inappropriate for the illness that is his actual condition.

Medical treatment is, on the whole, a private good. Similar mistakes, though, are possible with collective goods, jobs, and social relations. In a survey to determine the relative desirability of different kinds of river crossings in a certain area, respondents may give valuations based on mistaken ideas about time savings or the kinds of vehicles that could be accommodated. When it comes to jobs, ignorance tends to be particularly great in any system with a great diversity of work activities. The individual's knowledge of the full range of relevant work activities, together with their environments, is likely to be very limited. Analogous considerations apply to opportunities to satisfy social wants.

Ignorance is certainly not a peripheral issue. Lack of knowledge about drugs or even food and cosmetics can be a threat to life. One's quality of life can be significantly impaired by uninformed choices about careers, about housing and environments, and about people with whom to interact. Although the effects of choices may not be irreversible, reversing them may involve substantial costs, in loss of purchasing power and established attachments or in forgone advancements in a more suitable career and forgone alternative relationships. And when there are permanent impacts on the individual, as in the case of permanent injury or loss of good health, the results of choices are irreversible.

Ignorance about the nature of opportunities creates a difficulty for the conventional concept of preference. According to mainstream economic theory, what is wanted is a particular good. This interpretation, however, does not allow that consumers may make mistakes about the nature of that good. Such mistakes become more recognizable in Kelvin J. Lancaster's (1966:14–23) theory of "goods-characteristics." He has emphasized that products generally have a variety of characteristics, and differentiation between similar products takes the form of alternative combinations of these characteristics. It is these combinations of goods-characteristics that consumer preferences actually refer to. The consumption of specific goods then becomes the joint consumption of a set of goods-characteristics. This conception of preferences can be designated as *characteristics preferences*. Preferences regarding complete products can be referred to as *instrumental preferences*. This distinction naturally applies also to services, environments, jobs, and relations. The wants for goods, jobs, and so on then are merely instrumental to more basic preferences, namely, characteristics preferences.

Assuming for now that the individual clearly knows his characteristics preferences, his purchases will be mistaken or suboptimal if they are not the best means to his ends, namely, his characteristics preferences. What from the perspective of conventional economic theory may have appeared to be an attempt to assess the rationality of ends thus turns out to be an assessment of the rationality of means for reaching given ends.

The distinction between instrumental and characteristics preferences also saves consumer theory from an awkward issue. If all preferences are treated as ends, then we have the difficulty that the increased consumption of one particular good, namely, information, changes not just the point in the individual's indifference space that represents his consumption pattern, but also the indifference contours themselves. This would mean that the structure of preferences depends on what is produced for consumption; that is, it is not exogenous to the system of production and distribution. However, when instrumental and characteristics preferences are distinguished, so long as information determines only how instrumental preferences are derived from characteristics preferences, the latter remain exogenous while the former change in response to better information.

Rational ignorance and interests

Ignorance has been referred to as a form of irrationality. But it is so only in an epistemic sense and from an ideal-observer perspective characterized by omniscience, or at least by complete relevant knowledge. From the individual's point of view, complete relevant knowledge is normally not possible. Epistemic rationality from the individual's perspective is more reasonably conceived of in terms of available information. Thus Oppenheim (1975:260–1) has defined an action as rational if, among other things, it makes full use of the "information available to [the individual] in [situation] S – in the sense, not only of his *actual* state of information, but of the evidence he *could* obtain if he exercised 'due care under the circumstances'" (emphasis in original).

However, the notions of availability and dueness in care are very imprecise and, moreover, hide an issue of constrained rationality. Is information "available" when it can be obtained from an obscure volume in a library or from the mind of some person who might be tracked down by many days spent on the telephone? Constrained rationality resolves this question by dispensing with the notion of availability (or merely using it in a broad sense and treating it as a minimal requirement) and putting cost–benefit comparison in its place. Individual *constrained* rationality thus is represented by a degree of informedness that results from an information search that is taken to the point where the marginal costs, in effort and expenses, have risen to the level of the marginal benefits that result from improved choices. There is consequently a rational level of ignorance (or epistemic irrationality) for the individual.[2]

Such a constrained-rational level of ignorance for the individual, however, does not mean that his consequent choices are best for his interests. His interests hinge on ideal-observer rationality. If this were not so and if, instead, his interests depended on what was rational *for him* to do, then his interests could not be advanced by society's provision of information to him in order to increase his constrained-ra-

---

[2] Cf. Simon's (1955 and 1957) model of "satisficing" as rational behavior, which may be regarded as based on an implicit cost–benefit comparison. Uncertainty about cost–benefit comparisons in information-search choices makes the articulation of individual rationality more complicated and perhaps even indeterminate, as when there is no basis for making probability guesses, but this difficulty does not affect the following discussion of normative rationality concerning interests. For a review of different descriptive conceptions of rational behavior, primarily with reference to firms in a market, see Elster 1979:133–6.

tional level of informedness. This would clearly be an inadequate conception of interests. Despite all its difficulties, we have to deal with ideal-observer rationality, recognizing that, for practical purposes, it is an asymptotic concept, that is, one that in practice can never be fully represented but only progressively approximated. To make this approximation it is necessary for those conducting the interest-regarding evaluation to identify not only the critical features of the true state of affairs, that is, those features that potentially affect the interests of individuals, but also the actual knowledge of individuals in order to determine the extent and nature of their ignorance. On the basis of such a determination, corrections can be made in the revealed preferences in order to identify the interests of the individuals approximately. It will also be necessary to determine how wants change in response to improved knowledge. Though such a process is onerous, it is not impossible.[3]

5.3   Limits to practical rationality

Limits to deliberative rationality

Irrationality in choice, from an ideal-observer perspective, has so far been traced only to limitations to *epistemic* rationality that conform with unlimited *practical* rationality for the individual. There are, however, also limitations to the individual's practical rationality itself. It is now necessary to distinguish between ideal-observer practical rationality and practical rationality constrained by the individual's limited capacity for or enjoyment of rational consideration and comparison of options. The limitations apply both to conscious deliberation and to intuitive choices. Deliberation and intuition are alternative approaches or means to practical rationality. This means that practical rationality should not be equated with deliberation. In Table 5.1 an overview is provided of the various forms of instrumental rationality that are involved in the preceding and current discussion.

Deliberation, like the acquisition and retention of information, involves costs that have to be traded off against the benefits of such rationality. The costs are the time, energy, and possibly counseling assistance necessary to take into account and compare the options and their characteristics or impacts. The comparison of options, from the ideal-observer perspective, is not only of the relatively simple kind,

---

[3] For examples of institutional implications of the ignorance of individuals – specifically, government intervention in a market system – see Head 1966:5 and Rothenberg 1968:332–4.

Table 5.1. *Overview of the various forms of instrumental rationality*

Type of rationality	Ideal-observer rationality	Constrained rationality[a]
Epistemic rationality	Perfect knowledge	Rational ignorance
Practical rationality[b]	Perfect decision making	Rationally constrained decision making
General rationality	Perfect choices	"Rational irrationality"

[a]Constrained rationality may apply to (i) individuals and (ii) society.
[b]Practical rationality may be based on (i) deliberation and (ii) intuition.

such as whether to buy car A or car B, but of *all* options, and not only all options, but all possible opportunity *sets* (total combinations of consumption, leisure, work, physical environment, and social relations over the remainder of one's lifetime). Moreover, as Brandt (1966:264–5 and 1979:111–12) has emphasized, it is necessary not only to know of certain options and their characteristics, but to be vividly aware of them.

Another cost of rational deliberation is that extensive commitment to it is likely to preclude the satisfaction of particular kinds of important wants (and perhaps even some mental health needs) that are in some ways incompatible with such a commitment. The maximization of want satisfaction requires that rational deliberation be taken only to the level where the marginal benefits of further deliberation cease to exceed its marginal costs. In other words, an ideal observer will recommend to someone who is faced with deliberation costs that he pursue only limited practical rationality; that is to say, he will recommend a "rational level of practical irrationality."

The level of practical rationality is determined not only by the *extent* of rational deliberation, but also by the *structure* of deliberation. A rational structure of deliberation involves "investing" in deliberation to determine which kinds of choices deserve serious deliberation (and how much of it) and to devise decision-making aids, such as the repetition of previous choices (habitual choice) and the imitation of other people's choices, for choices that do not warrant independent deliberation. (Cf. Rothenberg 1966:231–2.) There are thus strategic choices of rules of thumb to be made. Errors, from an ideal-observer perspective, can occur both as a result of quite rational decision-making strategies and in the formulation of such strategies themselves.

Limits to intuitive rationality

The comparison of opportunities or the adoption of a strategy of choosing may not be based wholly on conscious deliberation but may be a partly or wholly unconscious process, with merely the conclusion of "I'd rather have A than B" becoming conscious. Experiences and nonexperiential knowledge are retained by the human mind and used without themselves coming to conscious awareness in the emergence of a preference. To the extent that such an unconscious use of knowledge is practically rational it can be referred to as *intuitive rationality*. Intuitive rationality may be superior to deliberation to the extent that the quality of choice relative to the choice effort is better than the same relation for deliberation. To the extent that habitual choice and imitation are unconscious and are yet rational, they represent intuitive rationality.

The limits to intuitive rationality are not those of diminishing returns to effort, as in the case of deliberation, but are simply the irrational part of intuition. Deliberation may be regarded as a response to the irrationality of the intuitive faculty, as in choices where past experiences are not adequate or where strong immediate desires distort choices with important long-run consequences.[4] Impulsive choices are often later regretted. What is needed is the self-knowledge to determine in what kind of choices reliance on intuition is beneficial and in what kind of choices it is to be distrusted and supplemented or supplanted by deliberation.

Sometimes there is a direct conflict between articulated wants and actual choices. For example, a student who has consciously decided that the most important thing for him is to prepare for an examination may end up carousing instead. Such a discrepancy between actual choices and explicit wants is occasionally referred to as weakness of will. Consciously, the individual has one set of preferences, but at the subconscious or spontaneous level of conation, certain other impulses or "wants" prevail. Brandt (1979:60–4) has identified such spontaneous wants as irrational, because they involve a deficiency in the awareness of the consequences of the impulsive preferences. The student may in some sense "know" the costs of his carousing when he

---

4 For a brief discussion of how "inconsistency of ends" is explained by psychological theory see Rothenberg 1966:235n15.

turns to it, but they are not fully before his mind, and his intuition does not perform an equivalent task for him. Consequently, his rational want does not generate the motivation necessary to override his immediate want, which is based on restricted awareness, and it thus does not shape his actual choice. Such a choice cannot be taken to represent his interests.

Practical irrationality and interests

From the ideal-observer perspective, wants may be irrational not merely because of ignorance, but also because of deficiencies in intuitive decision making and, from the individual's perspective, quite rational cost–benefit limits to deliberation. These factors widen the gap between wants and interests. They also make it still more difficult to identify interests. Wants revealed in choices need to be corrected not merely for distortions owing to ignorance, but also for distortions owing to inadequate decision making. Experimental conditions conducive to rational deliberation may reveal a pattern of choices at variance with real-world choices, so that, if the experimental conditions can be trusted to reflect real-world conditions (other than real-world irrationalities), such variances can be taken as a basis for corrections of irrationality. Although such corrections can be expected to be controversial, they are necessary for the interest-regarding evaluation of economic policies and systems, where some policies or systems make it easier for individuals to choose rationally or protect them to a greater degree from irrational choices than others do.

5.4   Interests concerning the future

Uncertainty and unpredictability

The problem of irrationality is greatly increased once the future and its uncertainties are introduced. Both epistemic and practical irrationality are involved. Epistemic irrationality is aggravated by the difficulty of predicting the future, and this difficulty is complicated by the fact that the future emerges from the interaction of individuals on the basis of their respective conceptions of how best to provide for the future. Moreover, uncertainty and planning for the future introduce certain further difficulties for practical rationality. It is not self-evident what *the* rational response is to risky choices, to choices where there is insufficient information to have a probability distribution of possible outcomes, to preferences changing over time, and to the distribution of want satisfaction over time. Although it may not be too difficult to identify conditions for *making* rational choices, for example, possession of relevant knowledge and a situation in which calm deliberation is possible, the criteria for assessing the rationality of the *outcomes* of choices are problematic.

Interests concerning provision for the future are ideally represented by choices based on ideal-observer rationality, under which the future is fully predictable. That is, for our wants to represent interests concerning the future, we must accurately predict the future. This requirement applies not only to natural events, such as weather and geological occurrences, but also to the actions and interactions of individuals and of the social institutions that they staff and their aggregate outcomes. As in the previously mentioned cases of irrationality, only the approximation of interests is possible, and it would have to take the form of corrections to revealed preferences, where the corrections are based on obvious forms of irrationality.

Apart from the need to make corrections for mistaken predictions in revealed preferences concerning the future, this issue has also a more direct implication for the interest-regarding evaluation of economic policies and systems. The extent of predictability of the future may depend in part on the particular policies adopted and certainly depends to some extent on the economic system as a whole. Some policies and systems, such as those that discourage change and those that effectively provide for the collective planning of change, will tend to result in a more predictable future than others, such as those that are more tolerant of, or incapable of preventing, economic and social turbulence. Since the latter makes it more difficult for individuals to provide effectively for the future, we can say that they have an instrumental interest in the predictability of the future, and this is an interest that some policies or systems provide for better than others do. Predictability (or, more precisely, predictability for given information-search costs) is an approximate interest-regarding performance indicator that does not require the detailed correction of revealed preferences for irrationalities.

As far as the *general* pattern of interests in a society is concerned, it is reasonable for an evaluation to take the position that prediction errors will be random, unless there are specific reasons for believing that in certain instances individuals' predictions will largely lean toward one side or the other. To the extent that the random-error assumption is appropriate, we can provide different answers to the following two questions: (1) How well does the economic system fulfill the general pattern of interests of individuals in the society? (2) How well does it protect individuals from irrational choices or their consequences? In the case of random errors, poor performance with respect to the latter question does not make it inappropriate to use information about revealed preferences to identify the general pattern of interests and to rate the system's performance in satisfying the *general* pattern of interests as high.

The randomness or nonrandomness of errors made by individuals has to be assessed in deriving accurate predictions. However, although an ideal observer may be able to make accurate predictions, they may not be available to an actual planner or evaluator. Thus the evaluator perspective, unlike the ideal-observer perspective, involves constraints similar to those facing the individual, although the resources, specialization, and experience of the expert evaluator may allow him to reach a greater degree of rationality than the individual who is left to his own devices, at least in areas where the interests are not particularly idiosyncratic. The level of ignorance and the simplifications and shortcuts in the analysis of interests that are rational for an evaluator, who should weigh the information and processing costs against the benefits (improvements to policy or system design and evaluation), leave him to cope with a certain level of uncertainty in the identification of interests. If the uncertainty is such that it is possible to articulate a probability distribution of possible interests, what is the best way of representing interests? A plausible answer is the expected-value rule, according to which $\Sigma_j P_j V_j$, where j refers to possible outcomes, V_j to the individual's relative valuation of outcome j, and P_j to the probability of outcome j, is to be maximized. In the long run this choice rule will maximize total net benefits to individuals. However, it ignores risk aversion, and to argue that risk aversion by evaluators is not in the interest of individuals is contentious, to say the least. This, then, is one problem that remains in the identification of interests by evaluators, that is, by relatively informed and rational third persons.

When uncertainty is such that a probability distribution cannot be identified, it becomes even less clear what rule should be used to approximate best the interests of individuals. Either assuming that all possible outcomes have equal probability and then using the expected-value rule or, alternatively, using the minimax-loss rule of selecting that choice whose worst possible outcome is better for the individual than the worst possible outcome of any of the other available options would be a response to the problem, but there is no one rational rule. The evaluator here has reached a terrain without adequate guideposts. We seem to have an intractable conceptual problem in the identification of interests.

Interests, shortsightedness, and time preference

One area of want satisfaction in which irrationality typically involves a one-sided bias rather than random errors is that of the intertemporal distribution of want satisfaction. The bias is due to a general tendency by the individual toward shortsightedness. However, the irrationality of shortsightedness is not easily identified, and even if it is corrected for, we still have not identified interests because these depend not on the constrained rationality of individuals, but on ideal-observer rationality. These two points can be elaborated by reference to the time preference rate, which refers to the payoff in future benefits that an individual requires in order to forgo benefits in the present. Shortsightedness will raise the time preference rate, but a positive time preference rate does not reveal shortsightedness, since it may be positive for reasons that do not represent individual irrationality. A positive time preference rate may be a rational response (1) to certain kinds of uncertainty and (2) to a certain pattern of changes in the future.

(1) Uncertainty may apply to the pattern of want-satisfaction opportunities in the future as well as to the duration of one's lifetime. Uncertainty about the future increases time preference because (a) the individual cannot be sure that when he provides for the future he will then still be alive to enjoy the benefits,[5] and (b) even when the expected value of certain provisions for the future can be ascertained, the individual is averse to the risk of getting an inferior outcome and so requires a risk premium beyond the expected value to make the appropriate sacrifices in the present for benefits in the future. It has been argued that in order to derive a social time preference rate from the private time preference rates of individuals, this uncertainty factor should be removed, because society as a whole does not face the uncertainties concerning survival and circumstances that the individual faces. (See Samuelson's and Baumol's positions in Millward 1971:188.) The issue here, however, is not what is rational for society, but what are the interests of individuals. In terms of the constrained rationality of individuals, a risk discount of future benefits may well be rational. Interests, however, are based on ideal-observer ra-

---

[5] For a discussion of increasing time preference with increasing age, based on a rational probability calculation, see Millward 1971:168.

tionality, or approximations to it. In this perspective, the interests of individuals are to be identified in the absence of uncertainties.

In other words, the distribution of levels of want satisfaction over time that is in the interest of individuals is that which is rational in the absence of uncertainty. Time preference owing to uncertainty, then, is a symptom of the impairment of interests through the existence of uncertainty for individuals and their lack of protection from its consequences.

(2) The alternative source of a positive time preference rate that does not represent individual irrationality is the prospect of a certain pattern of changes in the future. No uncertainty needs to be involved here. One conventionally recognized reason for a positive time preference rate, consistent with rationality, is that the individual's level of want satisfaction (measured, for example, in constant money value) will be rising and that his marginal valuation of want satisfaction will decline with increasing levels. Another reason may be that the individual has children, so that the family's want-satisfaction level has to be greater now, when the children are dependent, than later in order to keep the adults' level of want satisfaction constant over time. These are considerations that an ideal observer would take fully into account so that their impact on the time preference rate could be taken to reflect the individual's interests in the rationalistic sense of the latter.

Thus a positive time preference rate may reflect the interests of the individual; but it may also be due to uncertainty considerations relevant to constrained rationality, not to interests; or it may be due to shortsightedness, which is irrational both from the ideal-observer perspective and from the constrained perspective of the individual. A time preference rate that is positive in the absence of uncertainties and of prospective or required variations in the level of want satisfaction is presumably to be attributed to shortsightedness, that is, to individual irrationality. But on what basis do we describe such time preference as irrational? How do we know that it is a "defect" in the individual's "telescopic faculty" (Pigou 1920/1932:24–5) that is wholly responsible and not simply a basic want by the individual for a higher valuation of present want satisfaction than of future want satisfaction? One possible test is regret in the future; but this introduces the conflict between current wants and wants in the future, which will be considered next.

Interests and regret

It has been implicit in the preceding discussion that to the extent that they are ideal-observer-rational, wants *in the present* represent the individual's interests in the present *and* the future. This assumption will be maintained, and any inconsistency between what an individual *currently* wants for himself now and in the future, on the one hand, and what *in the future* he will want, on the other hand, will be taken as a sign of irrationality. Such inconsistencies then raise the question what represents rationality, or, alternatively, the potentially more manageable question how we should correct for the apparent irrationalities.

This question will be answered for two distinguishable kinds of inconsistency: (1) the inconsistency between at the present time wanting *specific* things now and in the future, on the one hand, and in the future wanting different *specific* things to have happened now and to be happening in the future, on the other; and (2) the inconsistency between now wanting a certain distribution of *levels* of want satisfaction *in general* over the period from now into the future, on the one hand, and in the future wanting a different distribution of want-satisfaction *levels* over the same period. As shorthand labels, I will refer to inconsistency (1) as "constitutive intertemporal inconsistency" and to (2) as "distributional intertemporal inconsistency."

(1) In the case of constitutive intertemporal inconsistencies, the question arises (a) whether it is the future wants that are afflicted by irrationality so that the present wants need no correction, (b) whether the rational wants are the contemporaneous wants so that present wants represent only interests in the present, and future wants represent interests at that time, or (c) whether the later the wants are expressed the less susceptible they will be to irrationality, so that future wants represent not only interests in the future but also interests in the present. The cases for arguments (b) and (c) are at the same time arguments against accepting present wants as appropriate representations of interests for the future.

The case for argument (c) rests on the notion that we become more experienced and wiser as we grow older. In other words, our level of irrationality declines with age. If this is the case and if the individual does not suffer from imperfections in memory, then the best vantage point from which an individual can identify his interests is the highest age he reaches. (If the improvement of rationality with age is more significant than the diversity of interests between individuals, this notion provides an argument for a gerontocratic form of government, provided that the elderly oligarchs can be trusted to govern benevolently.) Deathbed regrets (not as feeling states but as judgments) then become the most important indication of irrationality and of how present wants need to be corrected to approximate interests more closely. An interest-regarding evaluation would then be mostly concerned with how well economic systems serve individuals according to their retrospective assessments of their lives.

Retrospective assessments, however, are clearly fallible, owing to the fading of experiences in the individual's memory. Thus Pigou (1920/1932:25) claimed that "our telescopic faculty is defective" not just in our concern with the future, but also when "we contemplate the past." Although a person may be wiser and more experienced in his old age, this does not mean that in every respect he is in a better position to identify his interests as a young person than he was when he *was* a young person. To the extent that current preoccupations and pursuits are essential elements in interests in the present and to the extent that the individual gradually forgets them with time, it is contemporaneous wants that best represent interests. As a matter of fact, a case can be made for treating retrospective assessments of interests with as much caution and suspicion as the assessment of one individual's interests by another individual. Just as individual B may not sufficiently understand individual A to know what is best for him, so the individual in life stage B may be too distant from life stage A to be in the best position to articulate his interests in life stage A.

Certainly the converse – generally treating present wants for the future as the best representation of interests in the future – does not make sense. Interests in the future are represented either by contemporaneous wants at that time or by such wants corrected for irrationalities that afflict them at that time.[6] Thus interest-regarding evaluations of how well different economic policies or systems provide for the future of individuals depend not on current wants for the future but on wants in the future, that is, on wants that have to be *predicted*.[7] However, to go beyond that statement and indicate exactly the basis

[6] One possible exception to the priority position of wants in the future over interests in the future is the case of a prior commitment designed to avert mistakes in subsequent choices. See Elster 1982:222 and Brandt 1982:180 on this point. However, though such commitments may in some special instances reduce irrationality in the choices of an individual, they are not a reliable guide to the individual's future interests, given the kind of person he will be in the future and the particular circumstances he will be in at that time.

[7] This position differs from Brandt's. Brandt (1979:247–53 and 1982:179–82) has argued that *the* objection to a want conception of interests is that because wants can occur at any time and apply to any time, the program to maximize want satisfaction is overdetermined and thus unintelligible. The criterion of rationality cannot resolve inconsistencies between wants at different points in time (1979:85–7). This position, however, relies on a conception of rationality that is more constrained than the ideal-observer conception that I have employed in the rationalistic formulation of interests. Brandt's conception will be discussed in the next section.

for the necessary corrections cannot be done by reference to a particular category of want, but requires ascertaining how adequate or inadequate the knowledge of the individual will be at that time, not only concerning his environment, but also concerning his own nature.

(2) Before we turn to the question of self-knowledge, the second kind of inconsistencies, that is, distributional intertemporal inconsistencies, have to be discussed. Taking such intertemporal inconsistencies concerning the preferred distribution of levels of want satisfaction over time as evidence of irrationality, we can say that a positive time preference is ideal-observer-rational only if the discounting of want satisfaction will still be approved by the individual in retrospective assessments in the future. If such consistency does not emerge, the question is whether there are objective standards for rationality in intertemporal distribution.

One possibility is to apply the analogy between different persons and different life stages to this problem and to apply a criterion of distributive justice to the intertemporal distribution for the individual. However, it is not clear which criterion of distributive justice is appropriate here. Presumably, it means that we demand neutrality between, or equality of concern for, the different life periods. But pure equality does not make sense because it rules out improvements in living conditions with increasing age, even when they do not require sacrifices at a younger age. The maximin criterion is not satisfactory either, because although it does not rule out the former situation as unjust, it nevertheless declares unjust any sacrifices at a younger age for improvements in living conditions later, even when the sacrifices are minimal and the improvements substantial. When we are dealing with the same individual, it does make sense to allow that improvements in the future may more than compensate for sacrifices in the present. Does this perspective mean that simple aggregation of want satisfaction across the lifetime of an individual represents ideal-observer rationality? Quite apart from one consequence whose acceptability is doubtful, namely, that an eighty-year-long life in poverty is equivalent to a forty-year-long life with twice as high a standard of living, it is not clear that the assumption of the diminishing marginal valuation of levels of want satisfaction (assessed in opportunity costs or real purchasing power) adequately explains the aversion of individuals to fluctuating living standards. The conclusion that it does not emerges from at least one argument, namely, that valuation functions are not stable over time but have their shape and movement determined by individuals' past experience with living standards. (See, e.g., Duesenberry 1949:76–89 and Heath 1974:197–9.)

It seems that we have no definitive objective criterion for rationality in the intertemporal distribution of levels of want satisfaction, but must ask whether the individual, *in his subjective consideration* of this question, has met the requirements of epistemic and practical rationality. What these requirements imply for the determination of ultimate wants, as the wants concerning the intertemporal distribution of levels of want satisfaction can be classified, will be explored under the issue of self-knowledge.

A certain position has emerged from this discussion of interests regarding the future. With respect to the structure of interests *in* the future, predictable wants in the future are a potentially closer approximation than present wants for the future, although in a variety of instances the latter may be used as a basis for predicting wants in the future. But this is merely an approximation, and a further rationality assessment is still required to identify interests. With respect to the intertemporal distribution of rational-want satisfaction, there is no obvious rule that emanates from the criterion of ideal-observer rationality. It does not seem possible to use the rationality criterion to make judgments about interests that do not require an exploration of the adequacy of the knowledge and decision-making processes that the wants of individuals are based on. This caveat applies also to the last issue area to be dealt with under the rationalistic conception of interests, namely, that of self-knowledge and irrationality in ultimate wants.

5.5 Limits to self-knowledge and irrationality in ulterior preferences

Self-regarding irrationality and ultimate preferences

The problem of knowledge applies not only to the current and future external environment of the individual, but also to the individual himself. The individual is prone to serious mistakes if, in spite of his knowledge of the objective nature of private goods and services, environments, jobs, and relations, he does not know the impacts that they will have on what he directly or ultimately wants and values (or wishes to avoid and values negatively). He may make mistakes because he incorrectly predicts the benefits he will derive and the costs he will incur in certain choices (e.g., in mental states he values). The reason is that ulterior preferences lie behind the expressed preferences, and because of inadequate self-knowledge, the former are poorly served by the latter. More significant, however, are the questions whether the ulterior preferences can be irrational and how interests are to be conceived when that is the case.

Ultimate preferences are those which do not derive from, or serve, other, ulterior preferences. If we are to be able to assess their rationality, however, it is necessary that they be nevertheless contingent on factual conditions, as well as internal consistency requirements, and so the ultimate, or at least potentially ultimate, preferences may be mistaken either because they are based on insufficient or erroneous knowledge or because they are inconsistent. Two different perspectives on the significance of this contingency can be identified. One is that ultimate preferences *are* contingent on beliefs and mental processes concerning the comparison of consequences; since these beliefs may be mistaken and the thought processes inadequate to the assurance of consistency, such preferences can be irrational. (This position is taken in Brandt 1979:ch. 6. Brandt has used the term "intrinsic desires and aversions"; I am treating "ultimate" and "intrinsic" as synonymous in their role as qualifiers of wants, desires, and preferences, and I am treating "wants," etc., as including aversions.)

The alternative perspective is that ultimate preferences are to be conceived in such a way that they are *not* contingent in this manner.[8] Even though they can then not be irrational, the problem of identifying ultimate preferences, in this strong sense of "ultimate," is such that we can speak only of *potentially ultimate* preferences. This point is made very well by Sen (1970:63) with respect to "basic" and derivative value judgements; it applies equally well to preferences:

We may *ask* a person concerned whether a certain judgment is basic to his value system. But since no one would have had occasion to consider all conceivable alternative factual circumstances and to decide whether in any of the cases he would change the judgment or not, his answer to the question may not be conclusive. Another method is to ask the person concerned to think of a series of suitable revisions of factual assumptions, and ask him whether in any of the cases considered he will change his judgment. The process never establishes basicness, thought it can establish that the judgment is nonbasic in any obviously relevant way.

---

8 This position is represented by Amartya K. Sen (1970:59–64), if we apply to preferences the distinctions that he used for value judgments; he treated "basic" and "ultimate" concerns as noncontingent. Oppenheim (1975:261), too, seemed to adopt this position when he wrote that "our proposed language thus rules out stating that it is in A's interest to adopt one rather than another intrinsic preference." However, Oppenheim's further comments are confusing in this respect; he conceded that the assertion "that the criteria of rationality and of self-interest do not apply to the choice of 'ultimate goals' does not mean that they pertain only to 'means'" (p. 261), without indicating what lies between means and ultimate goals.

It is interesting to note that some value judgments are demonstrably non-basic, but no value judgment is demonstrably basic. Of course, it may be useful to *assume* that some value judgments, not shown to be obviously non-basic, *are* basic, until and unless a case crops up when the supposition is shown to be wrong. In this respect there is an obvious analogy with the practice in epistemology of accepting tentatively a factual hypothesis as true, until and unless some new observations refute that hypothesis.

Potentially ultimate preferences have, in this respect, the same status as hypothetically basic value judgments. To the extent that they are contingent on beliefs and reasoning the preferences are not ultimate in this more demanding sense.

Regardless of whether we use "ultimate preferences" in the relatively broad sense that admits their contingency or in the restricted sense that rules out this contingency, the preferences that are relevant are those ulterior preferences which are contingent and those whose ultimacy in the restricted sense is only provisional. This actual or potential contingency means that they are susceptible to irrationality.

Self-knowledge as a requirement of rationality

An important form of irrationality to which ulterior preferences are susceptible is inadequate self-knowledge. Three recent writers who have emphasized this possibility are Connolly (1974), Michael F. McDonald (1978), and Brandt (1979). McDonald has referred to the case of the individual who may "get what he wants but doesn't like what he gets" (p. 109); the attainment of his life goals leaves him dissatisfied. It is a case of "self-regarding failure" (p. 109) and irrationality in ends (p. 112).

Similarly, Connolly (1974), who has been concerned to keep "the choice criterion . . . fully operative" (p. 69) in his proposed concept of "real interests," has conceived of the latter as represented by the hypothetical choice that would emerge from full awareness by the individual of "the factors entering into [alternative] experiences and helping to make each what it is" (p. 68). There are two features of this criterion that warrant emphasis in the present context. The first is that it requires self-awareness to the point where it "includes the agent's explicit recognition of any *desires or inclinations basic to his nature* that must somehow be confronted (that is, expressed, repressed, sublimated, deflected) in any social setting" (pp. 68–9). In other words, ultimate preferences can be irrational if they are not related to appropriate cognizance by the individual of his psychological predispositions and pattern of reactions to different kinds of sanctions. The second is that the notion of awareness requires not merely having the relevant information, but having had the relevant *experiences* (pp. 64–5).

Brandt (1979) has focused on the question of the rationality of conditioned wants and, unlike most political theorists, has stressed the significance of individuals developing in a state of immaturity. In this context he has provided a criterion for distinguishing between conditioned ultimate wants that are rational and those that are irrational. He has defined "a desire or aversion [as] 'rational' if and only if it is what it would have been had the person undergone *cognitive psychotherapy*" (p. 11). It is this notion of cognitive psychotherapy with which Brandt has given some meaning to the idea of being fully aware of the nature of one's preferences; it is, moreover, a quite strong interpretation because it involves changes in ultimate preferences. He has defined cognitive psychotherapy as the

process of confronting desires with relevant information by repeatedly representing it, in an ideally vivid way, and at an appropriate time. . . . I call it ["cognitive"] because the process relies simply upon reflection on available information, without influence by prestige of someone, use of evaluative language, extrinsic reward or punishment, or use of artificially induced feeling-states like relaxation. It is *value-free reflection*. [P. 113; emphasis in original]

What is the nature of this representation within cognitive psychotherapy? Cognitive psychotheray requires full awareness of the origin of a want and the consequences of the want in the present and the future. Wants, including ultimate wants, are irrational if they can be extinguished by such awareness; alternatively, though the wants themselves may not be extinguished, cognitive psychotherapy may alter their intensity, so that it is the degree of the latter that is designated as irrational (Brandt 1979:120). New wants may also be created by cognitive psychotherapy; therefore, by this definition of rationality, the absence of certain wants can also be irrational. The process is one of "changing through patient self-stimulation by true statements" – a process that has apparently been applied successfully as therapy in "making excessive alcohol consumption aversive, reducing the craving for the approval of other people, mitigating the aversiveness of being alone, reducing the aversiveness of being self-assertive in relation to one's spouse or employer, reducing the intensity of the desire to achieve in all situations, and reducing the desire to smoke" (p. 114). This suggests that conditioned wants and aversions can be reconditioned by certain forms of cognition.

It may be helpful to summarize quickly the theory of conditioning that Brandt (1979:100–9) has used. He has regarded two processes as basic: contiguity (i.e., associative) conditioning and stimulus generalization (i.e., generalizing from a particular cause–effect experience to a whole class of causes). Conditioning may take a variety of forms, including a child's identification with or imitation of models (e.g., parents). Deconditioning can occur by three causal mechanisms: (1) counter-conditioning, in which a new response is developed to suppress a previous conditioned response to a particular stimulus; (2) inhibition, which breaks the association between two stimuli (e.g., hunger and the bell for Pavlov's dogs), so that the conditioned stimulus (the bell) has an effect that diminishes and finally extinguishes with increasing experience of the unconditioned stimulus (hunger) in the absence of the conditioned stimulus (the bell); (3) discrimination between situations in order to reduce the generalization of responses from one situation to others. Cognitive deconditioning then requires that counter-conditioning, inhibition, and discrimination be accomplished by true cognitions, but ones that create vivid and repeated awareness.

Apart from the serious difficulty of actually identifying interests that are free of the irrationality indicated by dissatisfaction or regret, by inadequate self-knowledge, or by inadequate awareness of the origin of one's preferences, there are two difficulties with this conception of interests that need to be discussed. One is the question whether we are still dealing with a preference-based conception of interests at all, particularly when we are dealing with the interests of children and unborn generations, as we must when we consider how well policies with long-term effects or economic systems provide for individuals' interests in the future. The other is the question whether it is in the interest of individuals *not* to have their irrational preferences satisfied, assuming these preferences remain unreformed.

The hierarchy of preferences

Referring back to Section 5.2 and the concept of characteristics preferences developed there, we must now ask whether characteristics preferences can really be taken to represent ends. Even though they were distinguished from instrumental preferences, there is no prima facie reason why characteristics preferences, in turn, cannot be instrumental to still more basic wants. There may be a whole chain of instrumental wants between actual behavior and desired ends. This extension of the notion of instrumental preferences leads to what Rothenberg (1968:330) has called a "hierarchy of wants": "Just as some commodities are improper means to achieving certain ends, so some proximate ends are less important than, and are inefficiently addressed to attaining, more ultimate ends." (It should be noted that the notion of a hierarchy here is quite different from that involved in A. H. Maslow's "hierarchy of needs," which involves a lexicographic ordering of ends.)

In this hierarchy of wants, which, when weighted, becomes a hierarchy of preferences, mistakes of the following kinds are possible at the instrumental levels. (1) The individual may be unaware or not willing to accept that two intermediate wants, such as having an absorbing job and pursuing a strenuous night life, may be incompatible. (2) Although intermediate want B serves ultimate want Z better than intermediate want A does, the individual may be unaware of the possibility or superiority of want B. (3) The individual may not recognize that wants instrumental to ultimate want Z may affect other ultimate wants as well. Thus the pursuit of a promotion at work may result in a loss in the quality of work friendships, and this change may be unanticipated by the individual. (4) The individual may not, and in fact not be able to, weigh *all* the intermediate wants from which choices have to be made. Consequently, certain ultimate wants may be overemphasized while others are emphasized less than would be optimal for ultimate-want satisfaction. To the extent that the individual cannot mentally process the complex optimization calculations involved, his intermediate preferences will be less than optimal.

As long as rationality involves simply the question how well instrumental preferences serve ultimate preferences, the major task is that of isolating ultimate from instrumental preferences. That task in itself is highly problematic. However, drawing that distinction does not help us in a fundamental way, unless we can formulate ultimate preferences so that they are not dependent on beliefs and reasoning. Since we are unlikely to be able to do so, we have to concede that even ultimate preferences are prone to irrationality.

Given the general susceptibility of preferences to irrationality, what does rationality now require? It has to be applied to the question what is to be done. In particular, rationality judgments apply to two quite different questions: (1) What preferences is it rational to develop? and (2) what preferences is it rational to fulfill? These two different rationality questions also point to different conceptions of interests, namely, "developmental interests" and "satisfactional interests." Developmental interests are those preferences (as well as capacities) that it is rational for the individual to develop. Satisfactional interests are the rational want of the individual to have his preferences, with or without qualification, satisfied.

Developmental interests

Developmental possibilities become progressively more open-ended and indeterminate as we move in our consideration from a person near the end of his life, to an adult open to development and change in a limited way, to a child with some developed dispositions but also much openness to different avenues of development, to a newborn with certain constitutional predispositions that can, however, emerge in quite different personality traits, and, finally, to those who will be conceived and born in the future and whose genetic makeup is not yet determined. A rationality assessment of preferences in terms of cognitive psychotherapy may be appropriate for adults, but it seems less appropriate for children, and it is ineffective as a criterion for the developmental interests of the unborn. It seems quite beyond a preference-based conception of interests to identify the latter.

A qualification concerning the appropriateness of the cognitive-psychotherapy criterion to the conception of the developmental interests of adults is in order here. It requires in one way too much and in another way too little. Concerning the reversal of developments that have already occurred – reversals that are developments in themselves – cognitive psychotherapy will be warranted only if the benefits to the individual exceed its costs (in resources, effort, and pain); if they do not, then it will be developmentally rational for the individual simply to accept the cognitive-psychotherapy-irrational preferences. To put it the other way round, the cognitive-psychotherapy criterion may demand a development that is not developmentally rational. On the other hand, if, instead of considering the correction of earlier development, we consider the possibility of future development, the retrospective orientation of the cognitive-psychotherapy criterion demands too little. If the criterion approves of any preference that will not be extinguished or mitigated by later cognitive psychotherapy, then its implication seems to be that the development of that preference is to be approved in the first instance. However, the only reason why later cognitive psychotherapy does not alter it may be that the conditioning has been so deep that it is irreversible or too costly to reverse. This does not mean that it should have taken place in the first instance. A development is not beneficial simply because it is irreversible. It is quite possible that an individual, after his conditioning, feels that he would have been better off without it but that it is now best for him to accept it and live with it.

This difficulty applies to Connolly's hypothetical-choice criterion as well. This criterion is attractive as long as we can treat aging and the accumulation of experience as an expansion of the epistemic horizons of individuals. But we cannot always do so. Connolly (1974:82n38) himself has pointed to "the case of a rather contented person who is convicted of a crime and several years later comes to prefer the security and routine of prison life to freedom in the larger society." The individual, being fully aware of all the relevant facts, would normally not prefer to be conditioned by prison life when considering it as a possibility, but once it has occurred he may come to prefer to live with it. Of course, we can still say it was unambiguously against his developmental interests if he, at the same time, feels that he would have been better off without this conditioning experience. In other words, going to prison was against his developmental interests, but now staying in prison can be in his satisfactional interest.

However, another example given by Connolly (1974:72) suggests that such a solution to this problem of developmental interests is not always possible. He cited the case of a young woman who had joined the anti–Vietnam war movement and who said that if, before joining, she had been able to predict what was going to happen to her she would have decided against joining, but who in retrospect felt that it was the right thing to have done. It is really a changed person, in a sense a different person, who is expressing the latter preference, and such shifts in potentially ideal-observer-rational preferences make it unclear which ones indicate the individual's developmental interests. (Cf. Wall 1975:505 on the difficulty in Connolly's approach of distinguishing between mistaken interests and changed interests.) Thus there is an indeterminacy in developmental interests not only for the unborn, but also for contemporaries, including adults. (That indeterminacy applies as well to McDonald's dissatisfaction criterion, if we interpret it to refer to retrospective preferences rather than to mental states.)

Satisfactional interests

The remaining problem concerning the conceptualization of interests that is to be dealt with here is that of the satisfaction of preferences that are irrational. Normally, it is simply regarded as irrational to fulfill preferences that would not persist if the individual had better information or reasoning. However, if, given the constrained ra-

tionality of the individual, it is not rational for the individual to reform his preferences, should an economic system then respond to the
hypothetically reformed preferences or should it respond to the *actual*
preferences, even though they are ideal-observer-irrational? No clear
answer emerges from the notion of satisfactional interests. If satisfactional interests are those preferences which it is ideal-observer-rational to satisfy, then the ideal observer has to visualize himself with
the irrational preferences of the given individual and ask himself (1)
whether he will be better off having his actual preferences frustrated
and making choices (or having them made for him) to satisfy preferences that *would* be rational, or (2) whether satisfying his actual preferences is more important than fulfillment of hypothetically reformed preferences that he does not hold, or (3) whether he is best
off to strike a balance between these two solutions.

Brandt (1979:160–2) has made an argument for solution (1). According to him, even if a preference that could be extinguished by
cognitive psychotherapy has not been so extinguished, it is normally
rational to avoid the action motivated by the, in this sense, irrational
preference. The reason given is that the fulfillment of such preferences is not very satisfying; and in the case of aversions, "if the existence of irrational aversions tends to lead to unhappiness, so does
action based on them" (p. 162). However, Brandt has allowed an
exception in the extreme case of "an irrational desire that is so strong
that the individual would be made deeply unhappy, perhaps even
neurotic, by its suppression" (p. 161). I have two objections to this
position, at least as far as a preference-based conception of interests is
concerned. One is that it is not clear why preferences based on ignorance or inappropriate reasoning and their fulfillment should normally lead to unhappiness or why only in exceptional cases unhappiness should result from frustrating such preferences. Preferences
may be based on blissful ignorance, and their fulfillment need not
change this situation. The second objection is that the ultimate criterion has really become happiness rather than preferences qualified
with the requirement of rationality. If we remain wholly within the
framework of the latter criterion, then, while we can distinctly con-
ceptualize satisfactional interests, it is not clear whether it is ideal-
observer-rational to fulfill or frustrate ideal-observer-irrational
preferences.

Solution (2), simply to fulfill preferences regardless of their irrationality, seems simply foolish in many cases. For government to remove certain opportunities, such as those for experimenting with
addictive drugs, or to inhibit the more extreme forms of adolescent

bravado expressed through self-endangering acts, may violate current preferences, but may be justified as rational because of the serious and irreversible consequences involved. That leaves solution (3), which is a mixture of (1) and (2). We can visualize an ideal observer who takes the frustration of irrational preferences into account together with everything else, in identifying what it is satisfactionally rational to do. Beyond this very abstract criterion, however, it is difficult to see how to formulate rationality criteria for satisfactional interests that would be of use for the design and evaluation of economic policies and systems.

We thus seem to have an indeterminacy concerning satisfactional interests that compounds the difficulties raised earlier. These arose from the epistemic and practical irrationalities in the preferences of individuals and consisted of problems in finding appropriate remedies for them. One was that expert evaluators are by no means the equivalent of the ideal observer and are capable of making mistakes, about both the ulterior preferences of individuals and their situations, as well as of having less than full integrity. However, even if the preferences and environmental conditions of individuals were fully known, there are still important conceptual indeterminacies in the rationalistic conception of interests that have been identified. (1) When there is uncertainty about the future, different responses to it can lay claim to being rational. (2) It is not clear whether constitutive intertemporal inconsistencies in preferences are to be resolved by reference to contemporaneous preferences or to later retrospective preferences. (3) This indeterminacy applies also to distributive intertemporal inconsistencies; in this case, however, there are also other possible criteria of rationality, such as intertemporal equality. (4) A notion of interests that consists of preferences corrected for epistemic and practical mistakes does not provide a criterion for the formulation of the developmental interests of the young and the unborn. (5) Now we also find that when satisfactional preferences are irrational, it is not really clear what the rational response to such irrationalities is, that is, what is in the individual's satisfactional interest.

CHAPTER 6

The development of preferences and the evaluation circularity

6.1   Interests, preferences, and the evaluation circularity

The evaluation circularity

To recognize that preferences, including ulterior preferences, are not simply given, but develop in a particular social context, is to open the door to a problem area that is still more serious for the interest-regarding optimization and evaluation in and of economic systems, as they have been conceived so far, than are the problems identified in the discussion of rationality. The problem area is that of feedback effects from the institutions and processes of production and distribution to the preferences that serve as the basis for identifying interests.

The significance of these feedback effects for optimization and evaluation is here described by the term "evaluation circularity." It refers to the partial means–end inversion that is involved when the means (that is, the system of production and distribution or particular processes in it) that are to be optimized or evaluated with respect to the end (that is, the fulfillment of preferences that represent interests) shape the composition of this end. What is being evaluated determines, in part, the criterion by which it is being evaluated. It is as though the gauge to be used for measurement were to be calibrated, in the process of measurement, on the basis of characteristics of the particular object being measured.

The issue that the concept of the evaluation circularity refers to is more specific and limited than the general point that social ends are shaped by social processes. Clearly, the basic values of society are to a considerable extent determined by the particular structure and culture of that society. In a theocratic society the goal of piety will be promoted; in a capitalist society material prosperity and freedom in economic initiatives will be encouraged; and in a socialist society perhaps cooperation and communal enjoyments will be stressed. The assessment of the extent of piety, for example, in all three types of societies would be biased against the latter two types. This kind of fundamental bias in the *selection* of evaluation criteria may be unavoidable. It is an important issue, but it is not what the concept of the evaluation circularity specifically refers to. Instead, the evaluation circularity results from a certain open-endedness of the evaluation criterion such that the way the criterion is *filled in* is determined by the social system that is to be evaluated.

More precisely, the evaluation circularity involves two conditions, one a precondition consisting of open-endedness in the evaluation criterion and the other the condition that defines the evaluation circularity:

1. *The open-endedness condition:*
    The evaluation criterion is multidimensional and, in itself, does not specify the dimensions or the weights that make them commensurable.
2. *The condition of the evaluation circularity:*
    The open-endedness in the evaluation criterion is removed by applying data that are determined, at least in part, by the object being evaluated. (For a technical clarification of the evaluation circularity see the Appendix to this chapter. The comparability problem that is discussed in Chapter 7 also arises from the open-endedness condition and is related to, but distinct from, the evaluation circularity.)

The evaluation circularity and preferences

Preferences, when used as the basis for the evaluation of economic improvements, especially long-run ones, or of economic systems, give rise to the circularity, because, as will be shown, they are characterized both (1) by the precondition of open-endedness and (2) by the circularity condition. Condition (1) is met conceptually, since many preferences are possible and these are not specified by the criterion itself. Condition (2), that of the evaluation circularity as such, is met empirically, in that, as a matter of observation or empirical hypothesis, preferences are shaped by the particular economic system or those processes of production and distribution which are structured by the policies to be assessed.

The effect of the evaluation circularity on the preference-based conception of interests can occur at two levels. First, when ideal-observer-rational preferences are subject to the evaluation circularity, interests themselves are too. Secondly, when it is the divergence of actual preferences from ideal-observer-rational preferences that is subject to the evaluation circularity, it is not interests as such, but a crucial form of information about them, that is affected by the evaluation circularity. In both cases, the susceptibility of preferences to the evaluation circularity is relevant to the attractiveness of the preference-based conception of interests as an optimization and evaluation criterion.

The evaluation circularity in a preference-based criterion is referred to in economics as the problem of endogenous, as opposed to exogenous, preferences. That is to say, preferences are endogenous to – that is, internally generated by – some aspect of the process for satisfying them. There are two reasons for preferring the term "evaluation circularity" to the term "endogenous preferences." One is that reference to the evaluation circularity emphasizes the normative difficulty resulting from endogenous preferences. The second is that the evaluation circularity can apply to evaluation criteria other than that of the fulfillment of preferences. (Galbraith [1958/1969:143 and 1970:472] has used the term "dependence effect." It, too, seems to me less illuminating than "circularity.")[1]

The condition that defines the evaluation circularity, that is, (2), can, in the case of the preference criterion, be broken down into four more specific conditions that are all necessary: (a) that preference structures not be completely innate, (b) that preference structures not be completely autonomous or self-determined (in a certain very demanding sense to be indicated in the next subsection), (c) that the development of preferences in a social context not be wholly haphazard but be characterized by a distinctive pattern, and (d) that the social patterning of preferences be affected by the system of production and distribution.

The rejection of completely innate or self-determined preferences

With respect to condition (a), there is really no question that the pattern of human pursuits is not fully determined by a set of instincts. Even from a "biological perspective" human beings are merely "structurally limited" and characterized by "undefined impulses, which may be defined or specified by a wide range of objects. What these objects may be is not determined by man as an organism" (Gerth and Mills 1953:10; cf. Marcuse 1964/1968:18; Galbraith 1967:17 and 212; and

---

[1] Alfred Marshall, Frank H. Knight, and Friedrich A. von Hayek seem to have regarded the generation of wants as a laudable aspect of the evolution of civilization (Myint 1948:132–4; Hayek 1960–1/1975:8; Doyle 1968:589). Endogenous preference formation is also recognized in Pigou 1920/1932:82–4; Dobb 1969:227; Weizsaecker 1971:345–6; and Gintis 1972a:276 and 1972b:578–9, 585.

Boulding 1969:2). Even quite basic needs are subject to cultural molding. (For a persuasive argument to this effect see, e.g., Kapp 1961:esp. 148–55.) Thus the want to eat, an innate need and want, will vary according to choices about what to eat, how much to eat, and in which setting to eat. All these things are not fully determined genetically.

Condition (b), the lack of autonomy in preferences, represents the violation of a condition that one of the conceptions of consumer sovereignty discussed in Chapter 2 is built upon. According to Thompson's (1973/1977:90–1) conception, the consumer "is assumed to respond only to wants that he originates or needs which are given to him by his environment. He is, above all, independent. . . ." The emphasis on independence or autonomy is a response to the threat posed by the evaluation circularity to the attractiveness of consumer sovereignty, or any other preference-based constitutive conception of sovereignty, as a normative principle.

Lukes (1973:52) has defined autonomy as the ideal

according to which an individual's thought and action is his own, and not determined by agencies or causes outside his control. In particular, an individual is autonomous (at the social level) to the degree to which he subjects the pressures and norms with which he is confronted to conscious and critical evaluation, and forms intentions and reaches practical decisions as the result of independent and rational reflection.

This conception of autonomy, though it is very demanding, is still not sufficiently strong to assure freedom from the evaluation circularity. First of all, even if the individual is fully capable of rejecting social pressures and promptings, it does not mean that those considerations and possibilities that he takes into account in his critical evaluations and those that he neglects will not be determined by the pattern of pressures and norms. What we require is ideal-observer rationality, not the constrained rationality of the individual. Constrained rationality, apart from being a difficulty in its own right for the conception of interests, also sets limits to the pursuit of autonomy. Secondly, freedom from the evaluation circularity not only requires that an individual's pursuits be *now* subjected to critical evaluation, as in Brandt's cognitive psychotherapy, but demands that the individual's *past* development, which determines his current preferences, shall have been autonomous. This is a clearly impossible condition, given the immature state in which the most significant phases of our personality development occur.

Autonomy in this strong sense is therefore as inappropriate (in the form either of a descriptive assumption or of a prescriptive demand) as the assumption of innate preferences is. What remains to be considered is whether there are distinctive patterns to the development of preferences and whether this patterning is significantly influenced by the process of production and distribution (conditions [c] and [d]). To answer these questions, we must consider different forms of preference patterning.

Forms of preference patterning

There are various ways of classifying forms of preference patterning. We can classify them in terms of (1) the social context in which the patterning occurs (families, formal organizations, mass communication audiences, or diffuse interaction); (2) the intentionality involved in patterning (deliberate, nondeliberate but approved by tradition, or incidental); (3) the psychological motivation of the individual whose preferences are being patterned (aspiring and perhaps envying, learning, desiring to belong, or adapting to constraints – for a more elaborate classification of this last dimension, together with a very interesting discussion, see Elster 1982); (4) the temporal origin of patterning (past experiences, contemporaneous perceptions, or anticipations of the future); and (5) the psychological objects of patterning (beliefs, feelings, or preferences).

The next three sections of this chapter discuss largely the first classification principle, that which distinguishes between different social contexts. More or less all the categories of the other four classification principles, that is, the degree of intentionality, the motivation, the temporal origin, and the psychological object of patterning, are involved in each of these social contexts.

This classification can be compared with a much simpler one developed by Herbert Gintis (1972a:275–7 and 1972b:584–7) in order to facilitate his discussion of preference patterning and its normative implications. His is a threefold classification consisting of "associative," "cybernetic," and "institutional" patterning. "Associative patterning" is the process by which "individuals naturally develop their capacities to derive welfare from [i.e., come to prefer] those economic bundles that they have habitually come into contact with" (1972a: 275–6). "Cybernetic patterning" is the determination by "the expected future structure of availabilities of alternative economic bundles" of individuals' choices concerning the development of their capacities (1972a:276). "Institutional patterning" is "the direct social mechanism – family, school and media – through which values and goal orientations are internalized" (1972b:587).

Although "associative" and "cybernetic" patterning seem parallel categories, "institutional" patterning is not. Both of the first two involve "adaptive preference formation" (Elster 1982), that is, a process of adapting one's preferences to what has been, is, or is likely to be available to the individual; I will subsequently refer to them as "experiential" and "anticipatory" patterning, respectively. "Institutional" patterning, however, refers to the social context in which patterning occurs; it is a quite different classification principle and may well involve experiential and anticipatory patterning, which are two temporal-origin categories applied to a particular form of psychological motivation. Of course, other kinds of psychological motivation may also be involved in "institutional patterning," such as wanting to "belong."

Further distinctions, such as that between "cognitive" and "affective" patterning made by some sociologists, will emerge in the following discussion. The five-dimensional classification proposed here is designed to accommodate such distinctions.

6.2   The patterning of consumer preferences

Forms of consumer-preference patterning

In the economic literature three forms of social patterning, as it applies to consumer preferences, can be distinguished. (1) The forms of consumption that individuals have had experience with will determine their preferences, often in favor of repeating these or closely related experiences. Patterning may actually take the form of habit formation. Endogenous determination is involved because these past experiences were chosen on the basis of the means for want satisfaction then available, so that instruments for want satisfaction that have been used in the past come to shape preferences in subsequent periods. (2) Imitation is another way in which it has been claimed that preferences are endogenously shaped. "One man's consumption becomes his neighbor's wish. This already means that the process by which wants are satisfied is also the process by which wants are created" (Galbraith 1958/1969:140). (3) Advertising is widely regarded as a process of creating or at least molding consumer wants (e.g., Galbraith 1958/1969:142–2; Scitovsky 1960/1964:237; Dobb 1969:6).

Although these forms of patterning have the potential to improve individuals' pursuit of their consumption interests, they nevertheless create difficulties for the preference-based criterion of interests in the evaluation of policies and systems. One is that their reduction of the gap between articulated preferences and interests is selective in a systematic pattern. This creates a difficulty for the approximate approach to interest-regarding evaluation suggested in Section 5.4, namely, that even if preferences are not free of errors, the general pattern of preferences can still be used as an appropriate representation of the general pattern of interests in the system, as long as errors are random. That procedure would mean that although distribution in the economic system would be imperfect, production would conform with interest-regarding optimality (assuming that the calculus requirements are also satisfied). However, if the correction of errors has a distinctive bias, so that the remaining errors in the improved preferences are no longer random, then the general pattern of preferences is no longer representative of the general pattern of interests. For example, preferences articulated without reference to past experience may be improved by relying on past experiences with consumer products and giving preference to those products that one has been relatively satisfied with. But this process creates a systematic bias against new products even when they would, on the average, satisfy rational interests more effectively than old ones. In other words, choices based on experience or habit may produce a pattern of preferences for a certain balance between established and new products that has a bias against new products relative to the structure of rational interests. The evaluation circularity is involved in system evaluation to the extent that economic systems vary in the sequence in which products are developed (e.g., home computers before counseling on human relations) and in the degree of uncertainty involved in the purchase of new products (consider, e.g., the differences between a system emphasizing consumer protection and information and one emphasizing caveat emptor).

This problem is intensified when the patterning serves not only to correct preferences, but to distort them, in the sense that it increases the deviation of preferences from interests in a nonrandom manner. Finally, the patterning can apply to interests as such so that it exposes to the evaluation circularity not merely the representation of interests by preferences, but the interests themselves.

Habitual choices and habituation

Concerning preference patterning on the basis of past experience, two distinguishable processes may be at work. One is the reliance on habitual choices; the other is the habituation of preferences. (1) Habitual choices are used as a decision-making aid when information and the capacity for practical rationality are limited. Given the costs of determining the real efficacy of wants whose satisfaction has not been experienced so far, experienced forms of want satisfaction will be given an edge over unexperienced forms in the preference structures of individuals. (2) Though habitual choices are instrumental to ulterior preferences, the habituation of wants and preferences need not be limited to instrumental wants. It covers the range of phenomena from learned tastes to unconscious conditioning to physical addiction. The costs of changing habituated wants and preferences are more profound than those of changing habitual choices. In the latter case research or experimentation may be necessary; in the former case significant psychological adjustment accompanied by severe stress may well be involved.

These two cases both give rise to the evaluation circularity, but in different ways. The form of the circularity that is common to them is that of past opportunities for consumption shaping current preferences. What has been produced in the past partly determines what will be wanted in the present and future. Since what is produced depends on the particular system of production and distribution and the pattern of policies, the system and its policies shape in a distinctive way the pattern of preferences.

The difference between habitual choices and habituated ulterior preferences lies in whether it is interests themselves or only the revealed evidence about interests that is affected by this feedback effect. The latter applies to habitual choices. Whether this systemic bias applies to an improvement of choices or a distortion of choices resulting from habitual choices is immaterial as far as the evaluation circularity is concerned; probably both improvements and distortions are normally involved. The habituation of ulterior preferences, on the other hand, makes the evaluation circularity applicable to interests as such. It is then conceptually difficult to describe the shaping process as one of improvement or distortion without introducing a criterion from outside the preference-based and rationalistic conception of interests.

Imitation

Viewed from a rationalistic perspective, the purpose of imitation is, like habitual choice, simply to assist decision making. If it is reasonable to assume that certain other individuals are better informed about the consequences of certain choices, and if the more basic preferences of the individuals that these choices serve can be expected to be similar to one's own, then imitation of these choices can be expected to satisfy one's ulterior preferences better than one's independent choices. It is not even necessary that the persons being imitated be themselves informed, only that they be part of a chain of imitation (A imitating B, who is imitating C, etc.) that is initiated by appropriate individuals and proceeds without cumulative distortions.

In the case of status wants, there is a further reason why imitation is rational. To the extent that status can be obtained by engaging in certain appropriate consumption activities, imitating some of the consumption activities of individuals who have status may be a way of attaining some status oneself. People may be imitated because they are informed about consumption activities that bring social respect to the consumer, but in some instances it may be more a case of certain consumption activities' being endowed with status because they are engaged in by individuals who already have status for other reasons.

The major effect of imitation on the overall pattern of revealed preferences is one of reducing the interpersonal diversity in preferences. Does this reduction give rise to the evaluation circularity? On its own it does not; it is conceivable for imitation to occur without preferences being shaped by the processes of production and distribution. However, under certain conditions it can intensify the circularity that arises from another social process. Two conditions that will provide for such interaction are (1) that the models for imitation be determined, at least in part, by the economic processes, and that at the same time (2) the preferences of these imitation models be more tightly shaped by these processes than those of the imitators prior to the process of imitation. An alternative version of (2) is that the imitation models be selected by the system on the basis of the suitability of their preferences to the prevailing economic processes. While it is reasonable to assume that condition (1) holds, it is not clear whether condition (2) applies extensively to consumer preferences. (In the case of work preferences, on the other hand, condition [2] may well hold to a considerable extent, since the selection of individuals for high-status work roles will depend in part on their having suitable work preferences.)

Advertising

Certain forms of advertising may serve to reduce the ignorance of consumers about consumption opportunities and their nature. To the extent that advertising acts in this way, it does so in a manner that is not costly to the consumer in effort (although it may affect the monetary cost of the product). Under appropriate conditions it may also be socially efficient, since it is information distributed by those who have ready access to it.

However, to the extent that it occurs in a market context (and possibly also in certain other kinds of systems), there is an incentive for producers and distributors to present information that is selective in a biased way, as well as to provide misleading messages. Moreover, advertising goes considerably beyond merely providing information or misinformation. It emphasizes repetition, triggers unconscious associations, and appeals to fantasies and irrational fears in a manner that is incompatible with rational decision making (Reith et al. 1966:144–55; Galbraith 1967:217 and 1970:474). The susceptibility of individuals to such processes of persuasion, which is due to their limited self-knowledge and the costs of rational decision making, induces producers to bias their choice of goods to offer in favor of those that can be made appealing by such processes (Reith et al. 1966:37; Galbraith 1967:213 and 1970:474).

Galbraith (1958/1969:200–4) has argued that advertising in contemporary capitalism, apart from shaping preferences for certain kinds of products, has created a disposition in favor of private consumption and against public services. Presumably, political persuasion does not counter this effect of advertising, since much of it is devoted to the selling of personalities rather than programs of action and since it may be directed as often against public spending as in support of it. (In a socialist system, on the other hand, advertising might have the converse tendency.) Another effect of consumer persuasion is, according to Galbraith (1967:281), a bias in favor of work and consumption at the expense of leisure. (This argument is also sometimes offered in *defense* of advertising; see Doyle 1968:588.) Finally, the inducements to consume are seen as affecting the consumption–saving choice so that individuals are no longer reliable savers (Galbraith 1967:49; according to Galbraith, this creates a framework in which the relegation of saving decisions to the corporate technostructure through retained earnings becomes socially superior to private sovereignty in this sphere).

Advertising certainly contributes to the evaluation circularity. The pattern of information and persuasion provided by it is distinctive to the processes of production and distribution of particular systems, and it serves to shape preferences to conform more closely with producer aims. How significant the circularity produced or intensified by it is depends on how deep the patterning is. If the effect is merely one of increasing demand for one brand at the expense of other brands of the same good, the patterning is relatively superficial. However, if the more serious claims of the critics of advertising are correct, we have not only brand-choice patterning, but also the patterning of *forms* of consumption, for example, in favor of cosmetics and against books, and perhaps even life-style patterning that affects the choices concerning the trade-offs among consumption, leisure, work satisfaction, and social relations. If advertising has an impact on such choices in favor of certain consumer goods and generates a bias against other kinds of wants, it patterns, for better or for worse, preferences at a much more basic level. Even though these may still be only preferences that provide information about interests rather than interests themselves, the impact may be so profound that it becomes very difficult to extract an image of interests from them that is not shaped by advertising.

Moreover, advertising may shape interests themselves. It can do so in two ways. One occurs when advertising directly affects the kind of ulterior preferences that represent satisfactional interests. Even if it is not conceded that such a process occurs directly, advertising can still have this effect in combination with habituation. Advertising may initially impinge only on instrumental preferences; but the fulfillment of these preferences then leads to habituation, so that they become ends, in the sense that it is subsequently more rational for the individual to continue to fulfill these preferences than to reform them.

6.3   The patterning of producer preferences

Work roles and their impact on preferences

In their performance of work roles in the context of formal organizations for production and distribution, people are subject to two kinds of patterning. One is that of the internalization of roles that results from their performance; the other is the preparation for the future performance of roles available in the system, where the patterning is anticipatory.

Although both forms of patterning may apply merely to instrumental preferences and thus to the accessible evidence about interests rather than to the interests themselves, in this section I will be more concerned with the direct patterning of the interests. Moreover, in contrast to the consideration of satisfactional interests in the previous section's discussion of consumer preferences, here developmental interests will be just as important as satisfactional interests.

Before beginning the discussion of preference patterning owing to the actual or prospective performance of work roles, it will be useful to clarify briefly the sociological concept of "role" and to indicate its implications for preference fulfillment in the absence of preference patterning. Roles have been defined either as complexes of behavior that follow a regular pattern and are determined by the expectations of others (Gerth and Mills 1953:10–11) or as the patterns of expectations that apply to particular social positions (Dahrendorf 1957/1973: 18, 44). In either conception expectations that structure behavior are central. This pattern of expectations, enforced by various degrees of positive and negative sanctions (or incentives, as economists would describe them), is determined, not by the idiosyncratic personalities of the individuals in the related roles, but by these roles themselves. Roles are *institutionally* interconnected. They make the behavior of individuals with particular positions predictable to others in the same institutional framework and permit cooperation between strangers and even potential enemies (Moore 1965:57). In the extreme, roles are entirely determined by the institutional nexus and not at all by the individual incumbents. One can say then that we have here an institutional equilibrium theory, in which an equilibrium internal to the institutional system is reached when all roles are complementary.

This conception of the social function and determination of roles, when applied to producer roles, does not logically entail the patterning of preferences.[2] It is conceivable that individuals simply follow the rules for their roles, so that their behavior is determined by their roles rather than by their personalities, and nothing need be implied about any impact of these roles on their personalities. Roles may be no more than contracted rules of employment (Moore 1969:875; cf. Heine 1971:59 on "role detachment"). However, most role theories assume or assert that without some form of "role internalization," role performance is not actually possible.

---

[2] As a matter of fact, it is conceptually consistent with the economist's image of work activities and their allocation as *responding*, in a market setting, to preferences. Although the strong conception of roles makes them immune to the preferences of their incumbents, it does not rule out the conclusion that roles are determined by the system's demands on the institutions in which the roles (together with resource scarcities and available techniques) are located, and these demands may represent consumer preferences; it also does not rule out the conclusion that the roles are allocated to individuals in part on the basis of their role preferences, or that institutions with unpopular role sets will disappear or be forced to adapt their roles under the pressure of the labor market. Moreover, there is also a more flexible conception of roles in sociology that allows for a certain amount of "role negotiation" by the incumbent (Goslin 1969a:7–10; cf. Dahrendorf 1957/1973:40 and Heine 1971:145, 184).

Role internalization

In the sociological literature on the adaptation of individuals to work roles, the focus has been on two processes. One is the acquisition of knowledge about the expectations that the role involves and of the skills necessary to carry out the expected tasks. The other is the internalization of certain moral values, such as conscientiousness and commitment, that can take the place of the very great and, in some instances, unmanageable degree of surveillance and hierarchical discipline that would otherwise be necessary, particularly in roles whose performance involves a considerable degree of discretion, as in the case of managers and professionals (Moore 1969:874). The openness of individuals to assimilating role expectations, skills, and values will be a criterion in their selection to fill roles. Such internalization will not give rise to the evaluation circularity, as long as the role features that are internalized remain specific to the role to which they adhere and do not shape the individual's preferences among roles, including that between the role he occupies and other roles, nor preferences in such other spheres as consumption, leisure activities, and social relations. It is unlikely, however, that these conditions hold.

There are at least two reasons why they do not. (1) Skills, once acquired, determine what kinds of roles an individual can perform with relative ease. This ease, together with the sense of competence that the individual can obtain from effective role performance, will mean that to have a role that involves previously acquired skills will, everything else being the same, be in his satisfactional interest. This situation results in an interest-regarding evaluation circularity because the set of roles that provides individuals with skills will be distinctive to particular systems of production and distribution, and the latter thus pattern satisfactional interests concerning subsequent roles.

(2) The performance of roles generally involves certain forms of conditioning and habituation. A certain set of activities is performed very frequently, the individual becomes accustomed to it, and it becomes "second nature" to him. Such habituation and perhaps attachment, in the sense that the individual becomes "comfortable" with such activities, affect not only later preferences concerning productive roles, but also other activities, such as leisure activities and forms of consumption. Conditioning is also brought about by positive and negative sanctions that back up role norms. (The relative efficacy of different kinds of external sanctions is briefly discussed in Goslin

1969a:14–16.) How people come to feel about different activities and situations is thus determined in part by their experiences with productive roles. As in the case of consumer preferences, habituation can make the evaluation circularity applicable to satisfactional interests.

Two cases of work-related patterning of preferences may be mentioned as illustrations that are potentially significant for interests. One is a claim that is occasionally made about the lack of a want for self-direction in the work world. (See, e.g., Gintis 1972a:271–2 and 1972b:591n3.) The argument is that because the capitalist system does not offer workers experience with self-management in industrial enterprises, the workers never learn to trust their own capacity to exercise democratic control over management in such a way as to keep the enterprise viable while designing work relations and processes more to their liking. If workers feel that self-management cannot work, then they will want not to be associated with worker-managed enterprises and will have a preference for hierarchically controlled enterprises. It then becomes difficult to compare a system of hierarchically controlled enterprises in which the workers prefer that kind of work setting with a worker-managed system where the workers prefer this mode of work relations, having had experience with it and possibly not having actually experienced hierarchical work relations. This difficulty might affect only instrumental preferences that can be distorted by ignorance, but if, for example, the distrust of the viability of worker-managed enterprise reflects a correct assessment of inadequate worker skills to make it work, then the impact extends to satisfactional interests themselves.

A second example of work-related patterning is the situation where the monotony of the work process leaves the worker so unstimulated and deadened that when it comes to his leisure, he selects wholly passive kinds of activities. Again, there is a problem of evaluating a system in which passive leisure activities are preferred but are the outcome of role performance. If the habituation has any significant depth, it is not just instrumental preferences that are affected, but satisfactional interests.

It might be thought that even though work roles involve socialization, individuals in general can choose roles in such a way that they choose packages that include the socialization experiences that go with the roles. This would mean that individuals choose on the basis of preferences sufficiently ulterior so that socialization experiences are instrumental to them. There are three difficulties with this position. (1) If this is an accurate description of the process, it indicates

that developmental interests are, in this respect, autonomous compared to production and distribution. Satisfactional interests, however, are not, since the extent to which the developmental interests can
be fulfilled depends on the set of roles made available by the system,
and the chosen roles then shape the satisfactional interests of the
incumbents. (2) Ideal-observer-rational choices are unlikely to be
closely approximated by the constrained-rational choices of individuals. Consequently, developmental preferences are likely to be
poor indicators of developmental interests. (3) Because of the process
of anticipatory patterning, developmental interests, too, will be
caught in the evaluation circularity.

Anticipatory patterning

Certain choices, such as those concerning education and self-development in general, are preparatory in nature. They extend the individual's capacity to engage in certain productive activities or to obtain
intrinsic enjoyment from activities. This category involves developmental preferences and interests. Gintis's argument that such choices
and the preferences from which they derive are "cybernetically patterned" – patterned through anticipation, in my terminology – is
based on the proposition that "the expected future structure of availabilities of alternative bundles and the present nature of costs of
acquisition of capacities" will be "crucial to the individual's decision as
to capacity development" (1972a:276, emphasis omitted).

Whether or not to acquire a particular work capacity (e.g. the ability to en-
dure monotony, or learn a skill) depends on his being able to exercise it – and
with what economic benefit – in the future. Conclusion: In order to choose
which capacities to develop, the individual must know the expected future
prices or more generally the terms of availability (in case no market exists for
the entity) of all goods and work-activities instrumental to the exercise of his
capacities. It follows directly that . . . , by the very logic of rational choice
behavior in a market system, expected future prices are parameters of the
preference structure, and influence the development of preferences over
time.
    This observation can be simply stated: in a market society of rational indi-
viduals, use-values are affected by the structure of exchange values.
[1974:420, emphasis omitted]

It is true that the relation of capacity development to preference
fulfillment can be interpreted in such a way that preferences remain
free of the evaluation circularity. The question is whether such an

interpretation is reasonable. As Gintis has put it, "rather than *extending* the one-period model to a multi-period one, [this particular interpretation requires that] we . . . essentially telescop[e] a multi-period to a one-period" (1974:423). To make this reasonable,

we must assume that the individual at time t = 0 has full knowledge of (a) the future price structure . . . ; (b) the way any sequence of consumptions . . . affects his capacities; and (c) the impact of any path of capacity development . . . on his welfare [or, in our current framework, on his interests]. While (a) may be reasonably defended, (b) and (c) are wildly at variance with reality. [1974:423]

The point about telescoping a multi-period model into a one-period model translates into the terms of my discussion in Chapter 5 as postulating a current set of preferences that applies to the present as well as to the rest of the individual's lifetime. As long as current preferences, both for the present and for the future, are not only rational but also consistent with both constitutive and distributive intertemporal preferences in the future, developmental preferences are safe from the evaluation circularity. Any of the following quite likely conditions, however, will rule this out.

(1) Distributive intertemporal preferences may change over time. The preference-based and rationalistic conception of interests is unclear in this case, as was indicated in Chapter 5.

(2) Uncertainty concerning future circumstances and concerning the interest-regarding efficacy of future opportunities induces individuals to resort to socially provided "non-experiential belief systems to give content to capacity evaluation" (Gintis 1974:423, emphasis omitted). Such belief systems, because they are based on the experiences of others, which in turn are limited by the opportunities of the system of production and distribution, will be shaped by this system of opportunities. In this way, the developmental preferences that could provide the basic evidence for developmental interests are trapped in the evaluation circularity.

(3) Once skills have been acquired, they will affect the ease or difficulty with which any further skills may be acquired subsequently. Therefore the capacity for further development in the future is determined by developmental choices in the present. To the extent that the individual does not fully understand these connections, his current choices, which will shape his future developmental possibilities, and thus his developmental interests, will not be completely autonomous, but will be guided by the system of production and distribution. In other words, the developmental interests themselves are caught in the circularity.

6.4   Cumulative socialization

Basic socialization and the evaluation circularity

The patterning of preferences is not merely a process that influences preferences that are, nevertheless, based in an essentially autonomous personality; the personality itself is in large part shaped by the social environment, which, in turn, owes much to the system of production and distribution. In other words, it is people's "character structures" that are endogenously shaped, and not just specific preferences about consumption and work. By what processes does this shaping occur?

Individuals are socialized into their society in a cumulative manner; that is, they have not just one role to relate to and internalize, but a series of roles, both at one time and over their lifetimes. They hold a whole series of roles covering different spheres, such as consumption, commitments to voluntary organizations, and relations to the polity, and these will change over time, so that the individuals move through a sequence of roles (or role sets). "Role development is thus cumulative; new roles building upon, modifying, and elaborating previous roles, each of which has resulted in the individual acquiring certain skills, dispositions and values that contribute to his ability to learn a new role" (Goslin 1969a:10). In this way the individual's self is shaped by society. His character is acquired "from the roles he has learned and appropriated," and those roles are determined by "the repertoire made available by his social environment" (Heine 1971:33). Though "as an individual gets older an increasing proportion of his behaviour may become independent of external control," it is simply "based instead on internalized dispositions" (Goslin 1969a:16; see also p. 14).

There are some institutions of which one of the primary purposes, or even the central purpose, is to socialize individuals in preparation for roles in other institutions. Such institutions are commonly referred to as "socialization agencies," and they are exemplified by the family and the school. They can be said to provide *primary socialization*, whereas socialization through the performance of adult roles is often referred to as *secondary*. Primary socialization is childhood socialization, which is conventionally regarded as primary in the sense that through it the basic character structure emerges.

The process of primary socialization

It is the helplessness and dependence, together with the absence of a fixed personality structure, of the infant that make childhood socialization not only necessary but also primary. The reasons for treating childhood socialization as primary have been summarized as follows (Zigler and Child 1969:503). It provides the individual's earliest learning experiences, its effects are likely to continue unless special conditions extinguish them, and it will shape later learning. Moreover,

the first learning is preverbal and for this reason may be expected to be more broadly generalized and less susceptible to later extinction or verbally mediated control. Furthermore, this same helplessness of the infant may well mean that he is often subject to greater drive intensity than commonly occurs later in life. If this assumption is correct, it should have two implications. First, drive reduction, when it occurs, is likely to be especially great and produce especially strong learning. Second, the occurrence of extreme drive states should set the stage for the learning of intense acquired desires, or what might be called emotional learning, and this sort of learning is of special importance for the formation of those internal characteristics that are of central concern in the study of personality.

The emotional element in learning is, furthermore, accentuated by the intimacy of the familial setting in which it occurs. (Explanations in psychoanalytic terms, adopted in the 1940s and 1950s by such prominent sociologists as Parsons and Mills, focus on the child's identification with or "introjection" of parental figures [Heine 1971:61–72].)

The reason why the psychological internalization that children experience within the family actually involves cultural patterning is that the parents, siblings, and other relatives have already been shaped by their own primary socialization, their socialization through role performance, ideological socialization (to be discussed shortly), and a socially formed conception of the roles available to and appropriate for the child being raised. In Erich Fromm's (1955:79) rather teleological phrasing, the family acts as "the psychic agency of society, the institution which has the function of transmitting the requirements of society to the child." In later childhood and adolescence, the family in modern society is gradually displaced by other socialization agencies: schools, peer groups, public figures and experts, public authorities, and so on (Inkeles 1969:625). Education involves not merely role preparation, but also a certain amount of role allocation in that it provides credentials that are a prerequisite to the adoption of particular categories of productive roles. Since the socialization agencies, too, are the product of prior socialization or of structurally determined social processes, as in the selection of teachers and in the elevation of individuals to public prominence, a certain cultural uniformity is imposed on socialization and makes for what has been referred to as "social character": "the nucleus of the character structure which is shared by most members of the same culture in contradistinction to the individual character in which people belonging to the same culture differ from each other" (Fromm 1955:76, emphasis omitted; cf. Heine 1971:78–9).

The image of *a* social character in a particular society, however, overemphasizes psychological uniformity at the expense of structured diversity and its psychological correlates. Diversity in character is due not merely to the genetic diversity of individuals and random elements in their social environment, but also to elements of diversity in the social structure. (Cf. Kapp 1961:169–70.) This diversity or, more appropriately, differentiated structure of the social system is, in large part, due to the division of labor and the functions of the economic system. Occupational groupings and income classes, to the extent that they form reference groups, not only provide distinctive secondary socialization experiences, but involve distinctive experiences for children that shape their image of and aspirations in the world.

Primary socialization and its functions

In relation to adult socialization it was mentioned that endogenous patterning is not to be considered an evil to be minimized simply because it creates the evaluation circularity for the want-satisfaction criterion and thereby makes the latter defective as a conception of interests. The situation is the same for primary socialization. As a matter of fact, within the predominant paradigm in sociology, primary socialization is regarded as performing a central "function," namely, maintaining social stability. Of course, social stability or system maintenance is not the ultimate consideration or ideal in an interest-regarding framework; system maintenance is relevant here only insofar as it is instrumental to the interests of individuals. (Cf. Homans 1961, cited in Heath 1976:67.) Therefore, in the present context, the term "function" will be used in an interest-regarding rather than system-maintaining sense, and this is how the "functions" of primary socialization will be assessed.[3] Since no conception of interests alternative to that of preference fulfillment has been developed in the discussion so far, the following discussion will involve a rather loose

---

[3] The teleological nature of "function" creates no difficulty here as the analysis is normative and the end or criterion clearly laid out. For discussions of the use of the concept in descriptive explanations see Benn and Peters 1959:239–40; Ginsberg 1961/1968:155–60; Emmet 1966:128–34; and Mackenzie 1967:90–1. The different normative orientations of functionalist sociology and of economics have been discussed by Olson 1968:109–14 and Barry 1970:173–5.

notion that represents interests with respect to survival and making one's way in the social world; these interests are taken to apply across different kinds of systems.

Primary socialization can be said to serve *personal* functions first of all. That is to say, it can serve the preferences or interests of the individual who is being socialized. At least the following functions are included. (1) The child is helped to learn about his environment and how to draw on it for the satisfaction of his wants. This socialization applies both to the natural environment, whose constraints and possibilities for manipulation have to be learned, and to the social environment, in which it is communication and the prediction and eliciting of reactions that have to be learned. The child could learn by trial and error, but that would be very costly in want satisfaction, and partial reliance on the transmission of the accumulated lifetime experiences of parents and siblings, as well as of transgenerational experiences of the culture, can serve to reduce these costs. Most critically, the want for survival may be fatally violated in an unguided process of trial and error. (2) The child is helped to learn the expectations of others, which are important to him not only to satisfy his social wants, but also to avoid punitive actions resulting in private-want frustration for him, and to identify his rights to call on the help of others (or simply to identify their amenability) in satisfying his private wants. (3) The child is helped to develop an image of the hierarchy of his preferences, which, as was stressed in Section 5.5, is by no means self-evident. Parents, siblings, and other relatives, as well as the culture as a whole, have accumulated experience about which pursuits are satisfying (i.e., fulfill more basic wants) and which are damaging or frustrating. This socialization includes finding a balance between social attachments and self-reliance. The former involves the benefits of security, sociability, and a sense of social significance. The costs are a loss of independence; misdirected help by others not wholly cognizant of the individual's distinctive traits; vulnerability to exploitation, vengeance, and grief; and perhaps a sense of individual weakness. For self-reliance roughly the converse applies. (4) The child is also helped to develop a structure of habits, that is, a "particular character . . . which permits a person to act fairly consistently and to be relieved of the burden of having to make a new and deliberate decision every time" (Fromm 1947:67; cf. Kapp 1961:113, 168). (5) Finally, the individual is helped to prepare for the adoption and performance of available roles at a time when he is psychologically open enough for this preparation to be relatively easy, but when he is not yet sufficiently mature to make his own decisions to pursue or neglect such preparation.

Concerning the last two points it should be noted that individuals with idiosyncratic innate psychobiological constitutions and idiosyncratic experiences will be served less well than individuals with more conventional constitutions and experiences. The conception of a child's "interest" that guides socialization agents may, to a greater or lesser extent, be independent of the child's basic nature and consist instead of Barry's (1965:185–6) relatively objectivist notion of "interest" as generalized opportunities for want satisfaction. " . . . the observation of everyday life makes it apparent that much of what each parent does to the child is guided by reference to some image of 'what he must be like to get on in life and the "world" later' . . . " (Inkeles 1969:630). Thus the capacities whose development is promoted may be determined by standardized conceptions of success rather than by reference to the individual's distinctive capacities and dispositions.

The second type of interest-regarding function of primary socialization is *collective*. That means that the socialization of the individual has significance for the interests of others who, directly or systemically, relate to him. " . . . it is of general concern that children should be equipped to become reasonably social and useful men and women" (Benn and Peters 1959:293), and this means that primary socialization constitutes a collective good. It has this feature in at least three ways.

(1) In order for an elaborate system of specialization and exchange generating a high level of consumer benefits to be possible, education has to be such as to enable individuals to acquire sophisticated and differential skills. (A further potential benefit of such a system and the education that makes it possible is opportunities for specialized forms of self-realization.) Thus cognitive child socialization is a collective good.

(2) The predictability of the behavior and responses of others facilitates social life. Predictability includes, as one important aspect, knowledge of the incentives that individuals will respond to. The standardization of the responsiveness to incentives (e.g., a universal responsiveness to money rewards) increases predictability in this sphere and thus facilitates quid pro quo relations (although this standardization may be at the expense of certain categories of interests, such as those that cannot be satisfied by quid pro quo exchange). In this case, it is conative child socialization that is the collective good. It socializes the individual's perception of his interests.

(3) More generally, social order may be conducive to want satisfaction. Social disorder may result from a refusal to cooperate, from the eruption of violence, or merely from uncertainty about the social environment that can, among other things, discourage investment (which, in the case of agriculture, may be a sufficient cause of famine). Any of these will seriously violate the interests of practically everyone, so that social order can be regarded as a collective good. If social order can be protected only by maintaining the prevailing system of institutions, then primary socialization can serve social order through system maintenance. It can do this in two important ways. (a) It can instill an acceptance of and commitment to the prevailing institutions. This is normative socialization. (b) To the extent that commitment to the social system depends on the extent to which it satisfies preferences and moral values, primary socialization can support the social system by promoting preferences and values that conform to the capabilities of the institutions of the system. This is again a form of conative socialization that shapes the individual's perception of his interests and consequently his preferences.[4]

Primary socialization and the economy

The next question is how the system of production and distribution shapes the process of primary socialization. In part it does this by the process of anticipatory patterning. In this case it is not the anticipation of opportunities by the individual being socialized but such anticipation by those concerned with the upbringing and education of the child (e.g., parents and teachers). Their conception of what opportunities will be available, of the accessibility of these opportunities to the particular individual in his particular circumstances, of the value of these opportunities to the individual, and of the personality charac-

---

[4] Olson (1968:108) has argued that "a society will, other things being equal, be more likely to cohere if people are socialized to have diverse wants with respect to private goods and similar wants with respect to collective goods." The first half of this generalization, however, is unwarranted, since comparative advantage can be exploited for mutual benefit without a diversity of preferences *among* consumers, although it is necessary that possibly similar preferences of consumers encompass a variety of goods. Moreover, to the extent that scale economies are of importance, nondiversity, both among consumers and within each consumer's preference structure, is of advantage. However, the diversity argument applies to a number of specific instances, such as private goods characterized by increasing costs and, most important, productive roles. With respect to the second half of Olson's statement, the advantage of similarity in preferences applies only to *pure* collective goods; amenities in danger of or characterized by congestion are best utilized with some diversity in preferences, especially regarding the timing of the use of the amenity.

teristics necessary as protection against what they see as typical difficulties of life will determine what these socialization agents will guide
the child toward and prepare him for. These conceptions will be
based to a large extent on the socialization agents' own experiences in
the economic system and those of their peers.

However, primary socialization occurs also in a much less inten-
tional manner. Children will use parents as role models and, usually
unconsciously, imitate them. The personalities of parents will in part
have been shaped by the occupational roles that they have been performing and that were made available to them by the system of production and distribution; they will also have been shaped by the reference group that their economic situation has put them into. Similar
things will have shaped extrafamilial role models as well, such as other
significant adults in the neighborhood and peers. Reference groups
have characteristically similar experiences in the economic system. In
the market system the residential land market, constrained as it usually is by urban land zoning, tends to segregate socioeconomic classes
geographically so that peers tend to have a certain similarity in experiences, which are then transmitted to the new generation.

Finally, the reference group and possibly the work experience will
shape aspects of parenting other than conscious and unconscious role
preparation. The degree of permissiveness and punitiveness in child
raising seems to be related to socioeconomic class (Heine 1971:70),
and so may the degree to which parents are attentive to the indi-
viduality of their children. To the extent that the relation is one of
consequence rather than correlation, parenting is patterned by the
system of production and distribution. Certainly it is plausible to argue that authoritarian workplace relations tend to lead to insensitive
authoritarianism in the home, with possibly the added element of
hostility from the workplace setting being vented in the home environment. In these ways, the system of production and distribution
influences parenting and thus the character formation of the next
generation. (For more extensive and concrete discussions of class-
related socialization see Inkeles 1969:622–3; Zigler and Child
1969:495–501; Heine 1971:69–76; and Gordon 1972:45, 52.)

Certain features of the personalities of individuals that are subject
to primary socialization are of particular relevance to the system of
production and distribution. One is the manner in which individuals
are motivated to provide socially productive services and resources;
closely related to it is the question what features of productive roles
they are prepared to tolerate or even to value. The pattern of attitudes and motives that is promoted by primary socialization may

well be decisive in how individuals respond to the opportunities available to them as adults. Thus one basic question is whether they are taught to value money reward (as a generalized means to the satisfaction of certain kinds of wants), to value status or power reward, simply to be obedient to authority or to traditional rules, or to act out of a sense of what is good for the community as a whole or for specific persons other than themselves.

Of course, these forms of motivation are not all developed with equal ease and effectiveness. Altruism, for example, may require focused and persistent socialization. Even then it may remain so limited that it needs to be supplemented by incentives appealing to other motives, such as symbolic rewards giving status to the altruist and public exhortations to certain behaviors, which together appear to make up the so-called moral incentives that some socialist countries have from time to time relied on. (For a discussion of different kinds of motivation and their effectiveness in production and distribution see Grossman 1967/1974:23–30.) Nevertheless, different emphases in the pattern of motives are possible in different economic systems. In one system altruism in the commitment to and performance of productive tasks may be wholly absent, whereas in another system it may play a central role. There may also be a difference in motivational patterns between socioeconomic classes.

The willingness to perform particular roles will also depend on the individual's willingness to accept such features of work relationships as subordination to superiors, observance of rigid rules, discretion, self-reliance, the need to negotiate and compromise with others, repetitiveness or diversity in tasks, and the pressure to be punctual and to meet deadlines. (For a discussion of the "dispositional orientations" in the work world of the modern industrial system see Moore 1969:866–7.) It depends in great part on the early socialization experiences of individuals whether they will find such role features a source of stress or of satisfaction. In addition, further aspects of motivation that are worth mentioning are a willingness to delay gratification, the pursuit of achievement, and a willingness to take risks. These too are propensities that have to be fostered by appropriate experiences if they are to develop and if the economic system is to rely on them.

Clearly the kinds of roles that a particular system of production and distribution makes available and the kinds of incentives or appeals that it relies on will be reflected in the process of primary socialization. They will be transmitted through the experiences and anticipations of the socialization agents to the latter's conscious preparation and unconscious modeling for socialization subjects. We thus have a circular process consisting of the system of production and distribution contributing to the socialization process in such a way that its consequences are in general conducive to the continuance of the economic system. In general, this arrangement serves the interests of the individuals being socialized, but we no longer have a clear conception of interests on the basis of which the distinctive forms of the whole circular process can be evaluated. In other words, while primary socialization is *broadly* in the interests of individuals, it also makes the preference-based conception of interests inappropriate as a basis for evaluating particular kinds of primary socialization.

Ideological socialization and institutional legitimation

It should not be imagined that primary socialization is a process of complete patterning of dispositions and preferences in the service of system maintenance. What I am referring to is merely a tendency from which there will be numerous deviations.[5] Moreover, a pattern of wants and motives generated by early socialization will not be maintained if it is not reinforced to some extent by subsequent experiences. (See the discussion of unlearning and relearning under conditions of social change in Heine 1971:77–8. Cf. Inkeles 1969:616. For a review of disagreements about how basic and fixed primary socialization effects are relative to secondary socialization see Heine 1971:76–84.) Consequently, a system's maintenance usually requires ideological socialization, which directly promotes the attitude that prevailing institutions are serving the interests of the members or are serving some greater good.

This direct process of institutional legitimation involves a propagation not merely of prescriptive values, but also of beliefs about reality, concerning both the status quo and possible alternatives to it. When we receive "knowledge" from the family, from our role settings, and from pervasive processes such as political communication, we in fact receive images that are inevitably partial; they focus on some aspects

---

[5] There may well be differences between individuals in their susceptibility to socialization. Thus David Riesman (1950/1961:240–9) has distinguished three character types: conformists, the "anomic" or misfits, and the "autonomous," who are capable of fitting in but in a number of ways choose not to and can make this choice without great internal conflicts.

of reality while concealing others. Moreover, they may actually mis-represent reality. These images or beliefs are usually crucial to the moral values that help to sustain social institutions. Ideological so-cialization, apart from serving a collective function, has not merely the personal function of providing knowledge (which is violated to the extent that distorted representations are being propagated), but also the function of satisfying the apparent want of individuals for a more or less consistent view of the world and of social life (Weisskopf 1971:33), which may be possible only with a certain degree of distortion.

There are different processes by which ideological propagation can take place. At one extreme are diffuse processes, such as family so-cialization and peer-group networks. At the other extreme are cen-tralized processes, such as political propaganda. In between lie inter-mediate processes, such as more or less pluralistically generated mass-media images (including those of advertising) and role socialization (which may, for example, have the effect of legitimating the work-place hierarchy and undermining worker confidence and interest in making demands for worker control). The structure of institutions determines to a large extent which of the potentially competing im-ages will be given prominence and legitimacy. It does this through the structure of roles, some of which involve the task of articulating and reiterating the prevailing ideology; through the selection of indi-viduals for such roles; through the pattern of rewards (private or social) for conformity to the ideology; and through exhortation.

Where power is highly centralized, the holders of this power can consciously use ideology for the purposes to which they put their power. If they are self-interested, the purposes will be the maximiza-tion of their own want satisfaction regardless of the costs to the powerless, as well as the continuance of their power. The ideological shaping of individuals' conceptions of their self-interest and obliga-tions thus can constitute an exercise of power that does not involve observable conflict (Lukes 1974:22–3). Democratically harnessed au-thority, on the other hand, could use ideology to optimize overall want satisfaction, as by countering socialization that in the past has served an exploitative regime.

Where power is diffused, ideology may be determined by the rela-tionships among the different institutions. Institutional ideologies may be mutually reinforcing or competing (or both with respect to different aspects), but in either case the relative strength of different institutions will be important. (For a discussion of the structural manifestation of power, including the ideological process, see Lukes 1974:38–56.) The relative strength of institutions may depend on their traditional legitimacy (i.e., on historical ideology), on their access to the means of coercion, or on their current capacity to fulfill preferences.

It should be noted, however, that the content of ideology is not independent of reality; it must allow its adherents to make sense of reality, and it will not do so if highly visible elements of reality contradict the ideology or if the ideology contains readily recognizable inconsistencies. But these constraints still leave a remarkable latitude to the range of images that can be propagated.

Whether or not the source of ideological socialization is attributed to the economic subsystem of the social system, the *content* of ideological socialization will certainly be determined in part by the institutions of the economic subsystem. Politically controlled ideology will be greatly concerned with the stability of economic institutions. One reason may be that political power and economic power are vested in the same groups. Another is that a social system is normally so interrelated that changes in one subsystem will usually result in changes in complementary subsystems. Consequently, if those who control the political subsystem are concerned with its stability, part of this concern will be for the stability of the economic subsystem. Finally, there are situations where the economic and political subsystems are interrelated to the point where the coordination of the economic subsystem rests in the political sphere. These are reasons why ideological socialization will, in its content, reflect the institutions of the economic subsystem and therefore make circular the preference-based evaluations of systems of economic processes, or even of policies that shape them sufficiently to affect the nature of their ideological supports.

Even when, in an unstable social system, socialization does not serve to maintain it, but instead operates to undermine or change it, it is still subject to the evaluation circularity, as long as preferences and interests are patterned by the system of production and distribution. If, for example, reformers' or revolutionaries' ideas for change have been shaped by the particular frustrations and deprivations that the current system of production and distribution gives rise to, then their preferences will not constitute an evaluation criterion that is favorable to the system, but these preferences will not be independent of the system either. It is this independence that is needed to avoid the evaluation circularity, and that is undermined by socialization, rather than by system maintenance as such.

6.5   Attempts to rescue the preference-based approach

Five positions

In the literature in economics one can find a number of justifications for persisting with the preference-based approach to evaluation, in spite of the problem of endogenous preferences and the evaluation circularity that they give rise to. The justifications can be classified as follows. (1) The principle of want satisfaction is not really a normative principle, but is value-neutral. (2) Satisfying wants as they are is democratic. (3) It is necessary to break the chain of the mutual determination of wants and social instruments somewhere, and the "economic approach" is to do this by taking wants as given. (4) Individual sovereignty does not require individual autonomy. (5) Wants are changed by cultural development, but this is a desirable form of evolution.

(1) The first position seems to have been fairly widespread in welfare economics at one point.[6] However, there is no reason why preferences as the constitutive principle of evaluation and optimization should have a different logical status in ethics from the features of the calculus principle of optimization, for example, interpersonal distribution. They are all prescriptive and are in need of some form of justification.

(2) The second position can take two alternative forms. One is the claim that one of the characteristics that makes a system democratic is its responsiveness to people's preferences ("the sovereignty of the people"), and the discrimination among, guidance of, and overriding of preferences is arbitrary and authoritarian. (This position is articulated, but by no means held in its full-fledged form, by Scitovsky 1951/1971:243. A similar, though more fully developed, position is to be found in Flew 1977 and is criticized in Chapter 8 herein.) This argument seems to me circular rather than justificatory: A main justification for democracy is that it provides for general want satisfaction, leaving the latter (and thus also the former) still to be justified. Why have democracy if want satisfaction cannot be justified? (Hutt 1936:262 and Lerner 1972:258 have referred to an affinity or normative parallelism between consumer sovereignty and democracy, rather than a derivation of one from the other.)

6 It appears to be entailed by Samuelson's (1950/1969:421) comment that the determination of distribution-general optimality is "ethics-free." Among the critics of this position within welfare economics have been Paul P. Streeten 1953:209; Scitovsky 1960/1964:232; and Sen 1970:57–8.

A second version of the want-satisfaction-is-democratic argument is that the principle of want satisfaction is a generally accepted ideal; that is, it is democratic in that it represents the popular will. (For the articulation and criticism of this version see Nath 1969:2, 125–31.) The first objection here is that it is highly doubtful that the principle is in fact generally accepted in an unqualified form. Secondly, even if it is, it is likely that the acceptance is based on a lack of awareness of the problems that irrationality and socialization create for the principle when it is used in assessing economic institutions and policies with profound impacts, and such awareness might well alter this acceptance.

(3) The third defense of the preference-based approach can be termed the division-of-labor argument, or what Paul P. Streeten (1953:214–15) has referred to as the "economic-aspect defence." (For an example of this position see Lerner 1972:258.) It has been presented by Hla Myint (1948:211) as follows:

> To begin with . . . it is inadequate to regard life merely as a mechanical process of satisfying given wants. As Marshall has suggested we must take life as a continuous process of development in which wants give rise to activities and activities in their turn give rise to wants, in overlapping cycles of mutual causation. . . . However, in trying to come to grips with this essentially continuous process, our analytical apparatus has to break off the chain of mutual causation somewhere and take that as our starting point.

And where does one make the break? The answer is provided at an earlier point in Myint's book:

> . . . we cannot definitely say whether the individual's wants are more efficiently satisfied in one situation compared with another unless we have the common basis of an unchanged system of wants for the two situations compared. And welfare analysis is nothing but such relative comparisons of individuals' positions. Indeed as Prof. Hicks has suggested, the assumption of constant wants seems to offer the only logically satisfactory distinction between the "economic" and the "general" welfare. So long as we are considering the problem of given wants we are discussing economic welfare, whether or not these wants belong to the "material" side of life or are capable of being brought into relation with the measuring rod of money. Once we move beyond the assumption of constant wants, however, we are stepping into the realm of general welfare where the economist *qua* economist cannot make any authoritative pronouncements (cf. J. R. Hicks, "The Valuation of Social Income," *Economica*, May 1940, p. 107). [P. 139]

While conceding that "the particular half of the mutual interaction . . . captured [by welfare economics] can merely be in the nature of a half-truth," Myint further argued that as long as wants are reasonably stable and predictable, as on the whole they are, they can be taken as given, so that "there is thus still a very large scope for welfare economics based on the assumption of given wants" (pp. 211–13).

The crucial issue, however, is not the stability or predictability of wants, but the exogeny of wants, their independence from the means of their satisfaction. If the structure of institutions that optimally satisfies a stable pattern of wants has significantly shaped or even created these stable wants, then the fact that it now satisfies these wants better than any other institutional structure makes it preferable to those other institutional structures only for satisfying these particular wants, but not necessarily for the way it will pattern wants in the future. The latter must be evaluated as well. There is no reason why a continuous process of mutual causation should constitute an intractable problem; as a matter of fact, such problems of interaction can be regarded as the staple of economics, with demand–supply interaction being the paradigm case. It is true that part of this interaction problem is essentially moral and thus may require abandoning disciplinary segregation and delving into philosophy. But that is not new for economics either. The current ethical basis of welfare economics stems, after all, from utilitarianism, a school of philosophy. The issue at stake therefore deserves to be dealt with in the context of a dialogue with philosophy, as well as other disciplines to the extent that questions of fact regarding the feedback process need to be resolved.

(4) A fourth defense is to be found in a popular textbook of the late 1930s (Benham's *Economics*). The author

admits that in the world as we know it demand schedules are *not* wholly "autonomous" factors in the economic situation. . . . consumers' decisions as to what they *want* to buy are themselves affected by propaganda on the part of those with goods to sell. This difficulty, however, he explains away by an extension of his metaphor: a monarch, he says, is still sovereign if he allows himself to be advised and cajoled by his subjects. [Fraser 1939:545–6, emphasis in original]

The analogy, however, is misconceived. The sovereignty of the absolute monarch is of an *institutional* kind and is justified for the maintenance of social order; the effectiveness of the king's rule in maintaining order, not the expression of his personal will, is relevant here. Consumer, private, and personal sovereignty, on the other hand, are interest conceptions of sovereignty, and the expression of personal interest is critical here. Fraser also extrapolated that "Professor Hutt (though he does not deal with the point explicitly) might add that while in such cases the actual power is wielded by the propagandist, yet the 'ultimate' power continues to rest with the consumer" (p. 546).

(Cf. Hutt 1936:258–9.) But Hutt himself approvingly referred to John Dewey's conception of sovereignty "as being derived from 'the complex of social forces that actually get themselves obeyed at a given time'" (p. 259), and if consumer or general wants are institutionally shaped, then it follows that either there is institutional ultimacy or sovereignty or it is the interaction between institutions and preferences that is entitled to that status. (Fraser himself accepted these two defenses of consumer sovereignty as long as they were not used "as an excuse for ignoring the *de facto* influence of producers' propaganda upon consumers' preferences" [p. 546].)

(5) The fifth kind of defense, which might be labeled "evolutionary," attempts, not to evade the significance of preference patterning, but to affirm it normatively. In a critique of Galbraith's "dependence effect," Friedrich A. von Hayek (1960–1/1975:8) argued that "most needs . . . are . . . for things which civilization teaches us exist at all, and these things are wanted by us because they produce feelings or emotions which we would not know if it were not for our cultural inheritance." This argument gives the impression that these are experiences *in addition* to those of a less-developed civilization; but new experiences may in effect make the old experiences impossible. What has to be compared is the total set of experiences in one cultural stage or situation with the total set in another. Unless Hayek had a hedonistic comparison in mind, which I doubt, it is not clear by what yardstick a later and more elaborate stage of civilization is to be found superior to an earlier one.

The normative significance of the evaluation circularity

None of these defenses is persuasive. The evaluation circularity simply cannot be dismissed in any of these ways. As Barry (1965:77–8) has argued, "choosing an economic system is not merely choosing a machine for satisfying wants but rather choosing a machine for *producing* certain wants in the future. . . . To refuse the opportunity to choose is to opt for the *status quo* without taking the responsibility for doing so." The innocent acceptance of the principle of want satisfaction and the neglect of the preference-patterning effects of acting in accordance with it constitute an implicit approval of these preference-patterning effects, without moral scrutiny of this approval.

To claim or imply that economists as a whole have tried to evade the normative implications of the evaluation circularity would be quite misleading. Many have insisted that the wants themselves need to be evaluated. (See, e.g., Streeten 1953:215; Robinson 1962:50; Scitovsky

1962/1964:248–9; Mishan 1967:159–60; Dobb 1969:213; Weizsaecker 1971:371; and Gintis 1972b:596. Cf. Marshall's concern with a
"eugenics" of wants, referred to in Myint 1948:136.) One way of
evaluating wants would be to rely on collective judgments concerning
desirable preferences or desirable processes of preference patterning.
This response to the evaluation circularity is also a plausible answer to
the comparability problem that is to be discussed next. The approach
of relying on such collective judgments will therefore be assessed at
the end of the next chapter.

Appendix: The technical conditions of the evaluation circularity

The evaluation circularity characterizes an evaluation criterion that is
multidimensional and whose dimensions or dimension weights are at
least partly determined by the object being evaluated. Thus if Z is the
evaluation criterion, Z_1 to Z_n are its dimensions, and a_1 to a_n are the
respective weights of these dimensions, so that

$$Z = Z(a_1Z_1, a_2Z_2 \ldots a_nZ_n),$$

then, in the case of an evaluation circularity, the dimensions i (1 to n)
or the a_i's are not specified until after the relevant features of the
object being evaluated have been identified. (Whether it is the i's or
the a_i's that are not specified prior to the evaluation process is not
critical; all possible i's could be included prior to the evaluation with
the matching a_i's becoming zero for those Z_i's that turn out not to be
relevant to the particular object being evaluated.) Thus, in the case of
want satisfaction, the i's represent the different kinds of wants the
extent of whose satisfaction is to be ascertained, and the a_i's are the
value weights that allow the different forms of want satisfaction to be
aggregated into a single index of want satisfaction. The circularity is
made possible by the fact that the weights and perhaps the want
categories are not specified prior to the application of the criterion to
the economic system.

The prior specification of weights that is required for freedom
from the evaluation circularity does not mean that the weights have to
be constant nor that the way in which they change must be independent of what is happening in the social system to be evaluated. In the
case of preference fulfillment, marginal weights may, and can normally be expected to, change with changing levels or patterns of preference *fulfillment,* but as long as they change in accordance with a
valuation function whose coefficients are fully specified without ref-

erence to the particular social system, the evaluation circularity does not arise. What is at stake is the origin of the *structure* of preferences, not the margin between fulfillment and nonfulfillment resulting from choices in response to the available opportunities. (In terms of indifference-curve analysis, it is the indifference surfaces that need to remain unaffected, while the marginal rates of substitution may change in response to changing opportunities.)

Thus a "displaced want," such as a concentration on certain leisure pursuits because the work situation is not satisfying, need not necessarily be subject to the evaluation circularity; it may simply indicate limited opportunities and a preference for the combination of highly remunerative but unsatisfying work with leisure activities that the remuneration makes possible, over satisfying but poorly remunerated employment. For the evaluation circularity to occur requires a process that shapes the structure of preferences and not merely constrains the choices of individuals. This would be the case if the pattern of opportunities leads workers to place a lower value on work satisfaction than they otherwise would.

PART IV

Measuring want satisfaction

CHAPTER 7

The comparability problem of the want-satisfaction principle

7.1 The want-satisfaction principle and calculus requirements

Although the focus of this book is the constitutive principle of consumer sovereignty and alternatives to it, calculus questions that have therefore been largely omitted so far cannot be ignored altogether. If a constitutive principle is not measurable in some way, then no matter how attractive it is conceptually, it is useless for the optimization and evaluation of economic policies, institutions, and systems. Thus the measurability of want satisfaction has to be considered to determine the attractiveness of want satisfaction as a constitutive principle. This is an issue parts of which economists have explored in great depth. The treatment here will, therefore, be merely in the nature of a brief review of some important positions concerning the measurability of want satisfaction. The point of the discussion in this chapter will be to reveal the limits to the measurability of want satisfaction that arise from the subjectivity of want satisfaction as a constitutive principle.

There are various approaches to measurement. Some measures capture directly the magnitude of what is to be ascertained, whereas others are more in the nature of proxy measures that indicate the magnitude of certain symptoms, correlates, or causes of the variable that is of concern. Moreover, some measures are cardinal, whereas others are merely ordinal. Thus whether a variable is measurable or not is not usually a question that can be given an unqualified yes-or-no answer. In many cases it is a matter of degree. Whether the particular degree, and kind, of measurability suffices depends on the use to which it is to be put. That means it now has to be made clearer what relevant optimization and evaluation tasks the principle of consumer sovereignty or its alternatives are to provide guidance for.

There are essentially two tasks for optimization and evaluation: (1) the development of efficiency rules and the determination of conditions of efficiency and inefficiency; and (2) comparative evaluations, where the want satisfaction of one person, economic system, or time period is compared with that of another. Optimization that includes interpersonal equity involves both tasks. The first has led to the elaborate Paretian efficiency calculus. Comparative evaluation, on the other hand, has been dealt with in welfare economics under the term "welfare criteria" for the identification of economic improvements over time, but has been largely avoided as far as intersystem comparisons are concerned, and for some time this was true of interpersonal comparisons as well. How demanding the measurement requirements of these various tasks are depends partly on how restricted the situations or systems to be optimized or evaluated are. Thus the efficiency rules are simplest when there are no constraints other than those of resources and technology. Difficulties increase for the efficiency calculus when political and other institutional constraints or costs have to be included. The less that is held constant in the case of comparative evaluations, the more problematic they become. Comparative evaluations over time are least difficult when they apply to short-term changes with unchanged membership and preference structures. The mere diversity of preferences between individuals causes serious problems in the comparative assessment of their respective levels of want satisfaction. If there are changes in the preference structures, in the distribution of purchasing power, or in the individuals who constitute an economic system, further difficulties arise.

At the heart of these difficulties lies what I will refer to as the "comparability problem," which, like the evaluation circularity, arises from the condition of open-endedness of the preference principle. The comparability problem refers to the fact that when we are faced with different patterns of want satisfaction, we have difficulties determining which patterns represent higher and which lower levels of want satisfaction.

Not only does the comparability problem have the same conceptual source as the evaluation circularity, but the latter is often the cause of the former. The diversity of preference structures between economic systems is to a large extent due to differences in their respective instruments for want satisfaction, which have divergent feedback effects on the preference structures in the respective systems. Similarly, preference structures within a particular system may well change over time, and much of this change is usually attributable to changes in the process of want satisfaction.

Nevertheless, there is a reason for treating the comparability problem separately from the evaluation circularity. Conceptually, they are distinct. Theoretically, it is possible to have noncomparability without the evaluation circularity, and conversely, we can have the evaluation circularity without the comparability problem. The former applies when there are no feedback effects from the want-satisfaction process to the preference structures, but differences in preference structures between individuals, systems, or time periods occur for other ("exogenous") reasons. The converse case is where preference structures are identical, even though they are shaped by feedback effects from the want-satisfaction process; the latter process, of course, then has to be invariant as well. Although the latter case is empirically implausible, the point is that the comparability problem is conceptually distinct from the evaluation circularity and raises distinctive issues.

7.2   Possible measures of want-satisfaction levels

Prices as community values

The most obvious measure of want satisfaction, at least as far as consumer wants are concerned, is money. Market prices readily provide money measures for traded goods and services and, with the help of certain theoretical assumptions, even of some untraded goods, such as environmental benefits and leisure. Market prices thus can provide value weights for a great number of goods. They represent the relative valuations of individuals in that they indicate what individuals are willing to pay for different goods. Moreover, since markets equalize the prices for goods, these prices represent communitywide valuations. Uniform prices also give meaning to the level of income of individuals and households. Income represents the quantity of goods that can be bought according to the pattern of prices that prevails. Income has thus been referred to as a measure of "opportunities for want satisfaction" (Barry 1965:176, 184) and of the "means to welfare" (Nath 1969:142). The values in terms of which these opportunities are measured are determined not only by consumers' willingness to pay, but also by supply conditions that reflect production possibilities. They therefore reflect not only the communitywide valuation of the benefits from them, but also, at least approximately (with deviations owing to "market imperfections" and external effects), their costs to society. In this way, it is at least initially plausible that exchange values are appropriate as value weights for different kinds of want satisfaction, and that their total, that is, the money value of consumption expenditures, is suitable as a measure of the total level of want satisfaction, whether for an individual, household, or economic system. Income then represents the level of want satisfaction that an individual or household *can* attain.

The first limitation of such monetary measures of want satisfaction is that they both include too much and exclude items that should be included. Take, for example, national accounts statistics. The most typical representation of the level of want satisfaction of a country or region is Gross National Product, which includes not just consumption expenditures, but also capital spending and certain instrumental expenditures, such as those for national defense and pollution control. To count these as part of the final level of consumer-want satisfaction would be misleading, since they do not add to want satisfaction, but are rather designed to protect against harm or the loss of want satisfaction, or to provide for want satisfaction in the future. Such items can be adjusted for, as William Nordhaus and James Tobin (1972) did in their time series estimates of their "Measure of Economic Welfare" for the United States. (Their adjustments went further than this; one of them is indicated shortly.) Their purpose, however, was to compare the overall level of want satisfaction in one country over a few decades, not to compare it between countries, or between individuals.

On the other hand, a number of forms of want satisfaction are not reflected in market exchange and in the national accounts. Thus externalities are not traded, by definition, and collective goods are usually not priced as well. Although shadow prices can help to indicate benefits and costs to individuals beyond what they pay for in the market, there will often be no systemwide equilibrium values for some of them. In conventional market situations, the price that all consumers face leads them to adjust their consumption to the point where their *marginal* value of the good, that is, their willingness to pay for one more unit of the good, equals the price, and that is the same for all. (The exception is nonbuyers; their marginal value for the first unit of the good is less than the price for it.) In most cases of collective goods and external benefits or costs, in contrast, individuals cannot adjust their level of "consumption" in order to maximize net benefits to them personally, so that, at their unadjusted margins of "consumption," different individuals place different (positive or negative) marginal values on them. For each individual, a separate estimation would need to be made, on the basis, not of behavior, but of valuations articulated personally by individuals – a task that not only is gargantuan, but also is not reliable, given the distinctive information problems in the cases of collective goods and externalities and opportunities for strategic responses when individuals are aware of the policy consequences of the resulting findings. In the case of optional collective goods, such as broadcasting, where marginal values *can* be equalized, they are equalized at zero marginal value, so that the reliance on marginal values would imply that the community places no value at all on these goods. (The national accounts method of assessing such goods in terms of costs implies that the benefits equal the costs, if it is used as a basis for measuring want satisfaction.)

Social wants were identified as a distinguishable category of interests in Chapter 4. Some of these may be mediated by the market, in such forms as commercial clubs and prostitution, but many others are not. A particularly convivial society will provide greater want satisfaction than one that structures social relations for isolation and loneliness, but the difference will not be reflected in any obvious money measure. Perhaps shadow prices could be worked out for such social-want satisfaction, on the basis of observed trade-offs that individuals make between convivial situations, on the one hand, and earnings or other monetizable benefits, on the other; but it would be a daunting task, to say the least. Relativity wants create a particular problem, since in this case levels of want satisfaction become interdependent between individuals. Because of these difficulties, social-want satisfaction tends to be excluded from measures of *economic* welfare, often with the questionable assumption that noneconomic welfare is on the whole positively correlated with economic welfare.

Work wants, too, create difficulties for the use of the marginal values that prices represent. In a competitive market the negative marginal value placed by individuals on their work commitments is indicated by their wage rates. Thus their earnings are a measure of their sacrifices. That means that in the marginalist approach to valuation the negative valuation of sacrifices in the form of earnings largely offsets the positive valuation of consumption. People appear to be no better off than if they were idle and abstained from consumption. Clearly, that is not the case; otherwise at least some of them would choose the latter option. One solution is that of Nordhaus and Tobin (1972:484–6), who avoided this conclusion by, instead of counting work as negative welfare, counting leisure as having positive welfare (using the assumption that wage rates reflect not only the marginal negative value of work, but also the marginal positive value of leisure). They thereby implied that zero want satisfaction consists of continuous work, no leisure, and no consumption, rather than idleness with zero consumption. For interpersonal and intersystemic comparisons the zero point is actually not in itself important, as long as it is the same for everyone and we refrain from talking about a doubling of want satisfaction or other "ratio scale" assessments, that is, as long as we treat the measurement of want satisfaction like a temperature scale rather than a weight scale.

Surplus and Paretian analyses

A more straightforward way of showing how people increase their level of want satisfaction by working and consuming is through "social surplus analysis" (Millward 1971:60–73). In the case of consumers, the benefit they obtain from consumption is indicated not only by the price they pay for it, which indicates their *marginal* valuation of it, but also by the price they would have been willing to pay for the "intra-marginal" units of consumption. Accepting the assumption of the diminishing marginal value of consumption, the consumers' willingness to pay for the initial units of consumption will be higher than that for additional units. This phenomenon is reflected in the downward-sloping demand curve. The difference between intramarginal valuation and marginal valuation represents what is conventionally referred to as "consumer surplus." Similarly, there is a producer surplus, based on the notion that the producer's requirement to be compensated rises with the level of labor services or other inputs that he provides, so that the compensation he insists on at the margin is higher than that which he would insist on for intramarginal units of input. This is reflected in the upward-sloping supply curve. Such consumer and producer surpluses are thus an alternative and potentially more sophisticated measure of want satisfaction.

However, this measure involves such stringent ceteris paribus assumptions that it is applicable to only quite limited optimization and evaluation tasks. First of all, it can be used only to evaluate *changes* in want satisfaction, not levels. Thus it cannot be used to compare the *levels* of want satisfaction of different individuals and economic systems. In principle, the level of want satisfaction prevailing under a system of self-sufficient households could be used as a benchmark for measuring the social surplus resulting from the particular system of social organization (Winch 1971:135–6), but this analysis would have to be conducted "in a general equilibrium context and no usable body of theory presently exists for such a task" (Winch 1971:152; cf. the discussion of Alfred Marshall's conception of aggregate surplus in Myint 1948:142–9). Social surplus analysis can thus be applied only within partial equilibrium analysis. This means that, even when it comes to assessing changes in the level of want satisfaction, the applicability of social surplus analysis is quite limited. The changes have to be such that prices other than for the good to which the surplus analysis is applied remain constant (Millward 1971:67–9). It is thus useful for cost–benefit analysis for projects with limited impacts, but not for analysis of major changes in the economic structure.

Also required for the validity of this analysis is constancy in the marginal valuation of money. (This requirement, incidentally, also makes the estimation of producer surplus unreliable, since the effects on individuals' purchasing power tend to be more concentrated, so that changes in the marginal values of income are likely.) More important, when we use, without further qualification, either marginal or surplus valuation to compare want satisfaction between individuals, and not merely to assess aggregate improvements, we also have to assume that the value of a dollar of income or expenditure is the same for all individuals and households, regardless of their level of income and assets. And we have to take at face value the necessarily lower willingness of the poor than the rich to pay for most benefits, including imputed values for collective goods, and the lower level of compensation the poor require for sacrifices, including labor services and environmental damages. (Although in the case of traded goods the marginal values will be equalized through relatively more restricted consumption by the poor, this pattern is revealed when the complete marginal value [or demand] schedules of individuals are compared.)

The traditional utilitarian approach to this problem was, of course, to refer to utility, to assume that the marginal utility of income declines with a rising level in income, and thus to give the money income and expenditure of the poor greater weight per dollar for utility. Utility here, though, meant not just want satisfaction or the fulfillment of preferences, but satisfaction *as a state of mind*. Quite apart from measurement problems at this level (which will be considered in the next chapter), this kind of hedonistic approach represents an alternative to the preference principle, and not a particular version of it. It thus falls outside the want-satisfaction framework.

The ordinal approach of Paretian welfare theory tries to avoid this issue by confining its analysis to questions of aggregate improvements and of efficiency in the sense of the full exploitation of opportunities for such improvements. By assuming that improvements are unequivocal if, and only if, everyone benefits, or at least no one is made worse off while others benefit, or (in its still more diluted form) the gains are sufficient so that this outcome *could* be assured, some powerful conclusions concerning the requirements for the efficient allocation of resources and distribution of outputs, as well as for cost–benefit analysis, have been arrived at. But these conclusions have been achieved only by evading all questions of interpersonal distribution, both of want satisfaction prior to such improvements and of the improvements themselves. There is thus no need to compare the levels of want satisfaction of different individuals. All issues that do require such comparisons are designated as noneconomic and exiled to the realm of politics.

Even with respect to efficiency, this evasive maneuver has a very limiting effect. Efficiency is indeterminate in the sense that there is an infinite set of efficient outcomes, each of which corresponds to a particular distribution of purchasing power (or whatever other measure of want satisfaction is used). To make it determinate we have to identify the equitable distribution, and that requires the measurement and interpersonal comparison of want satisfaction. Moreover, it becomes technically extremely complicated when the efficiency frontier (or the optimum point on it) is not attainable and we have to evaluate comparatively different suboptimal situations. In other words, as long as the issues of the measurement and interpersonal comparisons of levels of want satisfaction are avoided, the guidance that can be offered for optimization and the evaluation that can be achieved are quite limited. Of course, one can implicitly accept the current distribution as equitable or, in the case of efficiency prescriptions, be implicitly indifferent to distribution and distributive effects, and thus focus exclusively on the efficiency side of optimization and evaluation. Such one-sidedness, however, is simply evidence for the measurability problems that afflict want satisfaction.

Price structures and comparability

The problems raised so far arise when we consider situations in which the prices for traded goods are uniform and constant. When the constancy condition is not met, as in economic changes that involve changes in the structure of prices, we can end up in the paradoxical position where a change from situation A to situation B is warranted by the price structure in situation A; that is, the gains measured in prices in A exceed the losses measured by the same set of prices, but a move back from B to A is justified by the new set of prices that prevails in B. In other words, in terms of the prices in A the aggregate level of want satisfaction is higher in B, whereas in terms of the prices in B the level is higher in A. To avoid such indeterminacy, additional criteria have been proposed; but none that avoids significant equity judgments, as the Paretian analysis was designed to do, turned out to be satisfactory. (For systematic reviews, see, e.g., Nath 1969:ch. 5 and Dobb 1969:ch. 6.)

This problem applies even more when we try to compare levels of want satisfaction in different economic systems. It is true that different countries or regions may be economically integrated with one another through free trade, so that exchange values will be equalized across these systems and exchange rates will reflect the relative purchasing power of the different currencies, but there is at least one reason why the price structures will not be completely equalized: For goods that have to be transported from one area to the other, prices will not be equalized beyond a differential that represents the transport costs. For some goods, the transport costs will be relatively so high as to rule out any demand in the potentially importing region. Moreover, free trade cannot be assumed to be ubiquitous; trade barriers in the form of tariffs, quotas, and prohibitions prevent the intersystemic equalization of prices.

When the price structures of different systems diverge from one another, it is not clear how the marginal valuations are to be made comparable. One way would be simply to establish the relative valuation of the different currencies on the basis of their exchange rates, with the currencies then being the common denominators within the various systems. Exchange rates are theoretically appropriate for this purpose when the relative price structures are identical and the conversion through exchange rates makes the prices absolutely identical in any particular currency. However, it is not clear what meaning is to be attached to relative valuations of currencies established on the basis of exchange rates shaped by trade that is affected by transport costs and trade barriers and by demand–supply pressures related to capital movements rather than just to goods whose consumption constitutes want satisfaction. When exchange rates are directly controlled, the difficulties are intensified. And, of course, in the case of self-sufficient systems that do not engage in intersystem trade at all, we have no exchange rates whatsoever. These are problems relating only to the comparability of different price structures; the other problems of unrevealed marginal valuations and intramarginal valuations, of course, apply at least as much to intersystem as to intrasystem comparisons.

The most fundamental problem, however, remains the implicitly or explicitly assumed equality in the normative significance of a dollar received or spent, regardless of the overall level of want satisfaction of the recipient or spender. In mental-state utilitarianism the (hypothesized) satisfaction engendered by money received and spent by individuals at different levels of income can be differentiated. This is not an option in the want-satisfaction framework of preference utilitarianism.[1] In that framework, it seems that only through value judg-

---

[1] Two attempts to treat it as an option have been shown to involve feasibility problems,

ments concerning the quantitative significance that is to be attached to a dollar of income or spending (or their hypothetical equivalents) for individuals in various kinds of situations can this problem be resolved.

7.3   Want satisfaction and normative judgments

Normative judgments and collective choice

Any measure of want satisfaction that establishes interpersonal comparability without referring to the nature of the wants has another important shortcoming. It is incapable of reflecting the difference in the level of want satisfaction of two persons with, for example, the same money value of purchasing power or assets but different want structures. Compare the level of want satisfaction of A, whose wants are the wants of the majority and therefore the ones that the production system primarily caters to, with that of B, who has idiosyncratic wants and has to pay relatively dearly to have them fulfilled. Is B not worse off than A? By most well-thought-out standards, that distributive judgment would depend on the nature of the wants involved. If his want is for exotic foods or an expensive hobby, most of us would say that B is no worse off than A. On the other hand, if his want is to overcome some idiosyncratic disability, such as a want for a wheelchair, then it is reasonable to say that satisfying this additional want brings B's lower level of want satisfaction closer to A's and does not put B ahead of A. (For a discussion of this distinction see Rawls 1975:552–3; Scanlon 1975:659–61, 663–5; and the brief review of "central concerns" in Section 8.4 herein.) In other words, the level of want satisfaction depends on the nature of the wants to be satisfied. How wants are to be assessed in this respect requires normative judgments about their significance.

The conclusion suggested by this rather brief discussion of a subject that economists have developed to an impressive level of elaboration is that want satisfaction is a concept that cannot be made measurable without additional normative judgments that are neither contained in nor entailed by the preference principle. That principle is concep-

---

implausible empirical assumptions, and crucial and unattractive ethical assumptions. One is based on individuals' ability to discriminate between different levels of want satisfaction and involves treating the smallest interval that makes a difference to the individual as equivalent, for valuation purposes, to intervals of this kind for others. The other derives utility scales from choices of probabilistic outcomes in gambles, where it is assumed that the individual is maximizing his utility according to such a scale. For a discussion of these two methods see Sen 1970:92–9.

tually so open-ended that it does not point to an obvious measurement criterion. It requires normative judgments to fill it out. That is to say, there is not only the normative step of proposing that economic evaluation and optimization should be conducted according to impacts on levels of want satisfaction, but also the further value judgments that the interpretation of "levels of want satisfaction" requires. And these additional normative judgments that have to be made are quite strong. This conclusion then reinforces the position that emerged from the problems of irrationality and the evaluation circularity. In both cases it was found that wants, or their satisfaction and patterning, have to be normatively evaluated, in one case on the basis of norms of rationality and in the other case in terms of either desirable processes of preference patterning or desirable outcomes of such patterning. Now we need such judgments also to make want satisfaction measurable.

Some welfare economists have responded to this set of issues with the concept of a "social welfare function." Such a function identifies the objectives or ends of a society and their relative importance. Social welfare functions do not have to be based on want satisfaction, but that is what is usually proposed. Those that are based on want satisfaction not only take into account the relative preferences of individuals, which then represent the objectives in the social welfare function, but also provide the normative element necessary to make different patterns of want satisfaction commensurable. As a minimum, such a function has to identify the relative normative importance of marginal spending by individuals at different levels of affluence. However, because of objections to assuming that equal spending means equal want satisfaction, such as that just given, *types* of spending may require also differential weighting or calibration relative to some zero point. Moreover, want satisfaction that occurs without spending will have to be both quantified and weighted through the social welfare function.

Such a social welfare function could conceivably also incorporate those normative judgments that are needed to deal with irrational preferences, with indeterminacies in the rationality criterion, and with the development or patterning of preferences. Thus different normative weights might be set on any level of spending at different stages in the life cycle of individuals, on different forms of want satisfaction, or on different processes of production and distribution that influence the formation of preferences. Certain kinds of preference development might be given positive weights and others negative weights. In each of these cases judgments concerning the interests of individuals would have to be made.

Where do these normative judgments that have to supplement the principle of want satisfaction come from? Two alternative plausible sources are an ethical principle and a community judgment. There is, however, no general ethical principle or set of principles that has universal appeal and can deal with all of the questions raised by the principle of want satisfaction. It seems that these goals can be met only through community judgments about the social weighting of the satisfaction and development of different wants.

However, we now have a new level of potential problems concerning rationality and comparability. The judgments of communities are not immune to irrationality. The compromises on which the judgments of communities, small or large, tend to be based are often at the expense of consistency or of rationality in some other, more demanding sense. To the extent that different communities, societies, or systems will weight wants differently and to the extent that this difficulty applies also to any particular system over time, we get intersystem and intertemporal noncomparability in the values to be attached to the satisfaction and development of the different wants. Our gauge for measuring levels of want satisfaction varies over space and time.

Moreover, these values can be expected also to involve the evaluation circularity. That is to say, not only are the wants themselves shaped by feedback processes from the institutional instruments for satisfying wants, but these processes may very well affect the communal selection of values concerning want satisfaction and formation as well. Thus, in a system of production and distribution in which cooperative relations are fostered as the central mode of instrumentality for the satisfaction of wants, widely shared basic wants that individuals attend to even when they have little purchasing power will probably be weighted more heavily than in a system relying on competition and incentives for individuals. In the latter, one can expect greater reluctance to deviate from the principle of equal importance for every dollar of spending, since competition and individualized material incentives are likely to influence communal representatives to stress the values of diversity and desert over the values of equality, need, and communal enjoyment that cooperative relations tend to promote. Whether or not this particular example is empirically valid, the point remains that economic organization and even certain kinds of policies will tend to affect the normative judgments that communal representatives will bring to bear on the measurement function by which diverse patterns of want satisfaction are made commensurable.

Moreover, power plays a role in community decisions and may very well impinge on judgments about how far to deviate from the unqualified satisfaction of wants and how to measure want-satisfaction levels. There is thus an opportunity for injustices to enter at this level of decision making. Democracy in community decisions may reduce this tendency, but can by no means eliminate it.

To refer the necessary normative judgments to community choices is therefore not a sufficient answer. An ethical approach, even if unanimity cannot be expected, is required, normally as a complement to community decision making. The former can then inform and provide criteria for the latter.

Normative judgments and the rationale of want satisfaction

The more crucial point, however, is that regardless of how the required normative judgments are made, rather than flowing out of or naturally complementing the principle of want satisfaction, they have to be inserted in it. The normative judgments do not just need to be made about such supplementary considerations as the distributive aspect of the calculus principle, but apply to the the very basis and nature of the wants. While all principles have to be operationalized by some criterion if they are to be turned into measurable evaluation criteria, we here have to go much further than merely finding a way of operationalizing a concept.

To illustrate this point, take piety once more as an example of a possible evaluation criterion. Piety might be defined as faithfulness to the duties owed to a divine being, with the duties defined differently by the different societies. In this case, the criterion of piety would be open-ended and subject to the comparability problem, and perhaps the evaluation circularity as well. However, piety could be reasonably defined in a manner that is by definition fully exogenous to the system to be evaluated, that is, filled out without observing that particular system; for example, it could be measured by the proportion of time spent on religious activities. Similarly, freedom and well-being, both of which are multidimensional concepts, can be defined, for the purpose of providing an evaluative measure, either endogenously or completely exogenously; and the latter would not be absurd (although clearly not without its difficulties). In other words, plausible criteria for operationalizing these normative principles, that is, for "closing" their open-endedness, can be devised such that we do not insert additional value judgments of a substantive kind. This possibility does not apply to want satisfaction. The latter is not merely a constitutive principle in search of a complementary calculus principle; it requires the insertion of substantive normative judgments to deal with the open-endedness and indeterminacy in the constitutive principle, quite apart from its deficiencies of neglected irrationality and feedback effects.

More concrete and conceptually more significant is the point that not only do such substantive normative judgments have to be introduced, but they tend to be incompatible with the basic rationale of the want-satisfaction principle. This principle makes sense *only* when formulated in the open-ended manner, which requires the criterion to be filled out endogenously. To do the opposite, to set up a system of wants, other than the actual preference structures of the members of the particular society, as the constituents of the criterion would have the effect of depriving the criterion of its essential rationale. Even if these normative judgments do not go as far as ignoring actual wants, but merely constrain and bias the way in which their satisfaction is valued, their insertion into the want-satisfaction principle subverts the principle's fundamentally open-ended and subjective character. Yet not to insert them leaves it open to the problems of ignorance and irrationality, of the evaluation circularity, and of noncomparability. This dilemma quintessentially reflects the shortcomings of the want-satisfaction principle and of the sovereignty conceptions that are based on it.

PART V

Human interests and deprivation

CHAPTER 8

Objective conceptions of human interests

8.1 Human sovereignty

Human sovereignty and alternative conceptions of human interests

In order for the representation of interests to be suitable to the more ambitious tasks of evaluation and optimization, interests have to be formulated so that they are free from the inadequacies that afflict the want-satisfaction principle when used in that role. That formulation should not be subject to irrationality, it should transcend the evaluation circularity, and it should be measurable in such a way that the levels of interest fulfillment can be compared across individuals, situations, and systems. I will use the term "human interests" for those conceptions that meet these requirements. Human interests are those interests that are not contingent on particular economic systems, but apply regardless of the structure and process of production and distribution. In that sense, they are universal. (The aim here is to attain a perspective analogous to Rawls's [1971:260–3] "Archimedian point" for evaluating social practices, i.e., an evaluation that is "not contingent upon existing desires or present social conditions.") When economic policies, institutions, or systems serve interests in this sense they will be said to serve "human sovereignty," in distinction to consumer, private, or personal sovereignty. An economic system in which human sovereignty prevails is a system that serves human interests before any other goals.

However, before these comments raise excessive expectations or suggest that the impossible is being attempted, let me quickly add that no effort will be made to move beyond certain limits to comparability and thus to the systemic noncontingency of interests. It is only comparisons among modern actual or ideal economies that are deemed to be of interest. By "modern" I mean actual economic systems that are part of the current world system by being connected through the worldwide exchange of goods, technologies, or ideas about social organization and also systems conceivable under currently known social mechanisms and methods of production. Stone Age tribes, theocratic societies, and science-fiction colonies are beyond the sphere within which the idea of human interests will be explored.

Reference to universal human interests, as well as the conclusion of the previous chapter, suggests that the feature in the earlier versions of interest sovereignty that needs to be seriously qualified or discarded is their subjectivity. The objective conception was identified earlier as one involving public criteria, such as standards of rationality, as opposed to the conception where the individual alone is the appropriate judge of his interests. However, now that a wider search for alternatives is to be undertaken, it is useful to distinguish between at least two kinds of "objective" conceptions and to reiterate that a spectrum, rather than a dichotomy, is involved here. (Cf. the discussion in Section 2.1 herein of the variety of conceptions of interests as falling along a continuum of subjective and objective notions.) The further distinction is between *intersubjective* and *impersonally objective* conceptions. The former refers to interpretations of interests that are based on interpersonal agreement. That agreement may, of course, involve social units of quite different sizes, all the way from a small community to all of humanity. Impersonally objective formulations consist of criteria that are independent of the preferences of particular individuals, either singly or as groups, but are based on some notion of human responsibility to a deity, to evolution, or to their own nature or some other notion of the good for human beings whose specification is not left up to them.

Furthermore, both subjectively and intersubjectively conceived interests may be either *unqualified* or *objectively constrained*. That is to say, preferences and agreements about interests, respectively, may either be accepted as they are or have certain requirements imposed on them, such as the requirement for rationality or for autonomy.

To avoid confusion, it is important to point out that the concepts of subjectivity and objectivity here apply to the articulation of the content of the constitutive principle for economic evaluation and optimization and not to the methods of evaluation or measurement. Thus want satisfaction is subjective, not because an observer cannot determine whether certain wants have been satisfied, but because the wants themselves, the end, are determined by the subjects. We are therefore really dealing with what might be called *constitutive subjectivity, objectivity, and intersubjectivity*.

Since an unqualified subjective conception of interests is not a reasonable formulation for economic optimization and evaluation, the following possibilities remain to be considered: (1) an objectively constrained subjective conception, exemplified by *personally articulated in-*

terests that meet certain rationality requirements; (2) an (either un-qualified or objectively constrained) intersubjective conception, represented by *collectively articulated interests*, which can be applied to the formulation of basic needs, as will be done later; and (3) an imper-sonally objective formulation, which does not derive from the views of the subjects whose interests are at stake. The more extreme pos-sibilities, (1) and (3), will be considered before (2) is explored as an answer to the difficulties of those two.

Rational want satisfaction reconsidered

In order to assess the option of the objectively constrained subjective approach, I will consider once more Connolly's and Brandt's versions of the rationality requirement applied to personally articulated in-terests. To reiterate briefly, Connolly's conception of "real interests" refers to what would be preferred if one had experienced the out-comes of the relevant range of options, whereas Brandt's conception of rational desires refers to those desires that a person would have after undergoing cognitive psychotherapy. Both are corrected-pref-erence theories of human interests.[1]

Wall (1975:505–6) has criticized Connolly's conception as follows:

... Connolly's definition of "interests," or rather, his criterion for deciding which of two policies is more in an agent's interest, does not enable him to accommodate two important features of the concept as it is used in ordinary discourse. First, his criterion actually precludes the possibility of using judg-ments about what is in a person's interest to justify or criticize choices. Since his criterion is a kind of *prediction* about what an agent would choose in certain counterfactual conditions, the concept is drained of its normative or eval-uative significance. Secondly, since the concept is analyzed in terms of the hypothetical choice of an *individual* – since it is *his* "privileged choice" between the two policies in appropriate counterfactual conditions which is the *criterion* of which policy is more in his interest – it follows that the agent cannot be mistaken about what is in his interest in this hypothetical choice situation. That is to say, Connolly's definition or criterion commits him to a subjectivist position.

---

[1] Brandt has made no reference to interests, and it is not clear whether he himself would accept his conception of rational desires as the best representation of human interests. On the one hand, he has argued that "the good" is replaceable by "the rationally desired" (1979:126–9) and that individuals rationally and intrinsically want for themselves things in addition to happiness and pleasant experiences (1979:132–8). On the other hand, he has raised a basic objection to preference theories and has argued that when it comes to choosing a "moral code" the choosers will be concerned with happiness rather than rational want satisfaction. In any case, his conception of rational desires is a plausible representation of human interests.

These points are equally applicable to a rational-desire conception of human interests such as Brandt's.

However, the first point has to be rejected because there *is* a fundamental normative judgment contained in this perspective. It is that want satisfaction represents human interests *if* the wants are fully informed and rational. It is only after this normative position has been taken that prediction becomes relevant.

Concerning the second point, it is true that this approach is fundamentally subjectivist (although objectively constrained). Wall considered this an incorrect approach to ethics.

Wittgenstein's celebrated argument against the possibility of private languages can also be construed as an argument against the possibility of private judgment (subjectivism) – i.e. judgment of a kind in which the individual whose judgment it is is necessarily the only authority on its correctness. Those who seek to found moral judgment on private or individual criteria, such as the criteria derived from the empirical inclinations and desires of the individual, implicitly deny that there are public criteria of correctness here. Consequently, such theories are not theories of moral judgment at all. [Pp. 507–8]

However, the public criteria are contained in the overall judgment that wants should be satisfied and, more important, in judgments concerning informedness and rationality. Wall's criticism of the "incorrectness" of Connolly's conception is therefore unpersuasive.

There is, however, a critical difficulty for corrected-preference theories when used in intertemporal or intersystemic optimization or evaluation: They are still subject to the evaluation circularity. Connolly's hypothetical privileged choices are made by individuals who have already been socialized and for whom it is rational to accept that their selves are socialized selves. Although Brandt's notion of cognitive psychotherapy moves toward a transcendence of socialization, it does so only partially. If a certain desire or aversion, without being psychobiologically constitutional or "native" in the most literal sense of that word, is nevertheless so deeply internalized that vivid and repeated visualization of its source will not extinguish or alter it, then it is rational in Brandt's framework; yet a person may, given sufficient detachment for assessing the question, come to think that he would have been better off without this deep-seated conation. It thus clearly does not represent developmental interests (while being probably too demanding as a criterion for satisfactional interests).

The inadequacy of these two corrected-preference theories is brought out more clearly when we ask how we are to evaluate economic policies or systems by considering how well they serve the interests of unborn generations. While it might conceivably be possible to predict the effects of these policies or systems on the preferences of future generations, these would at most be satisfactional preferences. Individuals cannot express preferences about their earliest development, and they will be mature enough to express reliable preferences in that respect only after their most formative development has taken place. There is thus no point in trying to predict developmental preferences. In other words, developmental interests are not considered in a sufficiently fundamental way in these rational-preference conceptions. If we were to modify Connolly's real-interest approach and Brandt's therapy-rational-desire approach to include such basic developmental interests, we would have to consider choices by those whose interests are at stake, but under the hypothetical conditions where socialization has not yet taken place. This consideration is equivalent to weighing the desirability of different possible lives. The problem is that we need a conception of "desirability" that in some acceptable way represents the vantage point of those who are to live those lives, and the different lives can be expected to generate different conceptions of desirability, given the socialization experiences and deprivations that characterize those lives.

Finally, even if these problems could be overcome somehow, the commensurability problem would still remain. There is no reason to expect that the rationality requirements we have considered, when applied to preferences concerning goods, services, environments, work, leisure, and social relations, would produce a uniform set of both marginal and intramarginal value weights across individuals, time periods, and systems.

8.2 Impersonally objective conceptions I: essentialist ideals

Welfarist and essentialist approaches

The opposite to the subjective conception of human interests represented by want satisfaction is the varied array of impersonally objective conceptions, either "welfarist" or "nonwelfarist." The term "welfarist" has been used to refer to "welfare, satisfaction, or people getting what they prefer" (Sen and Williams 1982a:3). I will take welfarist interests to refer to what people desire for themselves, or to enjoyable mental states, or to conditions promoting either of these two. That is to say, welfarist interests consist of self-regarding want satisfaction, happiness (or pleasure, enjoyment, or contentment), or whatever is instrumental to one or both of these ends. Although want satisfaction is clearly a subjective conception of interests, conceptions or welfarist interests that are impersonally objective are (1) happiness conceived of in such a way that it is determined by an observer rather than the subject and (2) conditions required for want satisfaction *in general.*

Before entertaining the possibility of a welfarist impersonally objective criterion, however, we must consider certain representations of nonwelfarist forms. What I have in mind are ideals concerning the good of human beings that go beyond want satisfaction and enjoyable mental states. They characteristically refer to some notion of the essence of human nature or humanity from which certain *aspirations* or even duties for individuals flow, by virtue of being appropriate to human beings. I will refer to such ideal notions of interests as *essentialist* conceptions. (The following discussion will, however, remain within the confines of a human-centered approach, so that religious or "biocentric" conceptions of human interests will be left out of the picture. Similarly, I am ruling out organismic approaches, which attribute to societies, cultures, or states certain interests that transcend the interests of its current and future members and make those interests of social units constituents of *ultimate,* as opposed to instrumental, human interests.)

Two popular examples of essentialist conceptions of human interests are self-realization and self-determination. Self-realization encompasses both self-development and self-expression. Self-determination usually involves not only some form of freedom from social (and, in some conceptions, also genetic) determination, but also rationality in the exercise of this freedom. It is important to note that what makes these goals or ideals essentialist is not claims for their general appropriateness, but rather claims for their appropriateness as *ends in themselves* specifically. Self-realization or self-determination may be wanted, or may make people happy, or may facilitate social arrangements that efficaciously serve want satisfaction or happiness; if it is these considerations that give them their value, they have merely *derivative* value and are not ends in themselves. To be essentialist these ideals must be ultimate.

Self-realization and self-determination

Self-realization is sometimes based on a naturalistic justification. That is to say, it is claimed that simply by observing human nature we can arrive at values appropriate to human beings. Thus Erich Fromm (1947:29), for example, argued that "all organisms have an inherent tendency to actualize their specific potentialities. The aim of man's life, therefore, is to be understood as the unfolding of his powers according to the laws of his nature" (emphasis omitted; cf. Maslow 1962:e.g., 3–4). However, as analytical philosophers have continually argued in this century, there is a fundamental objection to deriving an "ought" statement from a pure "is" statement.[2]

Even if one avoided the naturalistic fallacy and instead put forward as an a priori proposition that human beings should fulfill their potentialities, then there are still difficulties for self-realization, quite apart from such a (perhaps defensibly) truncated justification. First of all, there is an indeterminacy in the principle of self-realization. We have many potentialities but limited time and energy to realize them. Should we realize as *many* potentialities as possible or those that can be realized in the greatest possible *depth*? By what criterion are we to weight these various potentialities? The principle itself provides no basis for prioritizing them. (Cf. Nielsen 1962:172–3 and 1973/1976:118–22.)

A moral criterion other than and beyond self-realization seems to be required not only to deal with the multiplicity of potentialities of human beings, but also to screen out certain potentialities whose realization we would not want to approve, such as deception, murder, suicidal depression, and insanity. (Cf. McCloskey 1976:4, 6–7, and Porter 1980:126–30.) Using human distinctiveness as the criterion to give normative significance to potentialities not shared with other species, as Aristotle suggested, will not remove certain clearly undesirable potentialities, such as the capacity to commit distinctly human atrocities and to experience irrational guilt and alienation. And many potentialities that we share with animals, such as the capacity for nurturing and for enjoying physical movement, seem eminently worth fostering. Even if there were not this difficulty, to make human distinctiveness the criterion to distinguish between normatively positive and neutral or negative potentialities means to make the promotion of human distinctiveness, rather than self-realization, the ultimate value.

Moreover, the ideal of self-realization seems to imply a conception of human beings as having functions that they are born with or socially endowed with, rather than ones that they come to choose. As Kai Nielsen (1973/1976:122) has pointed out,

---

[2] The descriptivist attempt to do so (for an overview see Hudson 1970:249–330), even if it is accepted as successful in what it aims to demonstrate, has a particular difficulty in the context of the quest to transcend noncomparability and the evaluation circularity. The moral force of certain "is" statements is determined by the institutions that shape people's lives; consequently, if one takes "is" statements as the rationale for self-realization, then how self-realization is spelled out can be expected to be different in different systems.

for the very notion of man's having a function to have even a tolerably clear meaning, it must be the case that man is conceived on close analogy with an artifact, a functional part of the body such as the liver or heart, or with someone such as a policeman or barber who has a social role. But man *qua* man has no social role and he is too unlike an artifact or a functioning part of a body for that analogy to be helpful.

(Cf. Nielsen 1962:175 and Baier 1957:366–7.)

If, on the other hand, the various potentialities that are to be endorsed for realization are determined by the particular social systems, then, of course, we are right back in the problem of noncomparability. If economic institutions affect this determination we also have the evaluation circularity. Moreover, self-realization, as articulated within particular systems, should be suspected of being formulated to serve system maintenance, which, depending on the nature of the system, may be exploitative.

Self-determination is the other essentialist ideal to be briefly considered. It suggests itself as an answer to the problem of heteronomous preferences. If preferences are autonomous or self-determined in a particularly strong sense, we no longer have the evaluation circularity. Moreover, if self-determination is conceived so as to require rationality, as is usually the case, the problem of irrationality is also removed. Whether the comparability problem could be resolved depends on whether self-determination is one-dimensional and measurable. It seems to me highly doubtful that that condition can be met without appealing to conceptually distinct criteria.

Still more fundamental, however, is whether self-determination is sufficiently feasible to make it an attractive central principle of optimization and evaluation and whether it is unequivocally desirable, in the sense that we would want to maximize it. Doubts concerning feasibility arise from the earlier discussion of socialization, and especially primary socialization. If our earliest and probably most fundamental development cannot be self-determined, by virtue of our immaturity, it is only later choices that can be self-determined, but they are then determined by a self that has already been formed by the social environment. Perhaps we can be "unsocialized" by a process such as Brandt's cognitive psychotherapy. But, even if possible, this is too weak a conception of self-determination to avoid the evaluation circularity, since such a review of habituated preferences may lead to their retention simply because they fit the social and economic system well. Concerning its desirability, the maximization of self-determination might well involve serious sacrifices of such other values as social rootedness or spontaneity (or the value of happiness, which they can serve). Maximal self-determination may be too much at odds with any reasonable conception of welfare to be acceptable as a central ultimate value.

One obvious answer to at least some of these difficulties is to treat both self-determination and self-realization as derivative from welfare interests. Self-determination and self-realization then would be desirable to the extent that, and in the form in which, they promote happiness. In this role they would still be very important values, but they would no longer be essentialist or nonwelfarist.

This discussion was not meant to provide a definitive critique of essentialist representations of interests. All that it was intended to accomplish was to indicate that there are no alternatives to welfarist conceptions that get us out of the basic difficulties of the want-satisfaction approach without embroiling us in major new ones. It is therefore reasonable to return to the immanent approach to criticizing and reforming interpretations of interests. Since consumer sovereignty and its extensions belong to welfarist interest theory, this is what will now be explored in an impersonally objective version.

8.3   Impersonally objective conceptions II: happiness

Happiness as an objective conception

It may seem curious at first that happiness is presented as an objective representation of human interests. Its presentation as subjective is both common and, without doubt, reasonable; happiness is taken to refer to mental states that individuals find desirable (Wright 1963/1976:100–3; Montague 1967; Rescher 1972:36–7; Brandt 1979:e.g., 146). "Ultimately, a man is himself judge of his own happiness. . . . any third person judgment which may be passed on his happiness, depends for its truth-value on how *he himself* values his circumstances of life" (Wright 1963/1976:101).

However, a less open-ended conception of happiness, which refers to a particular kind of mental state, or, more accurately, a conception of the happiness–unhappiness opposites that refers to a particular spectrum of mental states, can be objective. This is so in the sense that it is not a matter of personal choice what happiness is. We may have to rely on the subject to do the observing, since the observational technology may not permit reliable third-person assessments, but objective happiness means that it is possible to explain to the subject what the objective meaning of happiness is and what he is supposed to look for when assessing his own happiness. Thus, in one psychological scale of happiness, various points on the scale were given such descriptions as "complete elation[,] rapturous joy and soaring ecstasy"; "feeling very good and cheerful"; "spirits low and somewhat 'blue'"; "utter depression and gloom[,] completely down[,] all is black and leaden" (Wessman and Ricks 1966:273). The subjective element for respondents is one merely of judgmental discretion, not really of significant choice. In other words, although the assessment may have to be subjective, the formulation of happiness is constitutively objective. This formulation has to be such that the scale for measuring happiness can, at least in principle, be applied in different systems and that the economic processes do not shape the scale.

It is important, however, to distinguish this kind of objective conception clearly from another that has been called "objectivist" (Kraut 1979:180–1), but is so in a morally evaluative form. The latter similarly refers to mental states, but it differs from the *pure* mental-state conception in that it adds objective, third-person criteria that do not refer to mental states. This "notion of happiness encompasses at least some of our ideals of the 'good' life, and a contented, or satisfied, or pleasure-filled life which departs too radically from those ideals will not be seen as a 'really' happy life" (Brock 1973:243). Whether the ordinary-language meaning of happiness contains such ideals is subject to philosophical dispute (Brock 1973:243; cf. the opposite positions of Barry 1965:41, who took a morally evaluative position, and of Montague 1967:101–2). My impression is that both morally evaluative and nonevaluative uses of "happiness" can be found in common discourse. In any case, the more basic question here is what kind of objective conception of happiness is needed for economic optimization and evaluation.

One feature of the evaluative conception of happiness is that its moral criteria create a serious problem for making judgments about degrees of happiness and unhappiness. For example, if positive happiness requires by definition that certain moral standards be satisfied, it is not clear whether an immoral person who is contented or generally cheerful is to be declared unhappy or whether a judgment of happiness or unhappiness becomes entirely inapplicable. Describing the person as unhappy seems to make the moral standard the decisive element in the definition of happiness and the mental state only secondary; that would be odd, to say the least. The alternative of making the happiness–unhappiness judgment inapplicable means that immoral persons are considered neither happy nor unhappy, but merely immoral; again, this use seems odd and is certainly unhelpful.

Instead of using a compound concept that creates difficulties for the application of the happiness–unhappiness continuum and that, moreover, sets up controversies about appropriate moral standards to build into the definition and would probably lead to intersystem variations in such standards, it seems more useful to use the concept in a restricted, mental-state sense. (If there are reasons why happiness cannot be the sole normative principle, it is intellectually more candid to supplement it by requirements stated as *separate* value principles and to acknowledge clearly conflicts and trade-offs between happiness and other principles than to conceal such normative tensions by packing the additional normative principles into the concept of happiness.)

Although it is possible for a person to be happy or unhappy just for a moment, for economic optimization and evaluation it is necessary to focus on protracted happiness or unhappiness. What is at stake, therefore, are happy or unhappy states of mind that either are also protracted or are some aggregation or average over time of varying degrees of occurrent happiness or unhappiness. Intensity and duration are the only calculus dimensions needed for the assessment of a person's long-term happiness. The practical problems of measurement are left for later.

Assuming that mental states can in fact be assessed in terms of happiness and that it makes sense to aggregate these assessments over time, then we do have in happiness a constitutive optimization and evaluation principle that provides commensurability and is free of the evaluation circularity. Its use as such a principle requires, of course, that the happiness scale be calibrated prior to its application in particular systems.

The happiness principle is also free of the third affliction of the want-satisfaction principle, namely, irrationality, but this is not quite so obvious. Certainly, when the pursuit of happiness is irrational, the resulting happiness or unhappiness itself is not made irrational. The situation is simply analogous to the use of inefficient means to reach ends to which the rationality criterion is inapplicable. But what of the case where happiness (or unhappiness) is based on false beliefs? Beliefs are a cause, rather than a constituent, of happiness (cf. Davis 1981:119), and therefore irrationality here too characterizes the means and not the end. Just as moral criteria should be kept separate from the conception of happiness, so the ideals of truth and understanding should not be inserted into it. Thus happiness in a fool's paradise is neither rational nor irrational; its disadvantage is not that it is somehow a lesser form of happiness, but only that its future is not very secure. Happy people who do not know that some disaster is about to befall them are nevertheless still happy at this time.

It may appear that irrationality is treated differently with respect to happiness than it was with respect to want satisfaction, but that is, in fact, not the case. Most wants are instrumental to ulterior wants and are thus means rather than ends and subject to *instrumental* irrationality. To the extent that ultimate wants are involved, if they are ultimate in the strict, noncontingent sense, it was acknowledged in Section 5.5 that rationality judgments are not applicable, because wants then represent unconditional ends. (Ultimate wants in the more relaxed sense, where wants are contingent on beliefs or relationships among them, can still be subject to epistemic irrationalities and inconsistencies.) In the case of happiness we are dealing with an unconditional end. The correction of false beliefs does not change how happiness is conceived, though it does affect the set of wants that is to be fulfilled under the want-satisfaction criterion. Of course, it affects the efficient *fulfillment* of happiness, just as it affects the efficient satisfaction of wants, whether the wants themselves are rational or not, but that question is different from the constitution of the ends.

In the light of developments in utilitarianism in this century, it is perhaps somewhat curious for me to take a happiness theory seriously in this search for a conception of human interests. Although happiness theories in various guises have continually arisen in Western ethics since the early days of Greek philosophy, it is in response to difficulties that critics saw in mental-state utilitarianism that the preference theory rejected in this book has become the predominant one among utilitarian philosophers and welfare economists. However, since the preference theory of human interests has itself such serious problems, another look at the value of happiness is warranted.

Considerations supporting happiness as a central evaluation criterion

The best-known argument in support of the happiness principle is John Stuart Mill's (1861/1969). It consisted essentially of three elements: (1) that what is generally desired by people is desirable for people; (2) that people generally desire happiness (or pleasure, which in Mill's terms came to the same thing); and (3) that because every person should seek his own happiness, each person also has a moral obligation to promote the happiness of all. (It should be noted that Mill's conception of happiness was more open-ended and qualified than the one I am presently considering.) I will deal only with element

(2), that is, the psychologically hedonistic part, because, regarding (1), Mill did not claim to present a logical proof and, regarding (3), in our context here we are not concerned with how individuals should behave.

With respect to argument (2), it is frequently pointed out that people want not just states of happiness, but other states of being, activities, and achievements. One response is to insist that such other desires are, consciously or unconsciously, expected by the individual to be productive of happiness. This proposition could be empirically tested as long as we are dealing with conscious expectations. I, for one, would not expect it to hold for all identifiable wants of all persons. But a broader conception of the proposition, one that includes conditioning on the basis of past experiences and that is based on psychological theory and evidence, is more plausbile. According to it, "pleasure is motivationally basic, in the sense that all our intrinsic desires for a state of affairs S owe their existence to an experience of S having been pleasant, or something similar to S having been pleasant, or to the association of an experience of S with something else that was pleasant" (Brandt 1982:183; cf. Brandt 1979:ch. 5). It is possible that this is no more than a paradigmatic assumption with some evidence in support of it and that counter-hypotheses have not been systematically tested. I simply do not know. Nevertheless, the fact that psychologists have found it useful is itself a consideration in favor of it.

A second possible response to the criticism of psychological hedonism is to claim that wants that are not conducive to happiness (either of the person himself or of others) violate rationality, possibly because these wants have been patterned to serve system maintenance rather than the individuals' own most fundamental interests. For this proposition to amount to more than a sleight of hand, it, too, has to be empirically supported. Perhaps experiments in Brandt's cognitive psychotherapy would reveal a pattern. It would certainly not be easy to test it in a conscientiously unbiased manner. Even in the absence of bias, it is likely that there would be serious controversy over what the proposition entails. All this is not to denigrate this position, but to indicate that it is at present nothing more than a hypothesis, and one that is not easy to test.

Another version of the preceding objection to psychological hedonism is the assertion that people do not seek happiness, but that instead they pursue goals and that the achievement of these goals creates satisfaction or happiness "as a by-product" (Porter 1980:94). This version actually suggests another argument in support of happiness as the central ultimate value. Happiness, interpreted as "feeling good," might be taken to be the signal of our psychobiological constitution that not only are our most strongly felt wants being satisfied, but that such want satisfaction in fact is appropriate for us. In other words, "feeling good" is an indicator of the attainment of the good of our being. In this view, wants and their satisfaction serve the good of the subject, which is, if not constituted by happiness, then at least indicated by it. It should be noted, however, that this view is a welfarist version of essentialism. It might be based either on the naturalist argument that to see happiness as indicator of the well-being of human beings is purely a matter of observation or, alternatively and more plausibly, on the a priori argument that human well-being is the condition that is reflected by happiness. (Although, for the sake of simplicity, I earlier used the term "essentialism" to refer only to non-welfarist ideals, this use now needs to be modified, since there is no reason why happiness cannot just as well be seen as central to the human essence.) This, then, is another possible basis for the centrality of happiness.

Finally, there is an argument by Brandt (1979) that uses, as the criterion for the formulation of human interests, what we want for others when we are being rationally benevolent (as opposed to rationally self-regarding). The argument is that, first, commonsense observation suggests that when we are benevolent

what we seem to care about securing for other persons (e.g. our own children) is their happiness; and we seem to care about getting them what they want (or what they would want if they knew more, etc.) only to the extent that so doing will bring them happiness or avoid distress and depression. Second, the psychological theory of benevolence leads to the conclusion that what we are sympathetically motivated to secure for others is happiness and freedom from distress (although we may want desire-satisfaction because we believe it a means to these). [Pp. 248–9; see also pp. 139–48, esp. 146–8]

(The psychological theory, in very summary terms, is that sympathy is acquired by identifying, on the basis of the expressive behavior of others, the indicated *mental states* of others with mental states that one has experienced oneself. On the other hand, the objective satisfaction of a person's desires, apart from his *feeling* of satisfaction, cannot be expected to elicit sympathetic motivation in another person [Brandt 1979:148].)

If human interests are to be interpreted as what moral agents would agree should be the moral basis for designing, implementing, and evaluating institutions and policies, and if these are to be independent of their own distinctive characteristics, then, instead of using a self-oriented basis for identifying interests (as in Rawls's contractualism, where there may not be enough information behind the veil of ignorance to do that in any case), we may think of interests in more social terms, that is, in terms of what we recognize as each other's interests. In that case rational benevolence is an appropriate criterion of human interests, and if Brandt's argument is empirically valid, happiness is then the ultimate human interest. This other-regarding basis for determining interests is particularly appropriate where interests in other cultures and in future generations have to be identified and where no common means to the satisfaction of culturally and personally distinctive wants can be identified. (That Rawls's structure of primary goods is not universal is argued in Section 8.4 herein.)

These rather diverse arguments in favor of happiness as the central ultimate value in social evaluation suggest that quite different moral methodologies (to use Hare's [1973/1974:81] phrase to distinguish normative theories from metaethics and from practical ethics) are potentially capable of supporting it. One can arrive at it on intuitive grounds; one can extract it from an ideal-observer theory of social ethics; one can argue that universal prescriptivism leads to the organization of society so as to maximize happiness; and one can conclude that hypothetical social contracts under conditions conducive either to impartiality among self-interested agents or to mutual benevolence will make happiness central. All this is merely to make a case for the general attractiveness of happiness, not to provide a decisive argument for it. Before a fuller assessment can be made, we need to look at the conception of happiness more closely.

The affective and appraisal conceptions of happiness

In considering the pure mental-state conception of happiness, I will distinguish between two different versions of it, the affective conception and the appraisal conception. This distinction comes out clearly in Nicholas Rescher's (1972:36–7) definition of happiness as

a mixture of two prime considerations: (1) an assessment of mood patterns, some sort of "averaging" of the state of [the individual's] psychic feeling tone of euphoria/dysphoria over the recent past and the predictable future, and (2) an intellectualized appraisal of the conditions and circumstances of his present mode of life with a view to his content or discontent therewith.

(Cf. Brandt 1967:413–14.) Treating Rescher's two facets of happiness instead as different conceptions, we have two ways in which a person can be happy. (1) His feeling states are predominantly positive. (2) He is contented with his "total life pattern" (Brandt 1967:413), which can include not only his circumstances and conditions but also his achievements (Montague 1967:87–92). "Affective happiness" designates the first possibility and "appraisal happiness" the second. For a clear distinction between the two it is necessary to regard contentment or discontent in the appraisal conception not as a feeling state as such, but as referring to first-person *judgments* concerning the adequacy of the person's conditions and of his advancement toward his goals. The mental state in the latter case is an attitudinal or judgmental state rather than a feeling state as such.

Although it is reasonable to expect that appraisal happiness and affective happiness will usually be correlated, divergence between the two cannot be ruled out. Rescher has given the example of "the man who, from the angle of intellectual appraisal, finds no basis for discontent (he enjoys splendid health, is affluently circumstanced, has good family relations, etc.) [but] may possibly still fail to *feel* happy" (p. 37). Conversely, a man who is quite cheerful and enjoys life may, in a reflective mood, nevertheless conclude that he has been a failure because he has not achieved the goals that he set himself as a young man; but it is a relatively intellectual assessment that, apart from a momentary twinge of regret, does not alter his generally favorable feeling state. Because such divergence is possible, even though untypical, a choice has to be made about which of these two happiness conceptions is to be put forward as a representation of the fundamental human interest. (Nothing is gained by adopting a dual conception such as Rescher's. We not only then have to deal with the difficulties of both the affective and the appraisal conceptions, but we have the further problem of making appraisal happiness and affective happiness commensurable. How to do this has not been discussed in any of the writings that I am familiar with.)

As a constitutive principle for optimization and evaluation, affective happiness makes more sense than the appraisal conception, for two basic reasons. (1) As I will argue in a moment, affective happiness is normatively more basic. (2) The appraisal conception has subjective elements that are important here, and it is not immune to the evaluation circularity.

(1) My claim that affective happiness is normatively more basic than appraisal happiness rests on three points. (a) In the case of individuals who live from moment to moment and do not reflect and pass judgment on their general conditions, assessments of appraisal happiness cannot be made at all; the only way they can be described as happy or unhappy is in terms of the affective conception. (Cf. Davis 1981:112.)

Adoption of the appraisal conception of happiness would put us into the absurd position where we would have to say that such unreflective people, including young children, have neither happiness nor unhappiness and that expressing concern for their happiness would be nonsense.

(b) Although philosophers, to the extent that they adhere to a non-evaluative conception of happiness at all, tend to interpret happiness in appraisal terms, that is not the most basic use in common discourse. Let us imagine two opposite cases of divergence. In one a person judges his life, either his opportunities or his achievements, to be unsatisfactory, but his feeling state is not greatly affected by his judgment, so that in general he feels cheerful. In the other case the person judges his life to be satisfactory but most of the time feels anxious or depressed. I think it would generally be agreed that it is the second person who is unhappy, whereas the first is happy in spite of disappointments.

(c) The degree to which a rationally benevolent person will take another person's disappointments seriously as a reflection of his well-being will depend on their impact on his feeling states. If he acknowledges his disappointments but emotionally shrugs them off or is not preoccupied with them on an ongoing basis, then the rationally benevolent observer will not treat them as seriously affecting the core of the individual's well-being. (Rescher's [1972:37] example of "the man who sees himself as deeply unhappy [who] may yet continue in a euphoric state of 'feeling happy' (perhaps even through drink or drugs)" seems implausible, except in the transient state of "forgetting his basic misery." The fact that the man sees himself as deeply unhappy suggests a depth in *feeling* and not merely a *judgment* about the size of the discrepancy between expectations and attainments.) On the other hand, the depression or anxiety that affects an individual but is not (or at least is not recognized to be) connected with the conditions on the basis of which the individual appraises his life *would* be a cause for serious concern to a rationally benevolent observer. (If the disappointments are due to injustices, we may be concerned with them quite apart from their emotional impact; but it is then the injustices themselves, rather than the assessment of them by their victims, that should be the focus of the concern.) As far as well-being is concerned, it is the affective consequences of appraisals rather than life appraisals as such that constitute the core notion of well-being.

This emphasis on cases of divergence between appraisal and affective happiness must not blind us to the much more typical situation of the close relationship between the two. Affective happiness can thus be expected to reflect appraisal happiness to a considerable degree.

(2) The second reason for preferring affective happiness is that the appraisal conception contains important subjective elements and is subject to the evaluation circularity. It should, however, be noted first that these two features are not the same in the case of appraisal happiness as in that of want satisfaction. In this case we are not faced with multidimensionality. (Multidimensionality is possible, if, for example, appraisal is to be applied to one's opportunities and living conditions and also to one's personal achievements, or, alternatively, to various facets of one's life. But it can be avoided by limiting appraisal to the appraisal of one's life in general. This approach can be found in some of the "quality-of-life" research. See, e.g., Campbell, Converse, and Rodgers 1976:esp. pp. 7–11 and 32–7.) Without multidimensionality, commensurability is possible. However, there are reasons why this commensurability is not trustworthy and why appraisal happiness is subject to the evaluation circularity even without multidimensionality. The calibration for the single dimension we are dealing with is shaped by social processes that can be traced back to the economic system. Two such processes are what I will call, respectively, (a) the *expectations effect* and (b) the *face-saving effect*.

(a) Personal expectations are very much part of the individual's appraisal of his life. The appraisal cannot be conducted without them, since these expectations in effect provide the calibration for the assessment. These expectations are needed even to set the zero point that separates positive happiness from unhappiness in the appraisal. Whether one's life is good or not depends on what one expects a good life to consist of. Consequently, personal expectations are elements in the appraisal-happiness criterion. Personal expectations are shaped by economic processes either directly, through experiential patterning, for example, or through social expectations, generated by the experiences and views of others. In this way economic processes influence the calibration for appraisal happiness in distinctive ways. Moreover, even within particular systems, the expectations effect makes the assessment of appraisal happiness unreliable because expectations will vary between individuals and various groupings, including, in particular, socioeconomic classes.

(b) The face-saving effect consists of the social-psychological pressure to present one's circumstances in a more favorable light than one would in the absence of such pressures, possibly because one's circumstances are taken to be a reflection upon one's successfulness and worth. This effect creates a problem for the reporting of dissatisfaction. It may induce people to appraise their situations as satisfactory, even though deep down they are unhappy about them. We then have a problem of distorted revelation, and these distortions may be systematically patterned so that the revealed appraisal is subject to the evaluation circularity. (Cf. Townsend 1979:470–2.)

Problems in the one-dimensional conception of affective happiness

Taking these considerations as decisive for the rejection of appraisal happiness, I will now turn to the question whether affective happiness survives critical scrutiny to a significantly greater degree. In particular, (1) the measurability of affective happiness and (2) the assumption, adhered to so far, of its one-dimensionality have to be looked at.

(1) The most basic approach to the measurement of happiness is that of the public opinion polls on happiness (surveyed in Easterlin 1974). It involves asking a question such as the following: "Taken all together, how would you say things are these days – would you say that you are very happy, pretty [or fairly] happy or not too [or not very, or not] happy?" (Bradburn 1969:269, ch. 3; Easterlin 1974:99–111). Assuming for now that the respondents interpret this question in affective terms and that there is a single dimension of affective happiness, we have here a criterion that is constitutively objective, even though it relies on self-reports and is thus subjective in its assessment.

What is striking about these simle surveys, which use the three intensity categories, is that a remarkably high proportion of people, at least in the United States, characterize themselves as "very happy." According to one series of American polls, between 1946 and 1970 this proportion never fell below 39 percent; those who said they were "not very happy" were never more than 11 percent. Moreover, for the period 1946–52, for which that poll related the responses to relative incomes, it turned out that even among the poor one-third declared themselves to be "very happy" (Easterlin 1974:109–11).

Exactly what to make of these responses is not entirely clear. Clinical psychologists distrust the validity of self-reports. (For an extensive discussion see Bradburn 1969:ch. 3.) Self-reports may involve self-deception (Wright 1963/1976:102) or simply adaptation to perceived social expectations. A study (by H. J. Goldings) cited by A. E. Wessman and D. F. Ricks (1966:99–100) (a) discovered that most respondents rated their own happiness higher than that of the average person in the sample population, (b) presented "many indications in the American scene which suggest that feelings of happiness tend to be approved and feelings of unhappiness disapproved in the culture," and (c) concluded "that . . . the culture designates a preferred range for the avowal of happiness," so that there is good reason to suspect that a self-report of happiness may be a response to cultural pressures rather than a true report of the respondent's state of mind. (The mere presence of an interviewer seems to intensify this cultural pressure; one study, cited in Bradburn 1969:38, found that while a self-administered questionnaire yielded a "very happy" rate of 23 percent, an interview survey of another sample of the same population yielded 36 percent. On the other hand, the Goldings study also found that when individuals reported on their happiness in a setting of clinical rapport and trust, their avowals of unhappiness increased [Wessman and Ricks 1966:99–100].) Thus the expectation and face-saving effects seem to apply in a similar way to affective-happiness assessments as they apply to assessments of appraisal happiness. This finding certainly makes the measure untrustworthy. Whether the difficulty makes it prone to the evaluation circularity depends on whether the assessment standards and the social pressures are related to economic processes.

Those surveys, however, are quite crude. Moreover, it is not entirely clear whether the questions are meant to refer to affective or appraisal happiness. A more careful and more intensive type of survey that unambiguously refers to affective happiness was designed by Wessman and Ricks (1966). They developed a number of affect scales, with descriptions of the intensity level given for each of ten points on the scale. The scale relevant to happiness is the following:

XVI. Elation vs. Depression (how elated or depressed, happy or unhappy you felt today)
10. Complete elation. Rapturous joy and soaring ecstasy.
9. Very elated and in very high spirits. Tremendous delight and buoyancy.
8. Elated and in high spirits.
7. Feeling very good and cheerful.
6. Feeling pretty good, "O.K."
5. Feeling a little bit low. Just so-so.
4. Spirits low and somewhat "blue."
3. Depressed and feeling very low. Definitely "blue."
2. Tremendously depressed. Feeling terrible, miserable, "just awful."
1. Utter depression and gloom. Completely down. All is black and leaden. [P. 273]

The respondents were asked to do a daily rating of the high, low, and average for the day over a six-week period. "The subjects were told that probably the descriptive statements would not correspond exactly with what they felt, but were rather to be regarded as approximations from which they were to select those closest to their own experiences" (p. 29).

The Wessman–Ricks approach reduces susceptibility to the distortions that afflict the public opinion surveys by providing a much more elaborate scale with more specific intensity descriptions, by requiring a repeated answer so that insight by the individual into his feeling states is prompted, and by developing respondent confidence in the nonjudgmental empathy of the investigators. Although it is doubtful that distortions are removed entirely, this approach suggests that unless perfection is demanded, affective happiness can be measured in a reasonably acceptable manner. However, it is a very costly procedure. To evaluate carefully the performance of policies, institutions, and systems would require considerable expenditure of resources. Moreover, the approach is intrusive and, quite apart from being unwanted in many cases, may create a certain amount of anxiety, so that it may involve a direct cost in affective happiness. Nevertheless, such practical problems in the measurement of affective happiness do not necessarily count against the conceptual use of this criterion in a decisive way. The requirement of *conceptual* measurability is met in this case, and that of noncircularity is approximated. As long as this criterion is conceptually appropriate in other respects, it can be used as the basis for discretionary judgments where accurate measurement is not needed. Moreover, where such measurement is needed, it is possible.

(2) There is, however, a conceptual question concerning the assumption of the one-dimensionality of affective happiness. The objection has been made in the following terms:

The trouble with thinking of utility as *one* kind of conscious state is that there is no discernible mental state common to all that we regard as having utility – eating, reading, working, creating, helping. What one mental state runs through them all in virtue of which we rank them as we do? The truth seems, rather, that often we just rank them, *period;* often they are basic preferences, not resting upon further judgements about quantities of some homogeneous mental state present in or produced by each. [Griffin 1982:333]

The various kinds of affective states that can constitute the more general condition of happiness–unhappiness include such feeling-state spectra as fulfillment–frustration, love–hostility, ease–anxiety, confidence–fear, serenity–bewilderment, pride–shame, exhilaration–depression, and ecstasy–despair.

What does this then mean for the significance of the elation–depression scale? Is it simply one among several relevant affective dimensions, or is it some kind of resulting summary dimension? I must admit that I am torn on this question. On the one hand, I am inclined to think that I personally treat such specific emotions as anger, love, or fear as having significance for well-being (both my own and that of others) to the extent that they affect the elation–depression dimension, and that others do so as well. On the other hand, it may well be that, even though elation and depression constitute a definite affective dimension for particular points in time, an individual's assessment of his happiness *over a period of time* involves not only a judgment regarding the effect of different and fluctuating feeling states on the elation–depression dimension, but a valuation of these feeling states.

If it is conceded that happiness is multidimensional in this way, then it makes sense to define it, with Brandt (1979:253ff. and 1982:174), as preferred experiences, or, in accordance with my earlier argument, as preferred affective states. However, although Brandt has identified a single dimension in this conception in the form of "enjoyment," or the valuation of experiences, and has suggested a method for making it commensurable over time and between persons (1979:257–65), it is extremely difficult to operationalize. It involves identifying a sensation, such as thirst of a certain degree, on the basis of its physiological manifestations, in two or more physiologically similar (and perhaps similarly habituated) individuals and using it as the unit of commensurability by assuming the same valuation of the experience by the different individuals. With this procedure the relative valuations of experiences of different persons become commensurable. The task of actually applying this approach is daunting indeed. Even its discretionary use in thought experiments seems rather limited.

In addition, this mental-state preference theory is subject to the evaluation circularity. Focusing on the relative valuation of affective states, consider the contrasting evaluations of, respectively, serenity and exhilaration in contemplative cultures, on the one hand, and activist cultures, on the other. Since a society's system of cultural patterns and values and its system of economic institutions are interdependent, there is a form of evaluation circularity involved. It is not as fundamental as that for want satisfaction, since the effect of economic institutions on the valuation of feeling states is more subtle and marginal than their effect on wants for goods, services, jobs, environments, and social relations. And for intrasystem evaluation it may not be a problem warranting serious concern. Nevertheless, it is more serious than in the case of one-dimensional affective happiness.

In conclusion, it seems to me that either we accept the simpler one-dimensional approach to affective happiness or we reject it and by so doing also reject the possibility of any alternative formulation of a happiness criterion for economic optimization and evaluation.

Some basic difficulties for the happiness criterion

The attractiveness of the constitutive criterion of affective happiness, however, depends not merely on this question. There are other, more basic issues that also have to be settled before it can be accepted that affective happiness is the best optimization and evaluation criterion. First, though, let me quickly point out that one serious criticism traditionally leveled at utilitarianism is not relevant here. Since we are dealing only with a constitutive criterion, the issue of distributive justice does not arise in a direct way; the criterion remains open to alternative supplementary calculus principles that cover distribution. But that is not the only criticism.

One criticism to which happiness as a constitutive criterion is open is that we know so little about the macrosocial causes of long-term affective conditions that this criterion provides little reliable guidance in actual economic choices. It is true that careful observations are being accumulated about the effects of unemployment and relocations required by economic change on the mental health and psychological conditions of individuals. (See, e.g., Brenner 1976; Ineichen 1979:ch. 2; Jahoda 1982; and Kirsh 1983.) However, documentation is being provided only for limited aspects of the system of economic processes, and even for those, I suspect that it has not yet developed to the point where at least approximate predictive relations between economic developments and affective consequences, such as protracted anxiety and depression, could be agreed on for economic optimization. (With respect to pathological depression, an attempt is made to evaluate prototypical economic systems in Section 9.5 herein, but primarily for illustrative purposes.) Of course, this difficulty does not stand in the way of undertaking evaluations that involve the development of new empirical knowledge. For optimization, it makes the happiness criterion implausible *now*, although not necessarily in the future, when the appropriate knowledge base may be developed.

More serious for the long-term prospects of the happiness criterion are what Jonathan Glover (1979:82) has called "radical" policy and system implications in this context, by which he means the unconstrained pursuit of change to maximize happiness, including "social engineering." The latter may be taken to include changes in the preferences, aspirations, expectations, behavior patterns, and sensitivities of individuals and in the experiences that are conducive to their happiness. Without even considering changes to individuals, there are certain means of promoting happiness that we tend to view with suspicion, and some that we regard with revulsion or horror. Thus one way to promote happiness might be to offer diverting forms of popular entertainment or excitement to distract people from their otherwise miserable conditions. Psychotropic drugs of the future might make people's affective condition largely independent of the external environment. That possibility applies even more to the science-fiction images of self-operated electrodes in the pleasures centers of the brains of individuals (Smart 1973:20–1) and the experience machine that can simulate in people's brains any desired experience (Robert Nozick, referred to in Griffin 1982:333). The latter scenarios are also instances of changes to individuals. Such changes are involved as well in policies to contain the expectations of individuals, either directly through propaganda or through the creation of environments that accomplish this limitation. More extreme forms of change would be surgical interventions and a eugenics that selected for a predisposition to be happy. Even if the complementary calculus principle can be designed to rule out those policies that are exploitative and serve a privileged elite through happiness policies that are essentially diversionary, these implications still appear troubling.

These points, however, are not quite as devastating as they may appear at first sight. First of all, any normative ethic has to be designed for human beings as they are and for the kinds of opportunities and constraints that they *actually* face. Science-fiction scenarios are not really relevant, except as a conceivable challenge for designing an ethic appropriate to quite different conditions. (This is not to deny that the current rapid strides in brain research give thinking in this direction some urgency, but it is thinking about a fundamentally different situation from the current one.) Secondly, a principle for macrosocial evaluation can be asked to make sense under a quite broad range of situations, but to ask it to stand up under currently bizarre situations is not reasonable. (Cf. Hare 1976/1982:31–3.) Finally, if the science-fiction examples are used only to indicate the unacceptability of a principle on the basis of the intuitive unattractiveness of its implications, then that use is potentially misleading. Our intuitions, socialized as they are by our current modes of living, are probably no more trustworthy as judgments about the attractiveness of modes of living in a radically different future than the judgments of Cro-Magnon man would be about ours. If we insist on using our intuitions in this manner, we must stay reasonably close to the kinds of situations in response to which these intuitions arose.

As far as the currently possible forms of happiness policies, such as the containment of expectations, are concerned, these are not necessarily inappropriate, assuming they are not exploitative. Even if individuals are in some sense changed in the process, that effect is not distinctive to a happiness policy. Socialization is ubiquitous, and want-satisfaction policies, too, have their inevitable socialization effects. What may be distinctive to a happiness policy is that such changes of individuals are consciously assessed and taken into account in policy making and system design, rather than left as a side effect, usually unacknowledged.

This is merely to defend the centrality of the happiness criterion. It is not to claim that happiness can be used as a constitutive criterion in an unqualified manner. One set of issues that is very difficult to deal with on the basis of the happiness criterion alone is that concerning life and death. Thus a simple way of improving happiness would be to kill (painlessly and without creating anxiety) all those who are not able to attain happiness. Even on a calculus criterion of maximin distribution this would be the implication of an unconstrained happiness principle, at least for those people who, with the maximal effort of society, cannot be lifted out of long-term unhappiness. And it would be independent of the preferences of these unhappy individuals. It is true that such unpalatable consequences can be prevented through empirically contingent considerations, such as the impossibility of carrying out a coercive euthanasia program without creating anxiety, the fallibility of human judgments concerning happiness prospects, and the corruptibility of government. However, many philosophers regard such contingent considerations as insufficiently fundamental to match the depth of our intuitive objection. *If* we could assume infallibility, incorruptibility, and the avoidance of anxiety, should the happiness-promoting coercive euthanasia program be carried out? Is it ethically acceptable for a normative principle to be saved from undesirable implications purely by human imperfection? It seems that the happiness principle has to be constrained by other moral principles. (For an extended discussion of this set of issues, although not explicitly in terms of the distinction between constitutive and calculus principles, see Glover 1977. The issues of procreation and population policy also raise some problems for mental-state utilitarianism, but these affect largely the selection of an appropriate calculus principle, particularly with respect to intergenerational distribution.)

At least two reasons for not adopting an approach to economic optimization and evaluation that is directly and exclusively based on affective happiness have emerged. One is that our knowledge about the macrosocial determinants of happiness and unhappiness is so underdeveloped that the criterion can reasonably be used only to pose fairly basic research questions, on the one hand, and, on the other, to make generalizations that are either fairly obvious or quite speculative. The second reason is that to avoid intuitively unacceptable consequences the happiness principle has to be constrained by other moral principles, such as self-determination, the maintenance of a personal sense of identity (Glover 1979:85–6), and self-realization as ends in themselves. Related to this reason is the persistent claim of critics of mental-state utilitarianism that happiness is not the only thing that human beings want for its own sake, even when they are completely rationally considering only their own interests; Brandt's benevolent-observer argument, which stands in contradiction to this position, is an interesting challenge, but represents an alternative rather than an obviously superior vantage point from which to answer this question. Moreover, I do not consider the issue of the one-dimensionality of affective happiness entirely resolved. Consequently, even if affective happiness remains the central underlying value, as I suggest it should, other ultimate values have to be brought into the picture.

This means a form of value pluralism, although a weak one if happiness remains the central value and the others are supplementary. Since now different and complex ways of combining such principles are possible, it is doubtful whether one particular combination can be established as superior on the basis of arguments that are universally compelling. This difficulty suggests that the impersonally objective approach to the determination of a constitutive optimization and evaluation principle that has been explored in this section is best abandoned in favor of an intersubjective one.

8.4   An intersubjective conception: basic needs

Basic needs as evaluative criterion

The intersubjective or collectively articulated conception of human interests to which I now turn is that of basic needs. In contrast to the monistic approaches considered so far, the intersubjective approach to basic needs is relatively open-ended and potentially pluralistic. It allows the reconciliation of different value perspectives or at least compromises between them. At the same time, it is not (individually) subjective, either in the determination of interests or in the assessment of the fulfillment of these interests.

Unlike the happiness approach, which raises basically prudential questions once it is accepted, the basic-needs approach to be analyzed here is evaluative in a moral sense as well. That is to say, the question what interests are to be recognized as basic needs is not merely an empirical or prudential one, but also a moral one. Another feature that distinguishes it from the happiness approach is that it is usually formulated so that it refers much more directly to ascertainable outputs and outcomes of economic policies and systems. In other words, whereas the happiness approach is impersonally objective in its determination of interests, but has an unavoidably subjective element in the assessment of the fulfillment of interests, that is, of the degree of happiness attained, the basic-needs approach is intersubjective in its determination of interests, but, on the whole, impersonally objective in the assessment of the fulfillment of interests. Nevertheless, in accordance with the argument of the previous section, I suggest that basic needs should be formulated so that happiness is maximally promoted, with appropriate qualifications to avoid some of the undesirable implications of the happiness principle, such as those related to life-and-death issues. Actually, the notion of basic needs suggests a formulation so that unhappiness is minimized rather than happiness maximized (again with appropriate qualifications).

However, the basic-needs approach does not claim to be comprehensive in the way that the previous three approaches potentially are. The basic-needs approach to be analyzed here does not attempt to present the entire set of ends for economic policies and systems, but merely provides a *lexically primary* set of ends. That is to say, fulfillment of basic needs takes normative precedence over the satisfaction of other wants or the fulfillment of other ultimate ideals, but it does not rule out these other ends as secondary goals and criteria.

The conceptualization of human needs

Before I create the impression that there is a single, agreed-on conception of basic needs, let me hasten to add that there is not. But first some brief comments about the fundamental concept of human needs are in order. This concept is both normative and derivative. It has inherent normative force in that to recognize that certain wants or deficiencies of individuals or groups are "needs" of theirs is to acknowledge that there is some urgency in meeting them and usually also that society has a prima facie obligation to do so. The recognition of needs of particular individuals or groups constitutes a stronger claim on society than the recognition of individual or group wants. This is the case particularly with respect to social justice. To claim that certain needs should be met is to make an appeal for justice of a certain kind. The claim that certain wants should be satisfied, on the other hand, is, *as a justice claim*, contingent on other considerations, such as the contributions that the individual has made, which provide the real justification. At the same time, needs, unlike wants, are also a derivative concept in that a valid claim that something is a need of an individual or group has to refer, at least implicitly, to other values regarding what individuals should have or be in order, for example, to survive, to be productive, to flourish. A want can be an end in itself; a need cannot. Thus, in contrast to wants, human needs are normatively primary, but also normatively derivative. (That is the basis of the claims by Raymond Plant [1974:ch. 4] and Ross Fitzgerald [1977a] that appeals to needs are ambiguous when they do not make the normative underpinnings explicit and are misleading when they give the impression that they are founded wholly on an empirical basis.)

While this is the common core of various conceptions of human needs (whether recognized or not), there is a basic divergence between at least two views of human needs. One is essentialist, in that needs are identified as what is required for what is quintessentially human and as that without which harm will occur to the individual. How "harm" is interpreted has varied from "pathological consequences" (Bay 1968:242–3) to whatever is detrimental to "human flourishing" or "natural development" (Anscombe 1958/1969:193–4; McCloskey 1976:5–7) and constriction of rationality (Nielsen 1973/1976). Essentialist conceptions of human needs, as such, are subject to the objections raised against essentialist conceptions of interests in general.

The other interpretation of human needs is that they are what society agrees individuals should not be without. In this spirit, Benn and Peters (1959:144–6) argued for basic needs conceived of in terms of community standards. Joel Feinberg (1973) identified basic needs as things or conditions "in whose absence a person would be harmed in some crucial and fundamental way, such as suffering injury, malnutrition, illness, madness, or premature death" (p. 111). Although this definition sounds impersonally objective, Feinberg acknowledged the socially relative aspect of the concept by stating that "what *everyone* in a given society regards as 'necessary' [owing to habitual dependence] tends to become an actual, basic need" (p. 112). Similarly, Peter Townsend (1979) has argued that "people can be taken to be deprived if they lack the types of diet, clothing, housing, environmental, working and social conditions, activities and facilities which are customary, or at least widely encouraged or approved, in the societies to which they belong" (p. 413). The deprived "drop out or are excluded" from participation in one or more significant aspects of "the community's style of living" (p. 249). This exclusion concept of poverty or deprivation can be found in writers as diverse as Adam Smith and Marx (Atkinson 1975:189), Hegel (Sabine 1937/1963:654), and Galbraith (1958/1969:245).

This distinction between essentialist and conventionalist views of needs also parallels to a certain extent two different uses to which the concept of needs tends to be put. (1) The essentialist view is often used primarily to contrast needs with wants, with individuals presented as often desiring things that are not good for them. This approach is typically adopted by critics of the prevailing pattern of psychopolitical socialization, such as Herbert Marcuse. Needs in this sense, however, are the same as the concept of interests I have used in this work, qualified, of course, with the essentialist stipulations. (In the case of Marcuse, his formal definition of "true" needs is more like rational preferences than essentialist interests, but his use of the concept seems essentialist; however, in the context of actual social criticism that use is understandable, given the counterfactual nature of rational preferences.) (2) Although this latter use of the concept of needs is primarily constitutive, its conventionalist use represents in the first instance a distributive judgment. In its purely distributive sense, the concept is used by egalitarian adherents of consumer or personal sovereignty to refer to certain wants that are to be identified as normatively primary. These are wants that are held by those below a certain level of want satisfaction.

Basic needs as human interests

What will be adopted here is a mixed approach, one that is both distributive and constitutive. It is distributive in that it consists of *basic* needs, that is, needs that represent necessities in some sense. It distinguishes necessity interests from luxury interests. Given the normative priority of such interests, they represent that set of interests to which the principle of equality is applicable. However, basic needs, as used here, are not merely a calculus principle attached to the constitutive principle of want satisfaction, but are themselves also constitutive in two ways. The first is that preferences need to be corrected for various shortcomings; that is, a deeper kind of interest is involved.

Secondly, the nonfulfillment of particular kinds of interests is to be recognized as constituting specific forms of deprivation, rather than some aggregate "neediness." This approach then provides an answer to the problem raised earlier about the relative priority of one person's interest in a wheelchair and another's interest in exotic foods. If it is a satisfactory conception of human interests, it provides us with the "final definition" of interests that was mentioned in Chapter 2.

This approach to basic needs is being put forward as a representation of human interests, that is, a conception of interests that overcomes the difficulties of irrationality, the evaluation circularity, and noncomparability. However, the intersubjective approach, being socially relative, seems to be hopelessly caught in the evaluation circularity. Let us consider now whether there is any way to adapt it to free it from this difficulty, without creating new difficulties, in particular the ones raised in the discussion of essentialist conceptions of interests.

Rawls's theory of primary goods

One approach to human needs that attempts to resolve this problem is the contractarian theory of "primary goods" proposed by Rawls (1971:esp. 90–5; 1975; see Rawls 1975:554 for his statement that "the theory of primary goods is a generalization of the notion of needs"). In order to achieve the necessary independence from existing wants and social institutions, Rawls asked us to imagine an original contracting position in which individuals find themselves behind a "veil of ignorance" that allows them knowledge only of the laws of human nature and social processes, not of the kind of society nor the particular position within any society nor the distinctive character and talents that a contracting individual will ultimately end up with. In this hypothetical situation Rawls argued that the contracting individuals will recognize only "primary social goods" as human interests. These are

things which it is supposed a rational man wants whatever else he wants. . . . With more of these goods men can generally be assured of greater success in carrying out their intentions and in advancing their ends, whatever these ends may be. The primary social goods, to give them broad categories, are rights and liberties, opportunities and powers, income and wealth. (A very important primary good is a sense of one's own worth; [but it operates at a different level].) [1971:93]

He continued: ". . . whatever one's system of ends, primary goods are necessary means. . . . [Knowledge of these provides individuals behind the veil of ignorance with the basis] to advance their interests in the initial situation" (1971:93). This approach "represents, in effect, an agreement to compare men's situations solely by reference to things which it is assumed they all prefer more of" (1971:95).

Although Rawls used the theory to derive his well-known principles of justice rather than as a basis for formulating human interests, its potential in the role of the latter is worth briefly considering. It could be taken to be a comprehensive rather than partial conception of human interests and would in that respect be superior to merely a basic-needs principle. However, it has a number of crucial drawbacks.

(1) Rawls's particular list has been challenged regarding its claim to be independent of particular institutional systems. Civil liberties, economic opportunities, political influence and power, and, finally, prosperity as the set of goods that "a rational man wants whatever else he wants" may be appropriate to the aspirations fostered by our particular social system, but are they the most important requirements for a contemplative life, or for a life in pursuit of change, excitement, and risk, or for the person who looks to society for guidance and for freedom from temptations that lead to corrupting or alienating experiences? Alternative lists of primary goods that are more basic have been put forward (see Teitelman 1972:550 and Barry 1973:31). To base the set of needs on a thought experiment about the preconditions for various possible life aspirations in different social settings is precarious, to say the least.

(2) There is also a problem regarding trade-offs between, and value weights for, the primary goods. It is difficult to see how a thought experiment concerning the original contracting position could generate universally acceptable trade-offs. In fact, Rawls avoided the trade-off issue by arguing that the primary goods are lexically ordered, with a complete set of civil liberties and political rights coming first, openly competitive access to the positions in society next in line, and finally wealth and power, the latter two being assumed to be correlated. However, apart from the difficulty of measuring liberty and dealing with trade-offs among liberties (see Wolff 1977:90–2), there has been considerable criticism of the priority that Rawls has attached to liberties in general (Barry 1973:ch. 7; Wolff 1977:ch. 9). Although Rawls limited the applicability of this priority requirement to societies that have surpassed a certain minimum level of material prosperity, it is highly doubtful whether even in those situations it is rational to commit oneself never to trade off liberties for other primary goods.

(3) Finally, as a conception of needs the theory of primary goods fails to take account of the distinctive disadvantages of certain indi-

viduals. With its emphasis on those general goods that are preconditions for the want satisfaction of all, it neglects special needs, such as
those of the handicapped or of families with a large number of de-
pendents, because the worst-off are identified according to primary
goods, that is, the instrumental interests of all, and not according to
their distinct needs (Barry 1973:55–8).

While the discussion of the happiness principle left doubt about
whether one could plausibly postulate particular ultimate ends that
are universally applicable, the foregoing critique also suggests that
one cannot plausibly assume that there is a universally applicable set
of means to want satisfaction that can adequately represent needs.
Can needs then be specified in a less instrumental manner?

The format for specifying basic needs

A distinction that is useful here is one made by Richard Thayer
(1973/1977:197) between "diagnostic" and "prescriptive" needs. Diagnostic needs refer to "a set of circumstances which is considered to
be undesirable and thus a situation in which there is need for help of
some sort"; prescriptive needs refer to "the help which is required to
alleviate" the problem. (A. J. Culyer's [1976:14–16] distinction between "normative" and "technical" needs is similar.) Difficulties at the
level of optimization and evaluation that is involved here arise primarily when needs are formulated in prescriptive terms. First of all,
the means for eliminating or alleviating particular diagnosed deprivations are often substitutable, in which case there is not a single prescribable means that can be referred to as necessary. Secondly, even in
the absence of such substitutability within systems, the prescribable
means available and appropriate in different systems can be expected
to vary with their different patterns of resources, skills, and habits.
The alleviation of status deprivation, for example, will depend on the
basis for according status; in some instances the prescriptive need will
be nothing less than the abolition of fundamental institutions, such as
untouchability, whereas in others merely socially productive employment may be sufficient. For these reasons, diagnostic needs are
more promising.

We can diagnose such needs or deprivations at various levels of
specificity, ranging, for example, from a general health deprivation
identified by the level of impairment in the individual's daily functioning to a sophisticated diagnosis using medical categories. But only
at a relatively general level can we expect to avoid the evaluation
circularity and the comparability problem, since more specific depri-

vations will in many cases vary with the social systems' particular patterns of social expectations, and these in turn will often depend on the economic system. In Section 6.1 it was pointed out that even quite basic needs are subject to cultural molding; this difficulty applies essentially to prescriptive needs and to diagnostic needs that are articulated in specific terms, rather than to general categories of diagnostic needs.[3]

Aside from these conceptual requirements dictated by the need to avoid the problems of noncomparability and circularity, the specification of basic needs of individuals, or of what constitutes harm to them, is relatively open-ended. It cannot be resolved in an impersonally objective manner. Nor can it be decided by the kind of thought experiment leading to universal and fixed intersubjective choices postulated by Rawls. But a more open-ended approach, where it is merely assumed that some set of needs can be agreed upon by representatives from quite different systems and societal segments within them and where a process to elicit this set is created, is plausible. (The process by which the members of the Organization for Economic Cooperation and Development arrived at a common list of "social concerns" [Christian 1974] holds out promise that agreement on such a set is possible even among a more diverse set of socioeconomic systems. This is not to say, however, that the OECD process fully met the requirements of rationality and noncircularity, nor that it was a sufficiently representative process.)

The collective determination of basic needs

The process of arriving at a set of needs still needs to be guided by certain criteria. Thomas Scanlon's (1975) notion of "central concerns" is helpful here. These central concerns are objective formulations of well-being in that, even though variations in individual tastes and interests are recognized, these concerns are independent of preferences. They derive from a normative consensus-based evaluation of

---

[3] The use of general diagnostic categories for the formulation of needs might even make it possible to avoid the trade-off problem that should normally be expected in the prioritizing of different needs. Rescher (1972:4–5) has argued that "welfare," the totality of those conditions that are basic requisites to well-being, does not consist of an average of those conditions, but is determined by the lowest point in a person's "welfare profile." To put this definition into the terms of the needs approach, a person's most serious deprivation determines his overall state of "neediness" and is independent of how well off he is in other respects, since the latter cannot compensate for the former. If this argument has any plausibility at all, it is only for a set of very broad deprivation dimensions.

various kinds of interests and not merely from the intensity of the preferences that represent the interests (Scanlon 1975:655–8). In other words, central concerns depend not so much on how strongly individuals feel about them when considering them in a self-interested way as on the moral importance that the collectivity attaches to them. It then becomes an intersubjective decision what kinds and levels of deprivation to recognize as central concerns and how to measure them and to weight them against each other. Ideas of what is needed for people to be happy may well be, and in my view should be, a central consideration in this decision, but essentialist images of what is required to be truly human may play a role as well.[4]

To avoid noncomparability and the evaluation circularity, the agreement has to cut across the different kinds of systems that are within the orbit of evaluation. At least the following two approaches to meeting this requirement are conceivable. (1) Representatives from different systems could be assembled and asked to identify those deprivations that they largely agree are of normative priority. The problem in this approach would be that representatives might not have sufficient cross-cultural empathy to be able to come to a fair agreement and that they might not be sufficiently impartial to be fair to people in situations different from their own. Moreover, the agreement might to a significant degree be susceptible to feedback effects that are common to the particular set of systems.

(2) A better approximation of the contractarian model, one that under ideal conditions could induce sufficient impartiality, empathy, and cross-cultural understanding, might result from selecting individuals who have had experience with more than one culture and discovering what set of needs they could agree on. (This approach also has some affinity with the test that John Stuart Mill proposed for the assessment of the superiority and inferiority of different kinds of pleasure. See also Glover 1979:90–1.) Their experiences, both intellectual and concrete, should be such as to have made them familiar with a maximal variety of cultures. Examples of such people might be anthropologists, certain kinds of travelers, and those whose circumstances have immersed them in two or more quite different cultures.

---

[4] If such collective decision making can be applied to needs, a reasonable question to pose is why it should not be applied at a more fundamental level, namely, in determining the values that underlie the formulation of needs. The answer is that it is often easier to obtain agreement on certain derivative values that lie at the confluence of different basic values, so to speak. (Cf. Barry's [1965:145] position on the normative centrality of negative freedom.) It seems to me that basic needs are potentially such confluent values.

They need to be capable of transcending, at least under appropriate reflective conditions, the distinctive perspectives of the particular culture into which they have been socialized. They also need to have the kind of sensitivity that would qualify them as rationally benevolent observers. The conditions for choosing the set of basic needs should be designed to promote thoughtfulness, open-mindedness to new information obtained from other members of the group, and vivid visualization, and yet to discourage nonrational pressures toward group conformity in the conclusions. Finally, some consensus rule less than full unanimity would probably have to be used. Although the chosen array of needs would obviously not be timeless, the accommodation of the diversity of systems and situations that prevail in the present would assure considerable stability to those needs. Moreover, a special effort could be made to anticipate the implications of conceivable circumstances in the future.

One reservation about this approach might be the suspicion that the conclusion would be distinctive to any particular group selected. This possibility could be tested by the repeated performance of such choice experiments with different groups. Only that pattern of basic needs that persists might then be adopted. A second reservation might be that such cross-culturally experienced individuals would articulate the concerns of a particular cosmopolitan elite rather than truly universal interests and needs, including those of individuals who are well embedded in their cultures. This worry might be partly allayed by the judicious and diverse selection of individuals for the process, but some of it would be sustained by the recognition of the limits to human empathy and integrity. A third reservation is that, since the formulation of needs involves not merely empirical understanding but normative choices, these choices would be made by individuals without any particular political legitimacy. In other words, these individuals could not be regarded as *representatives* of the various systems, nor would they have legitimacy as representatives of humanity as a whole. For these reasons the formulation of needs by such a group could have only advisory status.

Their formulation could, however, provide the basis for the articulation and adoption of a set of basic needs by politically legitimate representatives. Alternatively, a hybrid of the approach relying on system representatives and that employing cross-culturally experienced individuals might be used, by having the latter act as resource persons for the former and setting up a choice context in which the qualities of the second approach would be promoted.

"Central concerns" as basic needs

In order to avoid disagreement purely over what basic needs are supposed to refer to, further guidance may have to be provided to the participants in the collective-choice process. Scanlon (1975:661) has suggested that central concerns are to be distinguished from "peripheral" concerns by the criterion that the former are important to virtually everyone. In other words, they refer to deprivations that, if experienced, make practically anyone feel deprived. The justification Scanlon has given for this distinction is that peripheral concerns are "preferences that are plausibly thought of as subject to the control of the person who has them" (p. 665). ". . . the agent is 'responsible for' [them] not because he has in fact chosen to feel this way (perhaps he has not) but because it is merely a reflection of something about him, unsupported by objective reasons" (p. 665).

It has been objected by Griffin (1982:344) that certain nonuniversal desires, such as an intelligent child's for intellectual stimulation, are not something for which the person can be held responsible. What this objection suggests is that it is not *actually universal concerns,* but *rationally and empathetically revised central concerns* that should count. That is to say, the participants in the collective choice of interests to designate as basic needs must be willing and able to understand different kinds of persons and situations of persons and to view central concerns in sufficiently fundamental terms so that they apply in different ways to different persons and situations. (Cf. Scanlon 1975:660–1.) Thus, if instead of intellectual stimulation the central concern were mental and sensory stimulation, then sports, crafts, entertainment, and variety in jobs and environments would be part of the means for fulfilling this broader conception of a need, and these means would vary between individuals.

But suppose that it is collectively decided, by a process meeting the requirements set out here, that a certain interest is not a central concern. Not only do the individuals who have this interest feel it as a want that is more intense than the attributed basic need, but rational review of this want confirms it as a more crucial interest of these individuals – more crucial satisfactionally, and perhaps even developmentally. Why should there be social priority given to the fulfillment of the ascribed basic need over the idiosyncratic, but individually rational interest? Assuming that the generality requirement has been met in the specification of basic needs, two further answers can be offered here.

(1) The perceived priority of socially nonbasic interests over socially

basic ones may lie in the degree of their respective fulfillment. One reason why a hobby may be more important to a person than sufficient food is that he already has nearly sufficient food but has had no opportunity at all to pursue his hobby. In other words, as the degree of deprivation approaches zero, some trade-off between basic needs and other interests must be recognized. This view suggests that the lexical priority of basic needs over other interests holds absolutely only for *significant* levels of normatively recognized deprivation. Beyond that threshold, there is a trade-off range in which basic needs do not have absolute priority, though a tilting of resource allocation and of distribution in favor of such marginal basic needs is still justified. In terms of policy and system evaluation, this means that an exclusive basic-need criterion applies only to deprivation greater than this "significance threshold."

(2) Another answer to the possibility of some socially nonbasic interests being more important to certain individuals than socially basic needs is that the fulfillment of basic needs may be recognized as an entitlement that is exchangeable. That is to say, not only is the individual not forced to avail himself of the opportunities to fulfill his basic needs, but he might be allowed to exchange this entitlement for purchasing power to fulfill socially nonbasic interests. In this case, such trades in basic-need entitlements would have to be accounted for in economic optimization and evaluation.

Such collective determination of needs, of course, does not preclude social critics from nominating their own set of needs as what they think should be the collectively adopted set and conducting their evaluations of and prescriptions for social practices and innovations on the basis of such proposed needs. These would not be legitimated needs, but they might over time come to influence the formulation of the latter.

8.5   Objective human interests and freedom

Freedom of choice and individual sovereignty

Proposing that want satisfaction be subordinated to an objective conception of human interests often raises certain concerns. One is that the individual thereby will lose considerable freedom of choice and the ability to influence production. A second concern, to be considered subsequently, is that the process tends to lead to a loss of political freedom, by generating, or providing a rationale for, totalitarian regimes.

Because there are many formulations of objective human interests and because they can have quite different implications for freedom, I will here discuss these criticisms only as they apply to the particular formulation that I have offered. Since I proposed that the central value that should guide the determination of basic needs is the minimization of unhappiness, the concern about the loss of individual freedom and economic sovereignty must be related to the minimization of unhappiness. Thus one response to this concern is to show that freedom of choice is important to avoiding unhappiness in several ways. First of all, preferences are important prima facie indications of what makes people happy, or alleviates their unhappiness. Recognizing this fact also means that human interests are to be identified not only, nor even primarily, as developmental interests and that satisfactional interests, whether based on desirable or on unfortunate patterns of development, are extremely important. Moreover, the nonfulfillment of preferences, even irrational ones, leads to unhappiness if it creates *feelings* of frustration. Finally, the exercise of choice is conducive to the development of autonomy, which, even if as an end in itself it is regarded as rather peripheral for most policy spheres, is nevertheless very important for self-knowledge and rationality in individual decision making as well as for the contribution to well-being that results from the feeling of competence created by autonomy. Although these points may not apply to all cultures, the desirability of imposing freedom on such cultures is not self-evident; to make freedom the primary value in such settings requires justification in terms other than itself.

The basic-needs approach merely provides for the availability of the means to fulfill diagnostic needs and does not usually require that the individual *must* consume or make use of the good fulfilling the need. (There are exceptions, and these will be discussed shortly.) Moreover, whether or not consumption of this good is optional, it is usually only a broad type of good that is specified as a "need good," and within that category considerable choice is possible and should be promoted, both because it provides guidance for the fine-tuning of the production of particular need goods and also because of the reasons mentioned in the previous paragraph. Freedom of choice as such may well deserve to be designated a basic need in its own right. Thus within medical care there are strong prima facie grounds for leaving to individuals the choice of physician and hospital, and also whether to follow the treatment "prescribed." A basic-needs approach would usually take not the form of providing particular goods to particular individuals, but rather that of assuring that certain kinds of goods, (e.g., food or housing) are available at certain prices, so that they are not out of reach of those in need of them. Such policies, aimed at the broad pattern of supply, in no way displace consumer choice. A basic-needs approach may even offer more choice than a want-satisfaction approach, as when the availability of certain goods and their publicizing makes people aware that consumption of these goods is in their developmental interest, even though the goods were not wanted in the first place. Nutritional supplements and medical checkups are possible examples.

Although these arguments suggest that human interests conceived in terms of happiness and basic needs require considerable freedom of choice, there obviously will be certain limitations to choice. One reason is that limitation is unavoidable. Even if maximal choice were the constitutive principle of optimization and evaluation, choice would be still be limited, given finite resources, and we would be faced with trade-offs in the provision of choice. First, there are trade-offs between different wants of the same person, and a particular social arrangement may provide extensive choice for some wants while constraining choice for others. Thus compulsory income taxation restricts free choice in the disposition of income but makes available certain collective goods that would otherwise not be part of the range of choice available to the person. (For other examples see Connolly 1974a:170–1.) Secondly, there are trade-offs between a wide range of choice now and a wide range of choice later. Compulsory retirement insurance can be said to constrain choice now in order to assure a reasonably broad range of choice in the future. Thirdly, there are interpersonal conflicts in want satisfaction. The prohibition of theft restricts the potential thief in order to protect the range of choice of the owner.

Moreover, there is no one-dimensional measurement of the range of choice that would allow us to maximize the latter. Simply counting the number of options depends entirely on how the options are categorized. (Is a Datsun 710 with special hubcaps a different option from a Datsun 710 with ordinary hubcaps?) More important, however, is that not all options have the same significance. Some options may simply be useless or frivolous, and their nonexistence may not make anyone feel that it is a loss to him in any way. In order to provide some way of attaching significance to different options, one or more ulterior value principles are needed. An objective conception of human interests can serve as exactly such a principle. Thus the significance of various options can be determined on the basis of their contribution to meeting basic needs and reducing unhappiness. Of course, the principle of want satisfaction, together with a justifiable calculus principle, could perform this role as well, if it were not for its other deficiencies.

What is even more significant for a basic needs approach is that, apart from the social choice between alternative ranges of choice for individuals, restrictions of choice are attributable to considerations related to want satisfaction rather than to basic needs. One example of restricted choice that is now ubiquitous is compulsory institutional education for children. It is not left to the preferences of the children nor to those of their legal guardians. Its compulsory nature cannot derive from its assignment to the status of a need, since medical care, when it too has the status of basic need and fundamental entitlement, is not compulsory in the same way (except in the case of contagious diseases and mental illness, when either the interests of other members of society are threatened or the individual's capacity to make choices is considered deficient). The compulsory nature of education, in fact, can be explained better as a matter of want satisfaction than of basic needs. Education is important to the productivity of individuals, which, owing to the interdependence of the productivity of the various factors of production, affects the want satisfaction of *other* members of society; it thus has external effects analogous to those of immunization, and it is these external effects of want satisfaction that provide the rationale for its compulsory feature. A possible link with basic needs is that if society considers itself responsible for assisting the destitute, compulsory education will reduce the risk that individuals will become dependent on collective assistance. But this step, too, is to prevent a reduction in want satisfaction to the rest of society rather than to ensure entitlement to education as a basic need. Other instances of restricted choice, such as the constraints on the ingredients in foods and cosmetics or on the persons allowed to engage in medical or legal practice, can also be attributed to interests interpreted as preferences, on the grounds that in many forms of consumption the principle of "caveat emptor" is too costly in information and incurred risks to be preferred by buyers. Basic needs create entitlements, whereas choice restrictions arise from other considerations. This is not to say that certain other conceptions of human needs are not designed to rule out certain wants, but they are not inherent to a basic-needs approach.

It must not be forgotten, however, that consumer sovereignty consists not only of freedom of choice, but also of control of production through that choice. Under a basic-needs approach this becomes a little more complicated. There are, in effect, two processes of control of production. The first is collective and arises from the basic-need entitlements. Two possible strategies serve this process. A supply strategy would be for the collectivity to assure that, through collective provision or through incentives or regulations for private producers, the supply and prices of "need goods" are such that these goods are accessible to those in need of them. A demand strategy, on the other hand, would be to distribute purchasing power to individuals in accordance with their needs and the cost of the means to meet these needs. Usually the appropriate strategy will involve a mixture of purchasing power, entitlements to particular services with freedom of choice regarding the agency or type of delivery, and access to other collective services that are provided uniformly. In any case, this distribution of more or less closely specified entitlements also shapes the pattern of production.

The second process controlling production is consumer or personal sovereignty, exercised both within the sphere of basic needs and outside it. Within the sphere of basic needs, it is exercised to the extent that the form of the entitlement leaves discretion to the person with the need, and as was argued above, there are good reasons for making such discretion extensive in many areas. Outside the sphere of basic needs, of course, personal sovereignty is appropriate, qualified by rationality considerations concerning satisfactional as well as developmental interests. Both inside and outside the sphere of basic needs there is a strong case for substantial personal sovereignty as a determinant of the pattern of production in the actual operation of an economic system. Without it, there is the danger that both the general formulation of basic needs and the specific ways in which they are met may become disconnected from the basic interests of individuals as they interpret them in the light of their experiences.

The slippery slope to totalitarianism?

Occasionally, the fear is expressed that if some higher principle, even if centered on the good for human beings, displaces the principle of want satisfaction, the path will be opened to the introduction of totalitarianism. (For an example of such a position see Flew 1977.) My argument here will be that, at least for the kind of approach taken in this chapter, this is not a reasonable fear.

Flew's main concern was that "an emphasis upon needs, as opposed to wants, gives purchase to those who see themselves as experts, qualified both to determine what the needs of others are, and to prescribe and enforce the means appropriate to the satisfaction of those needs" (p. 213). The emphasis on needs takes this course by justifying the displacement of the individual's judgment by expert judgment, putting the expert in the position of "benefactor" and making his prescriptions "appear to be inexpugnably admirable and mandatory" (pp. 217–18). These steps then can be used to justify the totalitarian control of society by a small group of "Guardians," according to Flew. Such a process would, of course, be a blatant perversion of the basic-needs approach I have outlined.

Although objective approaches to human interests or needs are open to abuse of this kind, *want satisfaction* is not immune to it either. One argument that can lead to such abuse is that the coordination of want satisfaction cannot be achieved in an optimal manner without centralized control over production and distribution and that totalitarian control is needed to make this centralized control effective. Another argument is based on the opposite idea: that only the market system can effectively provide for want satisfaction. This view then can lead to the argument that the market system must be defended against its enemies and against the intrusion into the economy by government that is characteristic of democracy. Ergo democracy must be prevented, and totalitarianism is an effective way of doing so. These two sketches of possible arguments are presented not in order to insist that a commitment to the principle of want satisfaction *will* lead to totalitarianism, but rather to make the point that, if one is determined to justify a totalitarianism regime, it can be done in many different ways, including those that emphasize want satisfaction.

That a totalitarian regime cannot be expected to perform well in meeting basic needs finds some support in the discussion in the next chapter, although the question is not addressed there in this particular form. What is indicated there is that an oligarchic form of socioeconomic coordination will not perform well in preventing four forms of welfare deprivation if the empirical assumption is made that the oligarchs are essentially self-interested. Concerning specifically totalitarian regimes and their impact on the happiness of the populace, certain further considerations can be advanced. One is that in a top-down form of government, the governors, even when they are concerned with fulfilling the basic needs of their subjects rather than merely their own interests, easily lose touch with the actual "central concerns" of the populace. Even though there may be experts to monitor these concerns, the fact that the experts are accountable only to the governors and that there are no democratic representatives to monitor the experts may induce the experts to report what the governors want to hear rather than what is actually the case. Moreover, when the popular support for the governors is doubtful, there will be a tendency to subordinate the honest representation of reality in public discourse to images of reality that merely rationalize current practice. In general, it can be expected that the regime will pretend to itself and the public that the "central concerns" of the populace are being met, rather than be open about unacknowledged concerns and about deficiencies in the way acknowledged ones are being met. Finally, totalitarian regimes militate against both diversity and the autonomy of individuals. The first is important for the elaboration of basic needs to apply to the distinctive conditions of individuals; the second is important for effective decision making by individuals to meet their basic needs and other interests and also for their direct well-being.[5]

8.6   The calculus of minimizing deprivation

Basic needs and calculus criteria

Although this book is concerned with constitutive principles or criteria for economic evaluation, it was pointed out in Chapter 7 that a consideration about such principles is whether the calculus criteria that are compatible with them are acceptable. The basic-needs conception of human interests is no exception, and a few comments on calculus criteria compatible with basic needs are therefore called for. Since unmet basic needs constitute deprivation, the task here is to give meaning to the minimization of deprivation. (It should be noted, incidentally, that in contrast to W. G. Runciman's [1966:ch. 2] "relative deprivation," which refers to the *feeling* or self-regarding *judgment* of deprivation, deprivation as used here is objective in its method of assessment.) Given the distinction between basic needs and other interests, it is to be expected that different calculus principles will apply in the sphere of basic needs from those applicable to the realm of nonbasic, "peripheral," or "luxury" interests. With respect to basic needs, two extremes can be visualized: the minimization of the aggregate of deprivation and a radically egalitarian approach. Neither turns out to be attractive.

The aggregative approach to deprivation will lead to priority atten-

---

5 Anthropological evidence about two tribes, the Fore in Papua New Guinea (Sorenson 1977:106–15) and the Yequana in Venezuela (Liedloff 1975), points to the conclusion that important conditions for character development that is conducive to happiness are a very close mother–child relationship in early infancy, freedom from restraint, and a profound confidence in the child's ability to indicate and pursue his own interests.

tion to the least deprived, if it is easier to meet their basic needs than those of the severely deprived. Such an approach is therefore insensitive to the degree of neediness and fails to use the latter as a basis for establishing priorities for the fulfillment of basic needs. Moreover, it is highly dependent on the cutoff points that separate basic needs from other interests. Since the collective establishment of such cutoff points, whether within economic systems or across them, can be expected to be subject to disagreement, compromise, and instability over time, it is a disadvantage for a criterion to be so sensitive to it.

Concerning egalitarian approaches, it is necessary first to clarify how basic needs are related to equality. Basic needs are those interests that must be met in order to make individuals equal in certain respects that are collectively designated as significant. With respect to any particular dimension of well-being, individuals will vary in their degree of deprivation. To meet basic needs means to provide for need in accordance with degree of deprivation so that people are brought up to a norm applicable to all. Thus the elimination of deprivation is equalizing.

The approach to minimizing deprivation that I have referred to as radically egalitarian, however, introduces equality in an additional way. It means that no one may be ahead of anyone else in his fulfillment of basic needs. As long as there is one person who remains severely deprived, everyone else has to be similarly deprived, even though all of society's resources and effort would be unable to remove that person's deprivation. Such extreme egalitarianism is of no advantage to anyone and can well hurt the most deprived by rendering the less deprived unable to help them either by providing direct assistance or by engaging in activities that eventually benefit them.

A more reasonable interpretation of the relation between basic needs and equality leads to a maximin strategy. It gives priority to the needs of the most deprived. As long as it is possible to reduce their deprivation, no others are entitled to provision for their needs. When the most deprived have had their condition improved to the point where some other group becomes the most deprived, the latter becomes the beneficiary of the maximin strategy. This approach means that any benefits (e.g., medical training) going to other than the most deprived have to be justified exclusively as means of reducing deprivation for the most deprived. Such a strategy, although it does not prevent others from being deprived to a lesser extent, means that the concerns of a basic-needs policy are completely monopolized by the most deprived.

A lexical extension of the maximin strategy reduces the extremeness of this feature (Sen 1970:138n12). It requires that at the point where no additional help will improve the condition of the most deprived, the focus of the basic-needs policy must shift to the next most deprived, constrained, of course, by the condition that any help to them must not worsen the condition of the more severely deprived. Once this group has been helped to the greatest extent possible, the group next in degree of deprivation will be the focus. Thus a basic-needs policy can move on from a focus on the most deprived to the less deprived, provided this move is never at the expense of the more severely deprived. As far as evaluation is concerned, this means that policies or economic systems are assessed lexically, that is, according to what they do first for the most deprived, then for the next most deprived, and so on.

Trade-offs in the minimization of deprivation

Applied in an uncompromising fashion, the lexical maximin principle still attracts criticisms that have to be taken seriously. An egalitarian criticism is that it will not allow sacrificing even a minimal improvement in the condition of the most deprived groups for the sake of reducing inequality in general, such as by reducing the gap between the mildly deprived and the most advantaged (Sen 1974/1974:285–6). An aggregativist criticism is that the maximin principle will not permit trading off minute changes in the conditions of the worst-off for the sake of even immense gains for the rest of society. These considerations are particularly significant in the face of what has been referred to as the "deprivation monster," that is, severe forms of deprivation that will gobble up all of society's resources and effort without great reductions in such deprivation. If these deprivation-reducing efforts yield no improvements at all, then, of course, the principle requires moving on to other deprived groups, but if there are at least minute gains, then moving on is not compatible with the principle. This consequence of the lexical nature of the principle makes its uncompromising application inappropriate, but more complex calculus principles that approximate it can be designed so that they are reasonable and also consistent with the normative orientation of the constitutive principle of basic needs. (Cf. Scanlon's [1982:123, 127–8] position that under a contractualist approach, a focus on the worst-off is warranted because they otherwise have reasonable grounds for rejecting an attempted agreement, but as a maximin solution is approached, the societywide sacrifices of the arrangement become greater and the case for it becomes weaker. For a critique of Rawls's use of the maximin principle, see Barry 1973:chs. 9–10.)

Deprivation can be assessed for particular needs or, alternatively, for needs as a whole. The quasi-maximin strategy could thus be applied to each need category separately, as is suggested by the rationale for defining basic needs as central concerns, with the balance of resources (or the value weights) between the different need categories to be determined collectively. The alternative is to apply the quasi-maximin criterion to a single deprivation scale, where value weights that are collectively agreed upon determine how any individual's various kinds of deprivation are to be aggregated to represent his overall level of deprivation. The multiple-deprivation approach rules out trade-offs between various kinds of interests, implying thereby that any particular kind of deprivation has to be addressed in its own terms and cannot be compensated for by advances in some other area. The general-deprivation approach allows such trade-offs and compensations, although certain kinds of deprivation may require infinite compensation from other interests – that is, they cannot be compensated for in this way.

One can certainly cite examples of forms of deprivation that we consider as requiring alleviation in their own terms, such as ill health. A person who is seriously deprived only in health and advantaged in all other respects would generally be regarded as just as entitled to medical care and related support as another person with the same severity of ill health but also various other kinds of deprivation. And yet I wonder whether this view does not stem primarily from the avoidance of the complex discretionary judgments that trade-offs require or, alternatively, from a conception of health not only as an end in itself, but as a fundamental prerequisite to other fundamental interests. If health is treated only as an end in itself, or at least as immediately instrumental to happiness, and if any other interests that it may impinge on, such as consumption, social relations, and stimulating activity, are separately identified as needs, then we should probably take account of the fact that the individual who is afflicted not just with illness but also with other deprivations is in more urgent need of help than the person who suffers only ill health. Moreover, if nothing can be done about the illness itself, we may well be justified in giving priority attention to the multiply deprived person's other needs, even though his deprivations in these areas may be somewhat less than those of other persons deprived in the same areas. In other words, there is a case, at least at the theoretical level, for an approach that recognizes quite diverse trade-offs and opportunities for compensation, which can only be assured by the general-deprivation approach. On the other hand, social arrangements, and perhaps even approaches to evaluation, cannot exceed a certain level of complexity and require some resilience to error and abuse, and a general-deprivation approach may not do well by these standards.

One final point requiring comment is that in the earlier discussion of the urgency of needs, it was suggested that as deprivation with respect to basic needs becomes milder, they no longer warrant absolute priority over interests other than such needs, and that in a certain range of deprivation below a determined level of significance, need fulfillment may be exchanged with other forms of want satisfaction. Thus forms of ill health that are not progressive, do not cause pain, and do not impair the individual's functioning in ways collectively deemed important may not warrant immediate and free medical care, but might be subsidized in some ways because they fall into this trade-off range of deprivation and entitle the ill person to some assistance that would not apply to other kinds of want satisfaction. This then becomes another area of complex trade-offs, which might well require decisions on a case-by-case basis and is thus a consideration against making need entitlements exchangeable. But the difficulty may be outweighed by the advantages.

In Chapter 9 the basic-needs approach will be applied to pure forms of economic coordination for purposes of illustration. It may seem that the calculus issues discussed here have not been sufficiently resolved to take this further step. However, it is not possible to make the illustrative evaluation sufficiently precise for this indeterminateness to be significant here. Thus deprivation is discussed in terms that largely apply both to a maximin approach and to a more aggregative approach to minimizing deprivation. A general-deprivation approach is not possible because it would have been too ambitious within this framework to propose a comprehensive set of basic needs and to establish trade-offs between them. Therefore, even though the general-deprivation approach is to be preferred on theoretical grounds, the illustrative evaluation is conducted wholly in terms of specific forms of deprivation.

CHAPTER 9

Deprivation under market competition and other coordination mechanisms: an illustrative evaluation

9.1   Socioeconomic coordination mechanisms and deprivation

The nature of the illustrative evaluation

In order to show some of the implications of a basic-needs approach for economic evaluation, and particularly the more ambitious kind of evaluation that is involved when economic systems are considered, I offer here an illustrative evaluation of a set of prototypical economic systems. My purpose is not to provide a definitive evaluation, but merely to indicate the kinds of considerations that enter this type of evaluation. This caveat needs to be emphasized because there are some important limitations to the following discussion.

The first is that it is not actual economic systems that are being considered, but specifically prototypical mechanisms for the coordination of production and distribution. Actual economic systems are much too complex to consider in what is merely an ancillary analysis. Pure kinds of coordination mechanisms have a certain simplicity that makes it much easier to generalize about their effects. Other features of systems, such as the pattern of ownership, are not dealt with directly, although the motivational pattern is considered to a certain extent.

A second limitation is that the evaluation of the systems is not based on a comprehensive and integrated set of basic needs and on trade-offs between them. Instead, I have selected a small number of basic needs and their corresponding forms of deprivation and will provide a separate evaluation for each of them. I am not in a position to predict the set of basic needs that would emerge from the kind of collective-choice process described in the previous chapter. In any case, to apply a complex array of basic needs would not be manageable in the present context.

Finally, much of the discussion is unavoidably speculative. Since empirical evidence on the selected forms of deprivation and their systemic causes is largely unavailable, speculative generalizations, based on deductive theory or impressionistic observations, are involved to a considerable degree. They are not necessarily controversial and may be widely accepted, but many still need verification.

The forms of deprivation used as criteria to illustrate the evaluation perspective of basic needs are poverty, poor working conditions, social isolation, and psychological depression. They have been chosen because they parallel the conceptions of interests as they were progressively developed from Chapter 2 to Chapter 8. Poverty is deprivation concerning consumption interests; poor working conditions are deprivation concerning work interests, a category of private interests; social isolation is a form of deprivation concerning sociability interests, which are part of personal interests; and psychological depression is a form of deprivation concerning human interests, including developmental interests. That under most conditions these forms of deprivation represent typical causes of unhappiness, the miminization of which has been proposed as the central value underlying the formulation of basic needs, is I think self-evident.

Socioeconomic coordination mechanisms

Because of the historically close relation between market ideology and consumer sovereignty, the focus of the illustrative evaluation is on market competition. To make the evaluation comparative, however, market competition is assessed in juxtaposition to alternatives to it. Table 9.1 summarizes several classifications of socioeconomic coordination mechanisms. (Although the purpose of these mechanisms is to coordinate the various production and distribution processes of the *economic* system, or rather subsystem of the social system as a whole, it would be too limiting to refer to the coordination methods as merely "economic," since some mechanisms, or at least critical features of them, are located in other subsystems, such as the political and the "cultural." As a result I am using the term "socioeconomic" to refer to these coordination mechanisms.)

From the classifications of Frank H. Knight (1933/1971), R. A. Dahl and C. E. Lindblom (1953/1963), Gregory Grossman (1967/1974), and Brian Barry (1973) I have derived a sixfold classification. It is essentially the same as Knight's, except that I accept Dahl and Lindblom's distinction between market competition and bargaining as significantly different forms of exchange. The alternatives to market competition that are considered more closely here are democratic central control and oligarchic central control. Although bargaining is distinguishable from market competition, it is not considered separately because, for

Table 9.1. *Classifications of socioeconomic coordination systems*

Knight	Dahl/Lindblom	Grossman	Barry	This book
Anarchism			Altruistic collaboration	Mutualist anarchism
Exchange system[a]	Price system Bargaining	Market mechanism		Market competition
			Exchange/ contracting	Bargaining
Democracy or democratic socialism	Polyarchy			Democratic central control[b]
Autocratic or militaristic system	Hierarchy	Command	Hierarchy	Oligarchic central control[b]
"Status" and tradition, or the caste system		Tradition		Regulation by custom

[a]Two forms of the exchange system that he spelled out were handicraft and free-enterprise systems.

[b]These are priority formulation mechanisms, which can be complemented by alternative implementation mechanisms: command systems, incentive systems, guidance of voluntary commitment.

Sources: Knight 1933/1971:14–19; Dahl and Lindblom 1953/1963:pts. III–IV; Grossman 1967/1974:18–20; Barry 1973:166–8.

the particular forms of deprivation considered, its effects are not distinct. In its decentralized form, it is similar to market competition, and in its centralized form, such as Sweden's centralized form of collective bargaining, it is a hybrid of democratic central control, oligarchic central control, and market competition. (One distinguishing feature of bargaining is that it is likely to generate conflict, but this is not crucial to the following evaluation. For discussions contrasting bargaining and market competition see Polanyi 1944:ch. 5 and Scitovsky 1951/1971:ch. 2.) Customary regulation will not be considered either, since the variety of kinds of customs that can prevail make it too open-ended.

Mutualist anarchism is also omitted from the evaluation, because it does not make sense given the basic motivational assumption used in the analysis. The paradigmatic postulate of neoclassical economics that individuals are motivated by self-interest is adopted here. Although it is allowed that individuals may be socialized to develop other relevant kinds of motivation, self-interest is the starting point of the analysis. In this way it is possible to keep the predominantly deductive analysis fairly simple and also to determine system performance when the motivational pattern is such that it puts particularly great demands on the process of coordination. Mutualist anarchism, on the other hand, requires very extensive altruism, and by virtue of this assumed motivation, it would be concluded to perform much better than the other socioeconomic mechanisms, which are assumed to coordinate primarily self-interested behavior. Although I do not consider altruism as a central motivation in social life to be beyond the realm of the possible and do, in fact, regard mutualist anarchism as particularly attractive for small social units, out-and-out altruism among all individuals in large-scale social units is unlikely, and a coordination mode that collapses without it is not of serious interest.

The basic features of market competition, the focus of this evaluation, are atomistic decision making, flexible terms of exchange, and egoistic motivation. Since the discussion refers to pure systems, the pure market system is defined as one that is market-governed in all spheres. It refers not to perfect competition, but to a system governed wholly by *free* markets. It thus excludes central administration, price control, and reliance on altruistic motivation. (That certain minimal system-maintenance functions have to be centrally organized even in a pure market system will be taken for granted, but treated as peripheral and not considered in the analysis.)

By contrast, democratic and oligarchic central control rely wholly on central decision making. Whether the domain for coordination is the individual productive establishment or the whole economic system, the democratic and oligarchic forms of central control involve a distinct locus of authority. Within the limited domain of a firm it may rest with management, the stockholders, the board of directors, or a workers' council. Central control in systemwide coordination is taken to mean detailed central planning, including the central determination of prices or central allocation without reference to prices. When central control is democratic, its priorities are determined by the electoral process, that is, by the preferences of voters aggregated in some way, but their implementation is organized hierarchically; that is, it is a system of carrying out orders. Under oligarchic central control, on the other hand, it is not only the implementation of priorities, but also their formulation, that is controlled by the "center" of the system. (Incidentally, I am using the term "oligarchy" to include autocracy, purely for terminological convenience.)

Applying the evaluation to such pure models means neither that a social system *could* practically rely on any single one of them nor that any coordination mechanism could be implanted in any culture. Though such considerations limit the practical applications of this very simplified, sketchy, and often quite speculative evaluation, the discussion can nevertheless do more than merely illuminate the basic-needs approach to evaluation. The determination of the respective strengths and weaknesses of the different pure coordination mechanisms can point the way to combinations of coordination mechanisms that are promising for the fulfillment of basic needs and whose more detailed evaluation would be highly worthwhile.

9.2   Poverty

Subsistence poverty as evaluation criterion

Two quite different conceptions of poverty have to be distinguished: subsistence poverty and relative poverty. Subsistence poverty refers to some absolute standard of consumption deprivation, whereas the standard of relative poverty is comparative to the general standard of living in the particular society. Although relative poverty is the conception that is most appropriate to industrially advanced countries and is there, explicitly or implicitly, the basis of the various poverty thresholds that have been adopted, it is not suitable as a representation of deprivation with respect to consumption interests as these were articulated in Chapter 2. The reason is that it involves social interests, in the form of relativity wants, status wants, and wants for belongingness. Only subsistence poverty represents a pure, private form of consumption deprivation.

Subsistence poverty will be taken to refer to that range of consumption levels in which health, including survival, is either impossible or seriously jeopardized by starvation, inadequate physical warmth, or abnormal exposure to illness or lethal injuries. The criterion thus is really one of ill health. However, it refers only to ill health that is attributable to an inadequate level of consumption and excludes the health effects of medical care, environmental conditions that cannot be controlled by purchasing power, and other sources. To make this criterion precise would require a specific conception of health, together with a measurement criterion. (For a survey of health status measures see Culyer 1978.) Moreover, the relationship between consumption and health should be clearly established. For the purpose of the following sketchy evaluation, however, neither is necessary. The issue is the extent to which different socioeconomic coordination modes generate or prevent very low standards of living. No quantification is involved.

This formulation of subsistence poverty avoids the problems of noncomparability and circularity, even though subsistence poverty itself is not without its elements of relativity. The latter are involved because each socioeconomic system has its own pattern of consumption opportunities, and the level and pattern of consumption necessary to meet the underlying health standards will thus vary. However, as long as health itself is defined in a system-transcending manner, comparability is provided by this ulterior criterion. Health thus provides for consumption deprivation the anchor that is missing for want satisfaction, for which there is no independent value of well-being from which its weighting and measurement could be derived. Subsistence poverty here really stands for consumption-related ill health.

Not only is evaluation of subsistence poverty relevant in the poorer countries, but in an evaluation of pure coordination mechanisms, it is potentially relevant to industrially advanced countries as well. The virtual elimination of subsistence poverty in most of the latter is almost certainly attributable to the existence of particular distribution mechanisms, so that in the absence of such mechanisms subsistence poverty would prevail even in those affluent countries where it now does not exist.

Although poverty immediately prompts the issue of the distribution of purchasing power, subsistence poverty depends also on efficiency in production and distribution. The necessities for survival and adequate health can be assured only if there are limits both to inequalities and to inefficiencies in the production and distribution of such necessities. The absence of such inefficiencies might be called "subsistence efficiency." Given a particular level of productive resources allocated to the needs of the poor, subsistence efficiency refers to how well the resources are used to produce and distribute the goods and services that will meet the needs. Both of these dimensions of performance need to be considered.

Market competition and subsistence efficiency

The market mechanism has reasonably strong incentives built into it to protect it from crippling inefficiency. But it is not free from inefficiencies, including inefficiencies affecting the production and distribution of necessities. Thus monopoly power – for example, over critical inputs to food production, such as fertilizer or agricultural equipment – may keep food prices high. Certain critical collective or quasi-collective goods, such as flood control, irrigation projects, and sewage systems, would not normally be provided in a pure market system. Externalities like industrial pollution may reduce productivity elsewhere (crop yields, for example). They may also be a threat to the health of those not in a position to move away. Consumer ignorance may prove an additional threat to health, as in the case of negligence or cost-reducing additives in food processing.

As far as producer planning is concerned, uncertainty about the investment intentions of other producers can create an inefficient pattern of shortages and surpluses together with sharp price fluctuations or simply a reluctance to expand production (Scitovsky 1951/1971:229–37; Dobb 1969:148–9; Lindbeck 1971:99; Richardson 1971:436–41). Research and development, such as for agriculture, is a collective good that is not provided efficiently under the pure market system. These phenomena can easily lead to more restricted supplies of and higher prices for necessities.

Apart from persistent poverty, it is also important to prevent temporary poverty, particularly when we are dealing with subsistence poverty, which can mean starvation and illness. Temporary poverty may be due to unpredictable events or poor planning by individuals or both. This is a problem of intertemporal efficiency because, within the constraints of not making others worse off, the affected persons presumably would consider themselves better off if their consumption resources were appropriately redistributed over time. If the future were predictable, it would be possible to forgo some consumption in periods of surplus in order to increase consumption in subsequent periods. However, the future is not fully predictable. Not only is there the inevitable unpredictability characteristic of all coordination mechanisms, but, as in the case of producer uncertainties, the market mechanism generates uncertainties for households by leaving saving and investment planning to atomistic decision making, without a coordination process comparable to the price mechanism that applies to *current* demand and supply. Every household makes decisions for its future, and these decisions influence the future environment for everyone, but the household does not know what the future-shaping decisions of other households are. (Cf. Graaf 1957:103 and Phelps 1965/1970:504–8.) A farmer may thus plant a crop that turns out to be in oversupply; he therefore receives such a low price that he cannot keep his family from falling below the subsistence level. This problem applies also to decisions concerning savings. Given this lack of coordination of actions regarding the future and the lack of the kind of control over change that would make change more predictable, a family's current savings and investments to protect itself against future poverty will be subject to potentially disastrous error.

Even without such systemic uncertainties there is a further problem in redistributing consumption over time. "Life-cycle poverty" refers to a typical pattern of variations during an individual's lifetime in earnings levels and in the level of spending required to maintain a constant standard of living. The same level of income will represent a lower standard of living for a family during the children's dependency than before and after that period. Redistributing consumption from earlier life phases to later ones can be done by saving and is therefore in itself not a problem for market coordination. The uncertainty concerning the length of one's life can be dealt with by annuity or pension markets. Much more difficult are uncertainties concerning future family size, which is partly, but by no means wholly, under the individual parent's control. Moreover, early marriage and family formation may make the first phase of relative prosperity too short for adequate savings for the parenthood phase. Even if the postparenthood phase can be expected to be relatively prosperous again, it is unlikely that the credit market will make it possible to engage in forward redistribution from that phase to the parenthood phase in the absence of collateral that can be appropriated by the creditor in the case of default.

It may well be, of course, that life-cycle poverty is attributable as much to individual shortsightedness as to a lack of institutional instruments for intertemporal redistribution. Shortsightedness may also be a cause of *lifelong* poverty if it affects early decisions concerning skill acquisition. The market mechanism does not provide a corrective when people neglect the future in their vocational-preparation choices and in their choices concerning savings for old age. The danger of later poverty may make some people more responsible about their futures, but this seems to be an unreliable effect, and much poverty under pure market coordination may occur simply because there is no institutional protection against a quite natural, or at least common, tendency not to visualize the distant future as effectively as the present or near future and therefore not to provide for the former as effectively as for the latter.

Among other instances of temporary consumption deprivation, natural disasters are particularly critical, especially when they destroy food supplies and people's shelter and threaten their health. While these problems cannot normally be attributed to the market system (although there are cases, such as that of the lack of flood control, where the nature of the consequences is due to market failure), the market system can be assessed by considering how well it protects individuals against the resulting subsistence deprivation. One way in which the system *is* responsive is that it allows the victims to use their savings to bid supplies of food, medicines, and other necessities away from other consumers that are not in the same plight. However, their savings may have to be quite substantial, because in such situations prices are likely to rise to exorbitant levels in the short run. Moreover, since the actions of entrepreneurs are not coordinated, the producer uncertainties already mentioned may make their response to the situation unreliable.

Income deficiencies in the short run might be overcome through credit markets and insurance markets. Both are potentially applicable to earning and consumption losses for reasons other than natural disasters as well. Credit markets, however, are not very effective for even the temporarily disadvantaged because of problems in the enforcement of repayment. Insurance markets may be quite effective in the case of natural disasters, but when it comes to other sources of earning losses, such as unemployment, they are prone to the phenomenon of "moral hazard," which refers to the situation where the uncertain events to be insured against are not sufficiently out of the control of the insured. Insurance protection against unemployment and low earnings owing to adverse market conditions provides opportunities for free riding, since the individual can slant his choice of employment in favor of high work satisfaction at the expense of employment stability or high earnings in the long run and can, when unemployed, not fully exert himself to find new employment. Determining the reasons for unemployment or low earnings (i.e., environmental conditions as opposed to personal choice) can then be contentious and costly. As a result, private insurance is unlikely to be provided under market competition for those contingencies, and in the absence of centrally provided insurance, individuals have to bear the full brunt of those earnings losses which are due to a pattern of events over some of which they have at least some control.

Unemployment itself is a form of inefficiency, sometimes referred to as "aggregative" inefficiency (Dorfman 1967/1972). In the market system it arises from an inadequate equilibration process between aggregate demand and supply. Flexibility in wages and prices cannot provide adequate equilibration, nor can a flexible interest rate assure it. A decline in prices and wages in conditions of unemployment has two opposite effects, that of increasing the purchasing power of money and that of reducing money income. The second effect may well be more important for consumer demand, so that insofar as investment decisions depend on the current level or trend in consumer demand, aggregate spending will be further depressed. Concerning the interest rate, although a decline will not actually aggravate unemployment in a similar way, it may be relatively ineffective in stimulating investment spending when investment profitability is much more sensitive to prospective consumer demand conditions. For equilibration at the full-employment level, the interest rate may have to be negative, but since the market mechanism cannot impose such a penalty on saving, saving will simply take place without being made available for investment. In general, then, the market mechanism cannot prevent unemployment. Unless the household has accumulated assets, unemployment, in the absence of the kind of insurance system that can be provided only with some form of central control, can precipitate subsistence poverty.

All these instances mean that, in spite of the market mechanism's efficiency-promoting incentives, serious inefficiencies do remain, and they are potentially important factors for subsistence poverty. However, the overall effect of pure market coordination on subsistence poverty depends at least as much, if not more, on the market's distribution of consumption resources.

Market competition and inequality

The market mechanism of coordination has both equalizing and "disequalizing" tendencies. Let us first look at the former. With respect to earnings, the neoclassical position on these tendencies has been neatly summarized by A. B. Atkinson (1975:79) as follows:

Given a perfectly functioning, competitive labour market, and all people and jobs being alike, there would be no difference in earnings. If there were any differentials, then everyone would flock into the higher-paying positions and equality would be restored through the competitive process. If all people were alike, and if the labour market were perfectly competitive, but jobs differed, then there would be earnings differentials such that everyone was indifferent about which job he did: i.e. there would be an equalization of "net advantages."

A miner would probably have to be paid more than a gardener for the miner to feel equally well off, considering their working conditions. The next modification of this picture is that of education and training, which are the focus of human-capital theory. To the extent that jobs require different qualifications, the costs of education and training (including earnings forgone during that preparatory period) have to be compensated for by higher earnings in order to make the various types of work equally attractive. Earnings inequalities here equalize the present value of "lifetime net advantages" (including nonconsumption interests).

This kind of process, which is equalizing if certain critical conditions hold, applies outside the labor market as well. If individuals own equal investment resources, the tendency of market competition to equalize returns to capital, owing to the movement of financial capital from low-return activities to high-return activities, will equalize investment income between individuals. Similarly, there will be equalization between the different kinds of self-employment and between self-employment in general and employee jobs. These equalizing tendencies serve to raise the lifetime consumption levels of the most deprived closer to those of the rest of the society.

However, this equalization is limited or reversed by important tendencies in the opposite direction. The conditions that under a pure system of market competition cause or increase inequalities and may thus push the worst-off into subsistence deprivation or hold them there include (1) chance events, (2) "imperfections" in market competition, (3) differential family size, (4) differential abilities, and (5) pecuniary effects of cumulative features in the inequality in productivity and purchasing power.

(1) The market mechanism provides considerable scope for chance because it permits a high level of change and turmoil. It is capable of accommodating sharp changes, since the system of flexible prices can make substantial adjustments to reflect new patterns of scarcities and surpluses. Such a setting, together with atomistic decision making, is prone to a considerable degree of unpredictability. Events that are unforeseeable at the time when decisions that make individuals dependent on them are taken normally affect members in a society quite differently, usually benefiting some and harming others. Some benefits and disadvantages will gradually be washed away by the equalizing process of market competition, such as the benefits to a scarce occupation or the redundancies in a surplus occupation, but the process may take considerable time and will not reverse the gains and losses that occur in this period. Moreover, the benefits and disadvantages may permanently affect a person's material or vocational assets; environmental damage, for example, may undermine real property values, or a change in market conditions may make a particular skill worthless.

(2) When there are systematic violations of perfect competition, such as monopolistic power, the equalizing processes of market competition are inhibited. Monopoly power can make the poor worse off

by holding down their wages and raising the prices of essential consumer goods.

(3) Even when there are equal earnings per member of the labor force and equal investment income per adult, differences in family size result in unequal standards of living, particularly between, for example, a childless couple and a family with many children and with one of the parents out of the labor force to look after them (or incurring the expenses of commercial child care services). The subsistence level of children of large families may be impaired not only during their childhood, but also during their adulthood, because they will be disadvantaged in the inheritances they receive and the resources that would allow them to undertake vocational preparation to enhance earning capacity. Such inequality may well be decisive in causing subsistence poverty in some instances, or it may compound other causes of such deprivation.

(4) Another source of inequality may be differences in mental and physical abilities. To the extent that they are genetic, these differences may provide for the intergenerational inheritance of inequalities. They may also be environmental in origin (debilitation by disease or maiming injury, for example, or neurotic behavior owing to stressful conditions). In this case, too, disadvantages will be transmitted to the next generation, since to some extent the environmental conditions that give rise to such disabilities are related to consumption levels of the parents, at least in a pure market system. There are, of course, physical and mental disabilities of a more random nature as well, such as birth defects, physical accidents, and emotional overburdening, which prevent individuals from being effective in market competition. Some of these, such as work-related injuries and the emotional stresses of poverty, are not actually random, but intensify deprivation.

(5) Once differences in productivity, property, and affluence exist, there are certain important cumulative tendencies in a market system, and these have detrimental repercussions on the productivity and purchasing power of the poor. People who have property can use it either directly for productive investments or as collateral for obtaining investment funds. Investments may be either in capital or in the acquisition of skills. The prospects for personal productivity resulting from the latter also enhance access to credit. The greater the individual's property or the more lucrative his skills, the greater will be his income and thus his ability to save and accumulate further property. Moreover, the rate of return on large properties tends to be larger than that on small properties (Meade 1964:44). Obvious reasons are

(a) economies of scale in the acquisition of relevant information and experience and the use of expertise, and (b) the rich person's ability to invest in ventures with both relatively high risk and high returns, and to protect himself by diversifying his investments, whereas the person with limited savings will find it wiser to confine himself to safer, low-return investments.

Not only does this situation contribute to inequality between moderate property owners and the rich, but the greater increase of personal and capital productivity and of purchasing power among the better-off than among the worse-off can have detrimental effects on the latter. It increases the effective demand of the better-off for finite resources such as land, thus driving up their prices and making them more inaccessible to the worse-off. The difficulty applies not only to factors of production, but also to consumption goods, such as housing. Their privileged access to capital also enables the better-off to supply markets at lower cost and may thus undermine the earning power of the worse-off. The fate of weavers during the Industrial Revolution in Britain and of the poorer peasants during the more recent Green Revolution in Third World countries, where productivity improvements were out of their reach but they suffered the price declines resulting from greater output by the better-off producers, illustrates this process. In this way cumulative developments in the inequality in productive endowments can jeopardize the subsistence of the worst-off.

Market competition, then, does not prevent the kind of inequality that normally puts at least some people, and in some cases substantial sections of the populations, below the subsistence level of consumption. Neither does it contain a remedial mechanism for direct redistribution. Although rich individuals are free to provide charity, it is not something that is promoted, let alone guaranteed, by the market mechanism, nor is the motivation that the market mechanism relies on and thus reinforces conducive to such activity.

Central control and self-interest

Centrally controlled systems have mechanisms with which to avoid the indicated sources of subsistence poverty. They can provide for better coordination between producers in their investment plans and reduce instability and unpredictability; they can publicly provide employment, credit, and insurance in situations where the market system does not; they can make saving for old age compulsory; they can

respond to natural disasters in an organized, rapid, and nonex-
ploitative manner; and they can provide for outright redistribution.

Although it is apparent that centrally controlled systems *can* prevent the kinds of inefficiencies and inequalities that market coordination is prone to, it is not clear that they *will* do so. Moreover, other
kinds of inefficiencies and inequalities may arise. Such systems lack
the constraints and incentives of competition and therefore can dete-
riorate into a pattern of massive inefficiencies. Whereas markets provide, in the form of prices, information about current supply conditions relative to demand, at least in the present, and incentives to
producers and consumers to respond to these conditions, central control requires that the controlling center obtain massive amounts of
direct information about production possibilities and consumer preferences and that the right orders be issued and obeyed. Not only does
this process leave substantial room for error, but if the functionaries
of central control are self-interested, rather than conscientious, they
may use misinformation and the subversion of instructions for private
ends, with blatant or subtle corruption resulting. A system of central
control can protect itself against corruption, but only with a potentially very costly process of monitoring.

Central control also lacks the equalizing forces of market competition, which put at least some limits on inequalities. Though central
control has access to a number of distributive mechanisms – such as
taxes and subsidies, the determination of earnings and of the prices of
consumer goods, and the redistribution of land and capital – these
mechanisms can be used for inequality as easily as for equality. Thus
the effects of central control, unlike those of the market mechanism,
depend in the first instance on the aims and determination of the
governors. These issues will be discussed primarily with reference to
democratic central control, but first let me offer a brief comment on
oligarchic central control.

Although an altruistic concern for the plight of the poor is possible
under oligarchic central control, much more likely is government
based on self-interest. From this perspective the oligarchs will be concerned not with the subsistence interests of the worst-off as such, but
only with how the survival and health of the worst-off serve the interests of the oligarchs. If they benefit from the worst-off in their
capacity as potential soldiers or as producers or, to include the power
interests of the oligarchy, simply as subjects, then it will be in the
interests of the oligarchs to protect the survival and, to a greater or
lesser extent, the health of the worst-off. If the oligarchs do not benefit in ways such as these, their rule cannot be expected to prevent

subsistence poverty. Moreover, marginal subsistence poverty may actually be in their interest if it keeps the worst-off under pressure to produce and without the resources to mount possible insurgencies. This summary leads to the unsurprising conclusion that an oligarchic system of central control, if guided by self-interest, cannot be expected to prevent subsistence poverty. It does not preclude that secure power, rather than being corrupting, might have a morally ennobling effect on the governors, but the aims would then become open-ended and systemic tendencies could not be identified.

In order to be able to determine the implications for subsistence poverty of democratic coordination, it is necessary to determine the attitudes and behavior of the electorate. If all the members of the polity are maximin egalitarians, democratic control will allow redistribution that approximates maximin optimality. The only difficulty arises over disagreements about the conditions that constitute maximin optimality and over the policies that will produce it. More interesting is the case where the citizens are wholly self-interested.

Assuming that democratic decision making is based on majority choices (rather than on pure or qualified unanimity rules of choice, as proposed in Buchanan and Tullock 1962 and criticized in Barry 1965:chs. 14 and 15), what are the distributive consequences? Anthony Downs (1957) has discussed this question in the context of representative government: ". . . the best way to gain votes is to deprive a few persons of income – thereby incurring their hostility – and make this income available to many persons – thereby gaining their support" (p. 198). Given that governments pursue the maximization of votes and that

the pretax distribution of income in almost every society gives large incomes to a few persons and relatively small incomes to many persons, a redistribution tending toward equality accomplishes the very political end government desires. Thus the equality of franchise in a democratic society creates a tendency for government action to equalize incomes from a few wealthy persons to many less wealthy ones. [P. 198]

According to Downs, the limits to complete equalization are set by disincentive effects, the belief of the poor that they too will be rich someday, and the resources of the rich to influence government in conditions of uncertainty (pp. 199–201).

However, it is questionable whether, assuming wholly self-interested citizens, the system is inherently inclined toward equality. Let us assume that the electorate consists of interest groups formed on the basis of income and that the income distribution is pyramidal; that is, the largest group (but less than the majority) has the lowest income, and with increasing income the groups become smaller. In this case it is true that the poorest group can form a coalition with enough other low-income groups to bring about complete equality, which will benefit all groups in the coalition. But in response to this development, or before its occurrence, the rich could form a coalition with some low-income groups, but excluding the poorest, which would make the low-income groups in the coalition better off than they would be under complete equality and would make the poorest worse off than they were initially. Or, by threatening to form such a coalition, the rich could induce the poorest to join them in a coalition that would require less than full equality.

In fact, the implicit assumption here that only the differentials between the groups and not their ranking in income levels will be changed is unfounded. Any group may try to become the richest. But no conceivable coalition of income groups is stable in the sense that it cannot be defeated by another possible coalition to which some of the groups in the previous coalition can be induced to defect by the offer of a higher income. Neither complete equality nor the equal division of income among the governing 51 percent is protected against new coalitions in which enough groups can make themselves better off so that they constitute new majorities. This fact neither rules out nor guarantees that one or more groups will fall below the subsistence level. (Barry's [1970:153] attribution of the equalizing tendency claimed by Downs to an implicitly assumed pyramidal income distribution is therefore mistaken.) The only conclusion that can be drawn is that any majority coalition is unstable when interest groups struggle directly over distribution.

Majoritarian democracy, considered purely as a decision-making procedure rather than as a society with certain ideals, does thus not have a definite egalitarian thrust, if we assume wholly self-interested behavior. Given that under democratic central control the other aspect of subsistence poverty, namely, subsistence efficiency, depends similarly on policy decisions, there is no reason to believe that it would fare any better than the distributive aspect. The problem of instability in policy making may diminish in a more complicated and realistic model of democracy that allows for various kinds of friction, such as bargaining costs and ignorance, and for the possibility of binding agreements. (The enforceability of the latter, though, is problematic, unless we supplement the motivational assumption concerning egoism with an assumption admitting promise keeping or loyalty as motivations.) These structural complications, however, do not point in the direction of greater equality. If anything, opportunities for the invisible exercise of power or influence, both by the representative governors and by their functionaries, will tend to work in the direction of inequality and exploitation. Some egalitarian pressures may come from a broadly based want for insurance against serious misfortune or a fear by the well-off of violence by the disadvantaged. In general, however, the pursuit of self-interest in a democratic framework does not guarantee that every group will be protected from falling below the subsistence level.

Egalitarianism and coordination mechanisms

What is needed to enable democratic coordination to assure the prevention of subsistence poverty, when feasible, is an egalitarian sense of social justice among the citizenry – not altruism in the strong sense, but a more qualified form that I will call "collectivistic altruism," which is to be distinguished from "individualistic altruism." The latter reveals itself in an individual's actions independent of what others do. Thus helping other persons or giving charitable donations to agencies that assist the disadvantaged represents individualistic altruism. Collectivistic altruism, on the other hand, limits itself to a willingness to advocate or even just accept general redistribution at one's own expense, but only if it is equally at the expense of all those in similarly advantaged circumstances. In other words, collectivistic altruists see redistribution as a collective (moral) good, but they are not prepared to incur sacrifices necessary for it if there are others who, although similarly advantaged, decline to make commensurate sacrifices. They will resort to collective coercion to ensure horizontal equity in redistribution. This step is not possible in a pure market system, but it is possible under democratic central control.

With respect to general redistribution, collectivistic altruism is probably much more prevalent than individualistic altruism. Moreover, the democratic process involves the justification of policies and the negotiation of compromises between interest groups, and these may foster collectivistic altruism to a certain extent, so that we find more of it under democratic coordination than under market competition or among governors exercising oligarchic control.

9.3   Poor working conditions

Working-conditions deprivation

In Chapter 3 it was indicated that work interests refer to those aspects of jobs that do not represent purchasing power. Deprivation concerning these interests can be conceptualized in two ways so that it will be free of the comparability problem and the evaluation circularity. The first is analogous to subsistence poverty. Such subsistence deprivation in working conditions refers to those working conditions that jeopardize survival and health. The criterion here really becomes one of work-related ill health. The other conception consists of first distinguishing between various dimensions of working conditions, next weighting these dimensions to make them commensurable through a cross-systemic process of valuation, and finally establishing on the resulting aggregate index of working conditions a deprivation threshold. The actual development of either of these two measures is not necessary for the following cursory discussion, but its possibility is indicated to show that the evaluation basis of that discussion makes sense conceptually. The focus is on the deprivation of the workers with the worst jobs.

To avoid confusion it is necessary now to draw a clear distinction between coordination for the economic system as a whole, including coordination between productive establishments, and coordination within productive establishments. (By "productive establishment" I mean units such as an industrial plant, a retail store, a restaurant, an office of self-employed professionals, etc., rather than a firm, which may encompass several such units.) The same coordination mechanisms are to be considered in the two contexts, but their performance capacities regarding deprivation in working conditions for the most deprived differ between them.

Working conditions and systemwide coordination

As in the case of consumption, market competition can have certain equalizing tendencies. Under perfect competition and full employment, jobs with poor working conditions will go begging owing to the loss of workers to jobs with better conditions (unless the former compensate for their deficiency by better pay). But such equalization will be constrained by the inequalities in the abilities of workers (as reflected in their highest attainable marginal productivity), and as was indicated in Section 9.2, the market system generates considerable inequalities in acquired abilities. Moreover, a tight labor market is not a consistent feature of market coordination; in the absence of a tight labor market the lack of alternative job options and the threat of unemployment will make workers captives of their jobs to a considerable extent, so that competition in working conditions will be seriously impaired. In general, those inefficiencies and inequalities of the pure market system that lead to less-than-subsistence earnings, as discussed previously, will also tend to lead to deprivation in working conditions, since workers' low bargaining power regarding their earnings will reflect low bargaining power regarding working conditions.

Central control has the capacity to prevent deprivation in working conditions by establishing appropriate standards in a manner analogous to the central determination of prices. If intraestablishment coordination is democratic, it can also be accomplished more indirectly by policies that make establishments with poor working conditions profitable enough so that productivity in output can be traded off for "productivity" in working conditions. As in the case of consumption deprivation, the utilization of these instruments depends on the concerns of those in power.

Under an oligarchic rule, assuming it is exercised in a self-interested manner, the governors will have no greater concern for deprivation in working conditions than they will have for consumption deprivation. The consumption interests of the oligarchs and possibly their power interests, which may require the financing of the machinery of coercion, will militate against incurring the opportunity costs involved in the improvement of working conditions. To the extent that protecting subsistence working conditions is in their consumption interests, whose fulfillment depends on labor productivity, and in their power interests, whose protection may depend on the survival and military fitness of the populace, they will do so. This interest of the oligarchs in the survival and fitness of workers may provide assurance of protection against subsistence deprivation regarding working conditions, but only for those whose fitness and productivity is important to the oligarchs.[1]

Concerning the *democratic* formulation of priorities, the points made about the maximin optimization of consumption apply to working conditions as well. If the citizens are wholly self-interested, a majority coalition working against the improvement of the worst working conditions is at least as likely to be in power as a coalition promoting such improvements. On the other hand, the process of democratic decision making may make citizens more sensitive to one

---

[1] The relationship between rulers and workers under oligarchic central control is similar to that of slavery. Slaveowners have an interest in their slaves because the latter are capital to them; employees are nowhere near as important to employers. Thus it has been reported about the Atlantic slave trade that the treatment and mortality rate of white sailors on slave ships was worse than those of the slaves themselves, though the conditions of the latter are, of course, notorious (Mannix and Cowley 1962:xi).

another and more concerned with distributive justice, so that moral considerations may enter the concerns of majority coalitions.

Working conditions and intraestablishment coordination

Intraestablishment coordination can take the forms that have been mentioned in reference to systemwide or interestablishment coordination. (1) The conventional form of coordination in the capitalist and state-socialist establishment is oligarchic, in that it involves central control by a few. (To the extent that labor unions participate in or explicitly constrain the management of the establishment, bargaining enters intraestablishment coordination.) (2) Worker-managed enterprises are democratic in the formulation of priorities, while the implementation of these priorities remains under central control within the establishment.[2]

The one form of coordination that has not been mentioned in this list of examples is that of market competition. The reason is that the establishment is a set of production relations that is removed from market competition. Although workers contract to perform a *general* type of work, the *specific* tasks that they perform are not contracted for; these are generally at the discretion of management, with worker choice being reduced to accepting management requirements or leaving the job and with little opportunity for task-by-task negotiation. One major reason for central control rather than market relations is that for a smooth but also responsive production process it is necessary to have a combination of stability in role relations within the establishment and flexibility in the role tasks that is not possible with market relations (at least not within reasonable limits on the costs of negotiation and on the losses resulting from delays in the replacement of role incumbents).

The extent to which the internal mode of coordination makes a difference for working conditions depends on whether the external or systemwide coordination system constrains the trade-off between working conditions and earnings. Central control of an extreme form makes the managements of individual establishments part of the cen-

---

[2] Democracy here refers to workplace democracy. It is, of course, possible to have two other forms of democracy in this context. One is consumer democracy, represented by consumer cooperatives, and the other is the "ownership democracy" of the capitalist enterprise with widely held shares, sometimes referred to as "stockholder democracy." As far as decisions concerning working conditions are concerned, self-interested behavior in the context of these alternative forms of democracy will lead to the same priorities as under oligarchic intraestablishment control.

tral bureaucracy and mere executors of central orders. Pure market competition means that every establishment will be under pressure to be no less efficient than the others. However, this system leaves a certain amount of leeway, since working conditions are part of worker benefits, and establishments as well as workers may choose different combinations of pay and working conditions. As long as there are enough potential earnings so that some of them can be traded off for better working conditions, deprivation concerning the latter is preventable. In effect, the pressure of competition acts to enhance a form of efficiency that includes working conditions as an output. Under conditions of imperfect market competition – as well as decentralized versions of hierarchical control that leave considerable discretion to lower levels of decision making, including establishment management – further scope for choice regarding working conditions is possible.

Within the limits of its scope for discretionary decision making about working conditions, internal oligarchic control, including control by boards of directors representing stockholders nominally or effectively, cannot be expected to do very well in improving the working conditions of the worst-off. Assuming a market environment, the approach will be the maximization of the material returns to management and those to whom management is responsible, that is, maximization of profits and management salaries, frequently with secondary maximization of working conditions for management and of management power. The maximization of management returns will be at the expense of both workers' earnings and their working conditions, so that it represents a force against the improvement of the conditions of the worst jobs. The secondary maximization of management working conditions has the same effect, except that intra-establishment conflict resulting from poor working conditions for the employees may threaten ease of management, which is one aspect of management working conditions. Management control may work in particular against good conditions for the worst jobs if respect for authority within the establishment is promoted by emphasizing status distinctions and if differences in working conditions are used to this end. Such consequences are also possible under internal oligarchic control in an environment of central planning that leaves this sphere of decision making to the discretion of the establishments.

Self-interested behavior and internal democratic control will, within the sphere of discretion allowed by the mode of systemwide coordination, curb management choices and in general act in favor of good conditions for the workers as a whole, but this does not necessarily mean that they operate to minimize working-conditions deprivation for the worst-off, since the latter may be excluded from the majority coalition that governs the establishment. However, internal democratic control may affect the balance between egoism and concern for others. The democratic process may induce an altruistic concern about the working conditions of the worst jobs in the establishment.

9.4 Social isolation

Social-relations deprivation and socioeconomic processes

To represent deprivation regarding social interests, social isolation will be used as the evaluation criterion. Social isolation is the lack of contact with other people, measured in frequency, duration, and intimacy. Social isolation is treated as a form of deprivation primarily because it characteristically leads to loneliness, which is an important form of unhappiness. It also means lack of access to help and emotional support from others in times of crisis. Of course, the absence of personalized social relations does not mean loneliness for everyone (not for the recluse, for example), and it is possible to be deprived in the opposite direction, by having insufficient privacy. (For a survey of views on conflicts between individual freedom and community see Plant 1974:ch. 2). However, the connection between social isolation and unhappiness is sufficiently universal so that the former will generally be recognized as a violation of a basic need.

Since social isolation is clearly a multidimensional category of interests, care is required in its conceptualization if one is not to fall prey to the evaluation circularity. The two possibilities for defining, in a circularity-free manner, deprivation that concerns consumption and working conditions are applicable here, too. Social isolation can, on the one hand, be defined as that form and degree of deprivation in social relations that tends to lead to illness of some kind. The other possibility is to establish a one-dimensional indicator of social isolation on the basis of intersystemic agreement about the relevant set and relative importance of different deprivation dimensions regarding sociality. For the more limited purposes of the following evaluation, the lack of family relations, friendships, and personalized work relations will constitute deprivation in social relations.

The processes of production and distribution affect social relations in a number of different ways. (1) Opportunities for social relations are directly "produced." Examples are personal counseling or psychotherapy, social clubs, community development, and physical community design. Personal counseling and therapy provide relationships themselves and also may help individuals to change their choices and behavior from patterns that isolate them from others to ones that are conducive to developing relationships. Social clubs, both cohesive ones with stable membership and open ones, such as bars, provide opportunities for personal contacts. This function may also be accomplished by neighborhood networks created by community development. Community design provides the physical structure for interaction between people that may promote either anonymity or sociality. (2) Economic processes also provide opportunities for social relations as a spin-off effect of productive activities. The performance and coordination of work tasks, supplier–customer relations, and the provision of personal services involve personal contacts that can develop from functional to personal relationships. (3) Socioeconomic processes also shape attitudes toward social relations. They affect people's awareness and articulation of their social-relations interests and pattern what people will offer each other and demand from each other. Sociality patterns that may be systemically promoted include self-sufficiency, competition, exploitation, and mutuality. These will clearly affect the extent and quality of personal relationships.

Effects of specific coordination mechanisms

Market competition is capable of producing a considerable range of social-relations opportunities. Personal counseling and therapy as well as social clubs may be commercially provided in response to effective demand. The architectural and land-use choices concerning community design will facilitate social relations to the extent that people are aware of and informed about the sociality effects of alternative community designs and to the extent that all significant spatial determinants of social relations (e.g., common areas conducive to personal encounters) are internalized, as by the large-scale residential developer. However, to the extent that they are not internalized in this way, they constitute externalities and tend to be neglected. Similarly, community development, being a collective good, will not be fostered by the pure market system, if self-interest is the predominant motivation, unless potential initiators and coordinators derive enough social-relations satisfaction from the necessary leadership activities to offset their sacrifices.

The social-relations interests of the most isolated individuals are probably fairly idiosyncratic. The explanation for extreme isolation cannot usually be found in poor sociability conditions for the population as a whole, but must be sought in the special conditions of the extremely isolated, either intrapersonal conditions, such as behavior that makes others feel uncomfortable with the isolated person, or social conditions, such as circumstantial isolation (as in the case of the old person whose family has moved away and whose friends have died) and stigmatization of certain individuals (homosexuals, for example). As far as isolation that is not the result of poverty is concerned, the market mechanism may perform quite well compared to other forms of coordination. It can induce some counselors and psychotherapists to deal with personal sociability problems; and it can attract entrepreneurs into the field of social-relations services and facilities (e.g., dating services and singles bars) for those who experience significant wants for social relations that are not fulfilled in other ways. Moreover, it can make it profitable to provide such services to stigmatized and otherwise disadvantaged minorities, for example, by creating gay clubs or day centers for the elderly (though when a certain form of stigmatization is universal in society, there may be no entrepreneurs available for catering to the social-relations interests of the stigmatized).

However, such market provision of social-relations services works only if there is effective demand for them. In fact, social isolation is often connected with poverty, since certain goods or services, like transportation, may be required for social relations and since the causes of social isolation, for example, social stigmatization, are frequently also the causes of poverty. For this potentially large group of socially isolated poor, important kinds of market-provided opportunities for social relations may not be accessible.

Some of these points apply also to work-related social relations. The market makes it possible for socially isolated individuals to choose jobs that provide opportunities for social relations and to trade off remuneration for them. Yet this does not apply to those whose earning power is so low that they cannot protect themselves from both consumption deprivation and social-relations deprivation.

A further difficulty arises when a person does not recognize that he is miserable because of his isolation or finds it too degrading to do anything about it. In that case, too, his social-relations interest does not become an effective want. This should make the market unresponsive to his interest. However, in at least one case, profit-making entrepreneurs will find it in their interest to respond to the interest of the isolated, even if it is initially not a revealed want. It is that of social-relations opportunities in the workplace. Even if people choose their jobs wholly on the basis of pay and physical working conditions and do not take the sociability payoff into account, it will pay the employer to encourage sociability if it will reduce conflict within the establishment, reduce labor turnover, or increase productivity. These may well be the results if the satisfaction of the unacknowledged social-relations interest gives the workers a greater sense of well-being.

Central coordination has, of course, the mechanisms to deal with problems of externalities and collective goods that affect social relations and also with social isolation that is due to poverty. It can also use collective knowledge to correct for mistakes that individuals make. However, little concern with the need for social relations is to be expected in the case of the oligarchic version of central control, especially with respect to the most isolated. As a matter of fact, in order to legitimize its authority, an oligarchy may accentuate status distinctions and thus create barriers to sociability. The democratic version is more promising, but when it operates on the basis of self-interest, the socially isolated are particularly unlikely to be part of the electoral majority whose interests determine government policy. Although common social-relations interests may be well provided for, those interests which are distinctive to the most isolated will tend to be neglected. Therefore, as far as the social-relations interests of at least the unimpoverished are concerned, the market may in some ways perform better than democratic central control.

This conclusion naturally changes when altruism is present in central decision making. It is very possible that democratic decision making creates greater sensitivity to the troubles of others than the competitive market environment does. If it does, democratic coordination will become increasingly able to alleviate all forms of deprivation. Moreover, it may affect the motivations that are brought to bear on interpersonal relations. If competition is limited and cooperative behavior extensive, individuals may be quicker to trust others and thus to become friends. Self-isolating behavior may be reduced and concern for others who are isolated increased. In contrast, market competition may penetrate the workplace to the extent that there is competition for promotions or wage advantages that can make for an attitude of mutual distrust and a certain callousness. It is this aspect of competition that has impelled certain social critics to denounce it as alienating.

9.5   Psychological depression

Depression as an evaluation criterion

To represent deprivation in human interests, which include interests concerning the individual's affective development, psychological depression will be used as the final evaluation criterion. Such depression refers to states of mind involving gloom, hopelessness, and listlessness. For the purpose of the following evaluation, it is pathological depression that will be considered. This conception is distinguished from "normal" depression (the "blues" and grief) by being abnormally protracted and by being accompanied by such somatic symptoms as lethargy and loss of appetite and sleep and such mental manifestations as self-blame, self-denigration, and helplessness. Since the latter are sometimes treated as causal factors in depression, to avoid confusion it is necessary to recognize that the clinical conception of depression refers to a syndrome of symptoms and causes. Obviously, depression is a constituent of unhappiness, or at least causally related to it in a very immediate way. The pathological definition of depression, which appears to be cross-culturally applicable, is not entangled in the evaluation circularity.

The evaluation of coordination mechanisms concerning this affective illness will be discussed at somewhat greater length than deprivation in interests regarding working conditions and social relations. One reason is that because it affects the individual's very structure of wants, depression is a particularly interesting criterion by which to evaluate coordination mechanisms. The second reason is that deductive reasoning from assumptions such as self-interest is not very useful in the prediction of human reactions, a process that is involved in evaluation regarding depression, and it is necessary to draw on inductive generalizations and empirical material. The focus here is on three issue areas that represent points of contact between socioeconomic processes and depression. (1) One is that of depression as a reaction to certain *current* life events or circumstances, which has been referred to as "reactive depression" (Schuyler 1974:6–9). Such life events can to some extent be related to the processes or coordination of production and distribution. (2) The second issue area is that of depression as a character disposition, which has been referred to as "characterological depression" (Becker 1977:17). This area represents developmental interests in a more profound sense. Environmental causes that stem from socioeconomic coordination are explored here. (3) The availability of curative experiences such as therapy is discussed as the third issue area.

Sources of reactive depression

The sources of reactive depression that are relevant for our purposes are the separation from or loss of persons of intimate significance or other anchors of one's existence, stressful personal circumstances, and conditions giving rise to a sense of helplessness and self-denigration. Loss and separation are central to the etiological literature on depression.

The first and probably most important cause of depression is the loss of attachments. All treatments of depression refer to the loss of an attachment to a mother by a child, of a spouse or a friend, as a probable source of depression; controlled empirical studies (Paykel, 1973, pp. 222–25) support the detailed clinical observations. More problematic are the extensions of the concept of attachment to nation, community, workplace – anything to which value is attached (Bowlby, 1969, p. 207). Yet for these, too, there is evidence that separations bear a relation to depression, although, of course, neither with persons nor with institutions, places, and symbols is the contingency relationship a necessary one – many of the separated do not suffer from depression. [Lane 1981:28; cf. Schuyler 1974:69–79; Rutter and Madge 1976:206–9; and Becker 1977:11–12 and 127–30]

More generally, "the work of several different groups of investigators has now clearly shown that the onset of depression in adult life is frequently preceded by acute life stresses" (Rutter and Madge 1976:209; cf. Becker 1977:127–9). To give more specific meaning to the notion of life stresses, I will use the term to refer to two kinds of causal factors that George W. Brown and Tirril O. Harris (1978:pt. III) have conceptualized: depression-provoking agents, that is, severe events and ongoing major difficulties, and vulnerability factors. The vulnerability factors that they have identified are the lack of an intimate and trusting relationship, for women more than two children under the age of fourteen at home, and lack of employment. Separation and loss and, more broadly, life stresses can be regarded as environmental conditions.

There are, however, also attitudes that are recognized as causes of reactive depression. Thus the cognitive theorist of depression A. T. Beck argued that there is a "negative cognitive set," consisting of self-denigration, helplessness, and hopelessness, which is the primary cause of depression and that sadness and apathy are secondary emotional changes (Schuyler 1974:73; Becker 1977:66ff). Reactive depression can therefore be broken down into two different emphases. One focuses on external conditions in the form of separation and loss and of life stresses, and the other concentrates on environmental influences on attitudes of helplessness and hopelessness and of self-denigration.

Reactive depression and environmental conditions

Loss by death is an important source of depression. To the extent that deprivation concerning consumption and working conditions affects the incidence of mortality, it also affects the risk of depression in the related survivors. Subsistence poverty can affect mortality by starvation and disease. Poor working conditions include the hazard of fatal accidents and disease. In these instances of the mortality effects of previously discussed forms of deprivation, the conclusions about the potential impact of the various coordination mechanisms apply also to death-induced depression in the survivors. Oligarchic central control has a high potential ability but very low intrinsic propensity to prevent this form of deprivation; under market competition both the ability and the propensity are limited; and democratic central control has a high ability but an uncertain propensity. This conclusion applies also, by and large, to the mortality effects of health deprivation in general, and thus to loss by death as a whole.

A more general form of loss is involved in interpersonal separations, as well as the loss of jobs and the loss of particular environments owing to migration to new places of employment.[3] With respect to attachments to persons, places, and organizations, Robert E. Lane has argued that compared to democratic coordination, the market system is disruptive. "The free labor market has the effect of attracting the young of both sexes from villages and close kinship networks to 'wage labor' situations" (1981:28); the effect is "the fracturing of affectional ties and the reconstruction of groups by work functions," a process that has historically created "psychic distress" (1979:41). Rather than referring to the market system loosely defined, as Lane has done, I am dealing with systems based wholly on the market mechanism. The general conclusion can be maintained, but the reasoning needs to be somewhat more specific.

Under market coordination without central control, there are reasons to expect a relatively high rate of both layoffs and geographic mobility. With respect to the former, fluctuations in aggregate demand that are characteristic of market coordination because of instability regarding general investment prospects result in a cycle of expansion and contraction in employment. Moreover, instability is

---

[3] There has been some controversy about the causal factors involved in the impact of migration on schizophrenia (Dohrenwend and Dohrenwend 1969:40–1; Ineichen 1979:47–8), but with respect to more limited disturbances, including depression, there are indications from empirical studies that migration and its associated experiences play a causative role (Kiev 1972:12–13).

created by the market mechanism's lack of coordination of specific investment plans of different establishments. Inconsistent production intentions subsequently have to be corrected, with layoffs as a likely element in the adjustments. Such layoffs owing to a lack of investment coordination may make geographic moves for the dismissed workers necessary. Beyond that, the market mechanism has a tendency toward disruptive structural changes (such as changes in consumer preferences and new technologies) that will in many cases force migration. Since there is no feedback of the dislocation costs to the initiators of change, these costs remain external to the investment decision-making process.[4]

Central control, on the other hand, has the planning apparatus to avoid such coordination problems. Even under the pure oligarchic model, central planning to prevent waste resulting from investment uncertainties is likely, since such instability limits production and creates problems of administration. However, when it comes to structural changes that benefit some while harming others, it is not clear that the oligarchs have any particular interest in containing such changes unless it is the oligarchs themselves who are the victims. The pattern under democratic rule is again more promising. It is true that it may neglect to contain change and to compensate its victims if the majority coalitions do not represent the victims. But Lane's (1981:30) argument that "the democratic state is protective of both communities and families" applies to the extent that, for a majority of the population, structural change in general is more of a threat than a potential benefit, so that general policies to contain change and to cushion its effects, including depression, will be instituted.

With respect to life stresses in general, the ongoing difficulties and vulnerability factors that are most susceptible to impacts from coordination mechanisms are unemployment, poor housing, and general poverty. To the extent that unemployment is something that threatens the majority of individuals in society, majoritarian democracy can be expected to take protective measures against it. However, if the majority is fairly immune to unemployment and it is a minority that passes into and out of unemployment, then the conclusions that were

---

[4] Even structural *responses* can manifest this lack of coordination. Baumol (1963:11–14 and 1965:37–8) has presented a model according to which urban blight involves a cumulative process in which the exodus of some families reduces the earning opportunities and living conditions of those remaining, thus inducing their progressive exodus as well. Those leaving initially have no inducement to take into account the impact of their departure on those initially staying behind. Such an explanation is also applicable to regional decline. (For a brief summary see Stilwell 1972:33–4.)

reached concerning poverty are more applicable. These also apply to poor housing as a factor contributing to depression. In general, democratic central control is more promising than oligarchic central control and the pure market system, but in the absence of widespread altruism (at least of a collectivistic kind), it does not guarantee the minimization of depression that is attributable to socioeconomic patterns mediated by life stresses.

Attitudinal sources of reactive depression

Lane has argued that the market system involves conditions and attitudes that are conducive to feelings of (1) helplessness and (2) self-contempt. (1) The idea of "learned helplessness" has been developed by M. E. P. Seligman, who found that exposing animals to aversive experiences that they could not control or escape from handicapped them severely in learning to avoid and control such experiences when the opportunity was available, in comparison with animals not preconditioned in this way (Schuyler 1974:74–6; Becker 1977:69–71). He and others also found such evidence for human subjects and, moreover, concluded that "instructional sets that strongly emphasize chance rather than skill factors" are contributing causes to learned helplessness (Becker 1977:72). In the light of this mode of depression as learned helplessness, Lane (1981:30–1) has argued that "the market ideology of self-reliance, or achievement through one's own efforts, particularly when this is married to a doctrine of equality such that everyone, no matter what his condition in life, is expected to be a 'success,' sets up the conditions for depression when failure rather than success is the outcome of striving." Environmental conditions uncontrollable for the individual are liable to frustrate his aspirations, particularly in a market setting, with its high level of change and unpredictability. Such frustration can then lead to an attitude of helplessness. This applies especially to the poor, whose choices and control are particularly constrained by their limited resources, even in the absence of change.

Under centralized coordination of a democratic form, the individual also has a problem concerning control. His control over collective decision making is miniscule. The massive bureaucracy that is required by pure central control may be quite unresponsive to the varying needs of individuals and may be a serious source of frustration. As a matter of fact, centralized coordination, even when democratic, compares poorly with the control that the individual can exercise over a range of private choices under market coordination.

However, two considerations favor democratic coordination. One is that miniscule individual control in democratic decision making and over bureaucratic behavior is still better for collective conditions than the total absence of control that applies under market coordination. Secondly, it seems possible for individuals to identify sufficiently strongly with a collective unit, including at times the nation, so that collective control gives them a sense of participating in this control. This identification will, however, be limited to the extent that there are defeated minorities and the bureaucracy is unresponsive. Moreover, if democratic decision making goes so far as to regulate extensively individuals' private environments and their consumption patterns, the loss of control would probably be much greater than the gain in control, and the feeling of helplessness would be greater than in a total market setting, even for the poor under some conditions.

Oligarchic central control involves even greater lack of control for the regime's subjects and thus conditions conducive to depression induced by helplessness. This applies not just to national coordination, but also within the productive establishment; in other words, entrepreneurial control can be expected to make workers more susceptible to depression than worker control (although the independent question of individual discretion *within* jobs is probably still more important).

(2) Self-denigration comes from the discrepancy between the individual's performance and his expectations or standards. These standards are obtained from social settings, and to a certain extent they are shaped by the prevailing coordination system and the ideology that makes it work. In this respect, too, Lane (1981) has argued that the market system contributes to reactive depression. "All competitive systems, all achievement-oriented societies (as contrasted to ascriptive societies), all open societies pose problems of self-esteem to their members. Equality of opportunity only extends these questions to a larger population. These are, of course, the boasted attributes of the market society, but they take their toll in uncertain self-esteem" (p. 32). This is intensified by "normlessness, [or] lack of internalized social rules and standards . . . , for these operate not only to make for endless striving but also for an uncertainty regarding the conditions which should suffice to tell the individual that he has, at last, succeeded, that his self-esteem is no longer in jeopardy" (p. 34). Evidence in support of the notion that achievable norms are important to the development of self-esteem has been found in the study of children (pp. 34–5). Lane has also argued, again on the basis of empirical evidence, "that self-esteem is the product of the small cohesive groups

that surround the individual as a child, and perhaps also as an adult" (p. 32). The market system tends to break up small groups and undermine their cohesion so that "one never knows in the market when one has, indeed, 'arrived' since there are always others who have exceeded in accomplishments the self-critical individual" (p. 32).

Assuming that these attitudinal pressures would apply to a social system relying exclusively on the market mechanism, they contrast sharply with what Lane has argued applies to democratic coordination. According to him, although there is a difficulty owing to the uncertainty about what is expected of the citizen, the state has to "govern by rules" and thus "sets limits in a manner not to be found in the market" (p. 35). At the same time, representative democracy is supportive of self-esteem because "the politician in and out of office by inviting support tells people that they are important" (p. 33). These points have a certain persuasive force. It might be added that whereas the market ideology makes an individual susceptible to blaming himself, even when his defeats involve a considerable element of bad luck, defeats under democratic coordination do not lead as readily to self-blame, since the reasons for the defeats are visibly collective.

Lane's observation concerning meritocracies, which "by definition grade persons in a hierarchy, but . . . provide secure clues to where one stands and better defined criteria for estimating why one occupies the rank one does" (p. 32), might be applied to oligarchic central control. However, even though the governing elite will have an interest in a well-functioning administrative system, it has no particular interest in conditions promoting self-esteem. Individuals uncertain of themselves are much less likely to challenge the existing system, so that the oligarchs may promote hierarchies in which not only is the judging of individuals' performance emphasized, but their positions are insecure as well.

Child–parent relations and the disposition to depression

The following discussion is still more speculative than that of reactive depression. The concern here is with a disposition toward depression that can be related to the social environment. It represents an impaired capacity for happiness. The disposition is "characterological" because it is part of the individual's character (Becker 1977:17–24). The social-environmental factors in the disposition toward depression take the form of injurious childhood experiences. Among these are the death of a parent, extensive separation from a parent, emotional rejection or denigration by a parent, and parental depression and alcoholism (Becker 1977:112–16; Lane 1981:23, 29–30). The relation of some of these causal links to socioeconomic coordination mechanisms has already been discussed in the context of reactive depression; the mortality effects of different coordination mechanisms, for example, have been dealt with. To the extent that the frequency of children's extensive separation from parents is correlated with the extent of labor mobility, the earlier comments on the migration effects of coordination mechanisms are applicable. The focus of the following discussion, however, is the quality of parenting as it may be affected by coordination mechanisms – in particular, (1) parental knowledge concerning the requirements of children for the development of a capacity for happiness, (2) values concerning parenting, (3) stressful circumstances that affect parenting, and (4) the possibility of replacing injurious parenting by better substitute care.

(1) A parent's intuitive knowledge of parenting has to be supplemented by consciously acquired knowledge when the former is inadequate. Intuitive parenting will be based to a considerable extent on the parenting that the person received as a child. (See, e.g., Rutter and Madge 1976:233.) To the extent that parenting in the previous generation was confusing or injurious to the development of the children's capacity for happiness and vitality, it is an inappropriate model for parenting in the current generation. This situation will vary from family to family. In those cases where this kind of deficiency applies, explicit knowledge concerning parenting is beneficial. The question now is how the different coordination mechanisms perform in providing such knowledge.

The market mechanism has both strengths and weaknesses in this respect. Its strength lies in the incentives it provides in the form of pecuniary rewards to the providers of knowledge through personal instruction and print and audiovisual media. The rewards, moreover, offer incentives to provide the kind of knowledge that is of particular interest to the potential users. The drawbacks include, in the first instance, that knowledge has a considerable collective-good feature and so will not be efficiently provided for in a pure market system. (Copyright laws have to be centrally devised and administered and therefore are not a feature of a pure market system.) Moreover, there are mental costs involved in the learning process, and these will be particularly high for the educationally deprived. The parent may also be unaware of, underestimate, or take a shortsighted attitude toward the benefits to be gained from knowledge about child development and therefore may not express the demand for it that would be rational. Finally, uninformed parenting may also result from insufficient parental concern for the interests of the children. All these deficiencies characterize the market mechanism with respect to parental knowledge.

Central coordination can avoid the deficiencies of the market mechanism as it concerns parental knowledge by removing deterrents to its acquisition, by providing positive incentives for it, and even by adopting a coercive approach, such as through compulsory parent education. It can also assure the development of knowledge about parenting conducive to affective resilience. That is the potential of central control; the question again is what tendencies there are for actualizing this potential. Under oligarchic control there is no reason to expect any particular concern for parenting that would be conducive to the development of a capacity for freedom from depression.

What will tend to emerge from democratic coordination is not entirely clear. If the assumption of self-interested behavior is not qualified, there is no explanation for normal parenting behavior. Assuming that parents' egoism takes the extended form of being concerned with the well-being of only their own children (this is a version of Mackie's [1977:84–5] "self-referential altruism"), it can be expected that majoritarian democracy will provide parental knowledge to the extent that collective-good features are involved. However, it may well neglect accessibility to such knowledge for the educationally and materially disadvantaged, and it can be expected not to attempt to correct for potential ignorance, uncertainty, and shortsightedness concerning the benefits of developmental knowledge, unless such correction finds subsequent public approval with a lag short enough so that political representatives are electorally rewarded rather than penalized. Correction based on children's affective developmental interests rather than parental approval will emerge from democratic decision making only if the latter induces altruistic behavior toward children in general; in that case it is possible that an enlightened majority will make resources available and possibly even require parental learning if parents are insufficiently knowledgeable. (This can, of course, also lead to a tendency to promote orthodoxy and inhibit experimentation and innovation, unless citizen altruism and functionary conscientiousness are complemented by open-mindedness about alternative modes of parenting.)

(2) Parenting is shaped not just by knowledge, but also by value orientations. Since different coordination mechanisms reinforce particular value orientations (and are reinforced by them), we can expect these value orientations to be reflected in parenting, with the parents acting as the "socialization agents" of the overall social system, which

includes the mode of coordination. The emphasis under market coordination on productiveness, competitiveness, self-reliance, and self-assertion can be expected to be reflected in child raising. Apart from restraining the development of altruism that is conducive to the prevention or diminution of depression-promoting conditions, such an approach tends to emphasize the judgment of performance and put into jeopardy the self-esteem of relatively poor performers, thereby putting them at risk of depression. Under oligarchic control the value orientation characteristically consists of an emphasis on respect for and obedience to authority. It will tend to provide a model for authoritarian and punitive parenting; although the literature that I have covered does not deal with the affective consequences of such parenting, it seems to me a reasonable hypothesis that authoritarian parenting will undermine, at least for some children, the development of self-esteem or the sense of environmental mastery or both and thus contribute to a disposition toward depression. Democratic coordination is more likely to coexist with a value orientation of mutual respect and friendliness, and such a value orientation will be conducive to parenting that is affectionate and concerned with building self-esteem and a sense of competence. Again, this is more of a capacity of democratic coordination, with the actual tendency being quite indeterminate.

(3) Another process through which coordination mechanisms can influence parenting is that of their impacts on the living and working conditions of parents and the psychological effects of these on the parents' approach to their children. Poverty and poor working conditions put parents under pressure and may impair their capacity to be attentive, affectionate, and appropriately tolerant toward their children. Such impairment can lead to childhood deprivations that manifest themselves in a disposition toward depression. (It may also result in hostility and generally aggressive behavior.) In this way, too, those coordination mechanisms that tend to generate poverty and poor working conditions may contribute to depression. In particular, it should be noted that oligarchic control can be expected to create worker frustration and hostility that cannot be expressed within the work setting and may consequently be vented within the family. Thus the internal organization of productive establishments can have an effect on children's affective development.

(4) The final point to be made about parenting concerns the extent to which coordination mechanisms provide for the removal of children from injurious parenting and for alternative care of them. (Orphans and abandoned children are also considered here.) The market

mechanism can provide for an adoption market, but it cannot assure that all parentless children will be adopted nor that children will be protected from injurious or even exploitative parenting, as when they are used primarily as servants. In general, the market mechanism has no significant capacity to protect children against absent or injurious parenting. Central control has this capacity, but the tendency to use it is doubtful both under oligarchic control and under egoistically motivated democratic decision making. Democracy with some degree of citizen altruism and conscientiousness among functionaries, however, can go some distance toward protecting children from injurious parenting – for example, by making physical child abuse a reason for transferring custody and by providing resources for good alternative care – and this responsiveness can improve the children's immunity to protracted depression.

Therapy

The remarks made earlier concerning the provision of social-relations counseling also apply to therapy for the treatment of depression. The market mechanism can provide therapeutic services and even generate a high degree of responsiveness to client demand for treatment of different kinds. However, it may not help those who are too depressed to seek treatment (unless they have families to organize it for them), and the variety of treatments offered may be more of a confusion than an opportunity for superior choice, because knowledge about treatment approaches and their effectiveness is likely to be lacking. Protection against charlatans is limited under market competition; client information by word of mouth is a poor basis for informed client choice in the case of infrequently used services. Moreover, the poor will not be able to afford therapy without jeopardizing their subsistence consumption. Finally, the development of diagnostic knowledge and therapeutic methods is handicapped under market competition because of their collective-good nature.

Under central control, it is possible to have professional licensing and monitoring and perhaps even a general referral agency that provides information about therapeutic approaches and their past successes. Individuals too depressed to seek help may be identified as ill and may be assisted in finding therapy. Therapy may be provided without charge, at least for the poor. Therapeutic knowledge and methods may be developed on the basis of collective funding. Of course, the oligarchic form of central control may be expected to make such provisions only to the extent that they will benefit the ruling group. As a matter of fact, political dissidents might well be subjected to depression-*inducing* conditions. Under majoritarian democratic decision making, egoistic citizens may provide for easily accessible therapy as a form of social insurance, but a majority of those less prone to depression may limit such arrangements. Moreover, the special needs of the poor may be neglected in this area, too. It is only when altruistic citizenship enters democratic coordination that it will focus on the rehabilitation of the most deprived.

Unlike the discussion of the other forms of deprivation, the discussion of depression has been conducted largely in aggregative terms, rather than with a focus specifically on the most depressed. The very general ideas considered here simply do not lend themselves to a distinction between the victims of severe depression and those of mild depression. Consequently, it has been assumed that system effects on depression in general reflect the effects on those most seriously affected.

9.6   Pure coordination mechanisms and deprivation

Although these evaluations of market coordination and alternatives to it, treated as pure models, are intended to be merely illustrative of the basic-needs approach and no more than exploratory in nature, a brief comment on what can be said by way of generalization across the four deprivation forms seems worth while. Such generalization is possible partly because the different forms of deprivation are strongly correlated. One reason is that they are often causes of one another. Thus poverty can cause poor working conditions, social isolation, and depression, and social isolation and depression can cause poverty. A second reason is that individuals can to a certain extent trade off the different interests and will presumably use this ability to achieve some sort of balance among them – that is to say, will avoid severe deprivation in one form by sacrificing other kinds of interests. Consequently, it is reasonable to expect that frequently a deprived individual will be afflicted by several kinds of deprivation. More important for the possibility to generalize across the different forms of deprivation, however, is that recurrent themes have emerged in this exploration.

With respect to market competition, the theme has been its incapacity to attend to the deprived, unless they have the economic power (earning power and purchasing power) to contract for such attention. Apart from this incapacity to undo deprivation, market competition has a general tendency to generate it in the first place. Its ethos of competition and self-reliance also constitutes conditions conducive to social isolation and depression. However, the process of competition does set *some* limits to inequality and thus deprivation, and for those with the necessary earning or purchasing power it can cater to quite idiosyncratic needs.

Central control has a characteristically broad range of capacities to prevent and remedy deprivation, but in its oligarchic form there is little pressure or incentive to actualize those capacities. Although the prevention of subsistence deprivation may be in the interest of the oligarchs, this may not apply to the most deprived, and forms of deprivation that are conducive to subordination may actually be promoted. Democratic central control can, in its impact on deprivation, vary widely. On the one hand, it may be similar to the effect of oligarchic central control in that the majority, if it is untouched by the more severe kinds of deprivation, may have no incentive to attend to them and may even employ them repressively; on the other hand, democratic central control may follow a full-fledged basic-needs strategy by bringing all the preventive and remedial instruments at its disposal to bear on deprivation. Where on this spectrum the system will be located depends on the political power of the deprived, which is usually slight; on the communality of needs; on the degree of altruism among the citizens; and on the conscientiousness of the functionaries. Needs that are widely shared may be served quite well, but more idiosyncratic ones, particularly of the severely deprived, may well be neglected. On the other hand, the democratic process may foster a certain degree of altruism, so that even the distinctive needs of the severely deprived may be attended to. Watchful government and citizen advisory committees within the bureaucracy can limit the rigidities and abuses that bureaucracy is otherwise susceptible to, if the electorate and its representatives are sufficiently determined.

These judgments apply only to systems that are based exclusively on single pure forms of coordination. Actual systems will normally consist of mixtures of these coordination modes. The various coordination mechanisms are, in fact, complementary in the sense that for different coordination functions in the economic system it is often best to use different mechanisms. Thus it may be optimal to have one mechanism within productive establishments, another between productive establishments, and still another to regulate certain system-wide phenomena, such as interregional and interpersonal distribution and employment policy. To judge the coordination mechanisms in a manner that is seriously enlightening, we need to evaluate with respect to basic needs their performance of particular coordination tasks within economic systems, rather than their performance as complete systems, as the limitations of the (for the task) rather brief evaluation in this chapter required me to do.

9.7   The preference and human-interest perspectives compared

The ultimate purpose of this chapter has been to bring out the implications of the basic-needs version of the human-interest approach to the evaluation of economic systems. Therefore, it will be concluded with a brief comparison of the preference approach that was critically analyzed in Parts I to IV and the human-interest perspective. The basic common feature is that they are both welfarist. They both take as ends the satisfaction of self-regarding wants, happiness, or conditions that serve one or both of the first two elements. This also means the rejection of conceptions of human interests that are both impersonally objective and essentialist.

The most important difference between the two approaches arises with respect to objectivity and subjectivity. The preference approach is subjectivist and accepts individual choices as the specification of ends. In its unqualified form, no adjustment is made for ignorance, irrationality, and preference patterning, and the problems of measuring want satisfaction are dealt with by limiting the tasks to which optimization and evaluation are to be applied and by using ad hoc measurement criteria that tend to be conceptually incomplete. The preference approach may be qualified by some objective constraints, such as certain rationality requirements, but they cannot resolve the comparability and circularity problems.

The human-interest approach in general is nonsubjectivist, but it may take an impersonally objectivist form or an intersubjectivist one. Although I find much merit in a welfarist approach in which happiness is the central value – a value that constitutively is impersonally objective – it cannot serve as an exclusive value. Basic needs as the alternative welfarist conception of human interests proposed here are formulated in an intersubjective, but system-transcending, manner. That is to say, basic needs represent an open-ended concept, like the concept of preferences, but the former are articulated collectively and cross-systemically. (For more limited tasks of evaluation and optimization, system transcendence may not be needed, but problems concerning interpersonal and intertemporal comparability and concerning rationality mean that some kind of intrasystemic formulation of basic needs is still needed.) As a conception of human interests, basic needs are partial but lexically primary in their entitlement to attention by society. They are best formulated so as to provide extensive scope to individual choice, but individual choice is treated as instrumental to human interests rather than as a definition of human interests in general and basic needs in particular. Basic needs have to be verified instead by reference to both the aims of individuals and the normative judgments of the collectivity.

Both evaluation perspectives are capable of attending to features of economic systems that tend to be neglected in a market-oriented perspective. Thus interests regarding the environment, working conditions, social relations, and, to a certain extent, even self-development can be included not only in the human-interest approach, but also in a broadly conceived preference approach. However, by formulating human interests in terms of basic needs, priority is given to the prevention of deprivation, and this is not an inherent element in the preference approach. (It could be inserted into the latter through an appropriate equity principle, but not without introducing notions that really are alien to the preference approach.) With respect to the interests of any individual, more fundamental is the point that whereas the preference perspective focuses on socialized wants, the human-interest perspective is concerned with developmental interests at a deeper level. It involves the evaluation of the pattern of socialization according to its effects on the human interests of individuals, both those currently alive and those yet to be born.

References

Andel, Norbert (1969). "Zur Diskussion ueber Musgraves Begriff der 'merit wants.'" *Finanzarchiv* 28:209–13.

Anscombe, G. E. M. (1958/1969). "Modern Moral Philosophy." *Philosophy* 33. Reprinted in W. D. Hudson (ed.), *The Is–Ought Question: A Collection of Papers on the Central Question in Moral Philosophy*, pp. 175–95. London: Macmillan.

Arrow, Kenneth J. (1951/1963). *Social Choice and Individual Values*. 2nd ed. New Haven, Conn.: Yale University Press.

Arrow, Kenneth J., and T. Scitovsky (eds., 1969). *Readings in Welfare Economics*. London: Allen & Unwin.

Atkinson, Anthony B. (1975). *The Economics of Inequality*. Oxford: Oxford University Press (Clarendon Press).

Baier, Kurt F. M. (1957/1966). "The Meaning of Life." Reprinted in M. Weitz (ed.), *Twentieth Century Philosophy: The Analytical Tradition*, pp. 361–79. New York: Free Press.

Balbus, Isaac D. (1971). "The Concept of Interest in Pluralist and Marxian Analysis." *Politics and Society* 1:151–77.

Bannock, G., R. E. Baxter, and R. Rees (1972). *The Penguin Dictionary of Economics*. New York: Penguin.

Barry, Brian M. (1964/1967). "The Public Interest." *Proceedings of the Aristotelian Society*, suppl. vol. 38:1–18. Reprinted in A. Quinton (ed.), *Political Philosophy*, pp. 112–26. London: Oxford University Press.

  (1965). *Political Argument*. London: Routledge & Kegan Paul.

  (1970). *Sociologists, Economists and Democracy*. London: Macmillan.

  (1973). *The Liberal Theory of Justice: A Critical Examination of the Principal Doctrines in "A Theory of Justice" by John Rawls*. Oxford: Oxford University Press (Clarendon Press).

Bator, Francis M. (1958/1971). "The Anatomy of Market Failure." *Quarterly Journal of Economics* 72:351–79. Reprinted in Breit and Hochman 1968/1971:518–37.

Baumol, William J. (1952/1965). *Welfare Economics and the Theory of the State*. 2nd ed. London: Bell.

  (1963). "Urban Services: Interactions of Public and Private Decisions." In H. G. Schaller (ed.), *Public Expenditure Decisions in the Urban Community*, pp. 1–18. Baltimore: Johns Hopkins Press.

  (1965). "Welfare and the State Revisited." Introduction to Baumol 1952/1965:1–48.

Baumol, William J., and A. S. Blinder (1979). *Economics: Principles and Policies.* New York: Harcourt Brace Jovanovich.

Bay, Christian (1968). "Needs, Wants and Political Legitimacy." *Canadian Journal of Political Science* 1:241–60.

Becker, Joseph (1977). *Affective Disorders.* Morristown, N.J.: General Learning Press.

Benditt, Theodore M. (1975). "The Concept of Interest in Political Theory." *Political Theory* 3:245–58.

Benn, Stanley I. (1960). "Interests in Politics." *Proceedings of the Aristotelian Society* 60:123–40.

Benn, Stanley I., and G. W. Mortimore (1976). Introduction to Benn and Mortimore (eds.), *Rationality and the Social Sciences.* London: Routledge & Kegan Paul.

Benn, Stanley I., and R. S. Peters (1959). *Social Principles and the Democratic State.* London: Allen & Unwin.

Bergson, Abram (1948/1966). "Socialist Economics." Reprinted in Bergson 1966b:essay 9.

  (1966a). "On Social Welfare Once More." In Bergson 1966b:essay 3.

  (1966b). *Essays in Normative Economics.* Cambridge, Mass.: Harvard University Press.

Boulding, Kenneth E. (1969). "Economics as a Moral Science." *American Economic Review* 59:1–12.

Bowlby, John (1969). *Attachment and Loss.* New York: Basic Books.

Bradburn, Norman M. (1969). *The Structure of Psychological Well-Being.* Chicago: Aldine.

Brandt, Richard B. (1966). "The Concept of Welfare." In Krupp 1966:256–76. (Also to be found in Timms and Watson 1976:64–87.)

  (1967). "Happiness." In Edwards 1967, III:413–14.

  (1979). *A Theory of the Good and the Right.* Oxford: Oxford University Press (Clarendon Press).

  (1982). "Two Concepts of Utility." In H. B. Miller and W. H. Williams (eds.), *The Limits of Utilitarianism,* pp. 169–85. Minneapolis: University of Minnesota Press.

Breit, W., and H. M. Hochman (eds., 1968/1971). *Readings in Microeconomics.* 2nd ed. New York: Holt, Rinehart & Winston.

Brenner, M. Harvey (1976). *Estimating the Social Costs of National Economic Policy: Implications for Mental and Physical Health and Criminal Aggression.* (Report to the Joint Economic Committee, Congress of the United States.)

Brock, Dan W. (1973). "Recent Work in Utilitarianism." *American Philosophical Quarterly* 10:241–76.

Brown, George W., and Tirril O. Harris (1978). *The Social Origins of Depression.* London: Tavistock.

Buchanan, J. M., and Gordon Tullock (1962). *The Calculus of Consent: Logical*

Foundations of Constitutional Democracy. Ann Arbor: University of Michigan Press.

Burkhead, J., and J. Miner (1971). *Public Expenditure.* London: Macmillan.

Campbell, Angus, P. E. Converse, and W. L. Rodgers (1976). *The Quality of American Life: Perceptions, Evaluations, and Satisfactions.* New York: Russell Sage Foundation.

Christian, David (1974). "Social Indicators: The OECD Experience." Paris: Organization for Economic Cooperation and Development.

Connolly, William E. (1974). *The Terms of Political Discourse.* Lexington, Mass.: Heath.

Culyer, A. J. (1976). *Need and the National Health Service: Economics and Social Choice.* Totowa, N.J.: Rowan & Littlefield.

(1978). *Measuring Health: Lessons for Ontario.* Toronto: University of Toronto Press.

Dahl, R. A., and C. E. Lindblom (1953/1963). *Politics, Economics and Welfare.* New York: Harper & Row. Harper Torchbooks.

Dahrendorf, Ralf (1957/1973). *Homo Sociologicus.* Rev. ed. London: Routledge & Kegan Paul.

Daniels, Norman (ed., 1974). *Reading Rawls: Critical Studies of Rawls' "A Theory of Justice."* New York: Basic Books.

Davis, Wayne (1981). "A Theory of Happiness." *American Philosophical Quarterly* 18(2):111–20.

Dobb, Maurice (1969). *Welfare Economics and the Economics of Socialism: Towards a Commonsense Critique.* Cambridge: Cambridge University Press.

Dohrenwend, B. P., and B. S. Dohrenwend (1969). *Social Status and Psychological Disorder: A Causal Inquiry.* New York: Wiley.

Dorfman, Robert (1967/1972). *Prices and Markets.* 2nd ed. Englewood Cliffs, N.J.: Prentice-Hall.

Downs, Anthony (1957). *An Economic Theory of Democracy.* New York: Harper & Row.

Doyle, Peter (1968). "Economic Aspects of Advertising: A Survey." *Economic Journal* 78:570–602.

Duesenberry, James S. (1949). *Income, Saving and the Theory of Consumer Behavior.* Cambridge, Mass.: Harvard University Press.

Easterlin, Richard A. (1974). "Does Economic Growth Improve the Human Lot? Some Empirical Evidence." In P. A. David and M. W. Reder (eds.), *Nations and Households in Economic Growth: Essays in Honor of Moses Abramovitz,* pp. 89–124. New York: Academic Press.

Edwards, P. (ed., 1967). *The Encyclopedia of Philosophy.* New York: Macmillan.

Elster, Jon (1979). *Ulysses and the Sirens: Studies in Rationality and Irrationality.* Cambridge: Cambridge University Press; Paris: Maison des Sciences de l'Homme.

(1982). "Sour Grapes – Utilitarianism and the Genesis of Wants." In Sen and Williams 1982b:219–38.

Emmet, Dorothy (1966). *Rules, Roles and Relations.* London: Macmillan.

Feinberg, Joel (1973). *Social Philosophy*. Englewood Cliffs, N.J.: Prentice-Hall.

Fitzgerald, Ross (1977a). Introduction to Fitzgerald 1977b.

Fitzgerald, Ross (ed., 1977b). *Human Needs and Politics*. Rushcutters Bay, NSW, Australia: Pergamon.

Flathman, Richard E. (1966). "The Concept of Interest and the Public Interest," ch. 2 of Flathman, *The Public Interest*. New York: Wiley.

(1975). "Some Familiar but False Dichotomies concerning 'Interests': A Comment on Benditt and Oppenheim." *Political Theory* 3:277–87.

Flew, Antony G. N. (1977). "Wants or Needs, Choices or Commands." In Fitzgerald 1977b:213–28.

Fraser, L. M. (1939). "The Doctrine of 'Consumers' Sovereignty.'" *Economic Journal* 49:544–48.

Fromm, Erich (1947). *Man for Himself: An Inquiry into the Psychology of Ethics.* Greenwich, Conn.: Fawcett.

(1955). *The Sane Society*. Greenwich, Conn.: Fawcett.

Galbraith, John Kenneth (1958/1969). *The Affluent Society*. 2nd ed. New York: New American Library.

(1967). *The New Industrial State*. New York: New American Library.

(1970). "Economics as a System of Beliefs." *American Economic Review* 60:469–78.

Gerth, H. H., and C. Wright Mills (1953). *Character and Social Structure: The Psychology of Social Institutions*, pt. I. New York: Harcourt Brace.

Gilpin, Alan (1966/1977). "Consumers' Sovereignty." In *Dictionary of Economic Terms*. 4th ed., p. 42. London: Butterworths.

Ginsberg, Morris (1961/1968). "Social Change." Reprinted in Ginsberg, *Essays in Sociology and Social Philosophy*, pp. 129–61. Harmondsworth, Middlesex: Penguin.

Gintis, Herbert (1972a). "Consumer Behavior and the Concept of Sovereignty: Explanations of Social Decay." *American Economic Review* 62:267–78.

(1972b). "A Radical Analysis of Welfare Economics and Industrial Development." *Quarterly Journal of Economics* 86(2):572–99.

(1974). "Welfare Criteria with Endogenous Preferences: The Economics of Education." *International Economic Review* 15(2):415–30.

Glover, Jonathan (1977). "Actual and Potential People," ch. 4 of Glover, *Causing Deaths and Saving Lives*. Harmondsworth, Middlesex: Penguin.

(1979). "How Should We Decide What Sort of World Is Best?" In K. E. Goodpaster and K. M. Sayre (eds.) *Ethics and Problems of the 21st Century*, pp. 79–92. Notre Dame, Ind.: University of Notre Dame Press.

Gordon, David M. (1972). *Theories of Poverty and Underemployment: Orthodox, Radical and Dual Labor Market Perspectives*. Lexington, Mass.: Heath.

Goslin, David A. (1969a). Introduction to Goslin 1969b:1–21.

Goslin, David A. (ed., 1969b). *Handbook of Socialization Theory and Research*. Chicago: Rand McNally.

Graaf, J. de V. (1957). *Theoretical Welfare Economics*. Cambridge: Cambridge University Press.

Griffin, James (1982). "Modern Utilitarianism." *Revue internationale de philosophie* 36:331–75.

Grossman, Gregory (1967/1974). *Economic Systems*. 2nd ed. Englewood Cliffs, N.J.: Prentice-Hall.

Hailstones, T. J., and M. J. Brennan (1970/1975). *Economics: An Analysis of Principles and Policies*. 2nd ed. Cincinnati: South-Western Publishing.

Hanson, J. L. (1965/1977). *A Dictionary of Economics and Commerce*. Rev. ed. Plymouth, U.K.: Macdonald & Evans.

Hare, R. M. (1973/1974). "Rawls' Theory of Justice." *Philosophical Quarterly* 23:144ff. and 241ff. Reprinted in Daniels 1974:81–107.

   (1976/1982). "Ethical Theory and Utilitarianism." In H. D. Lewis (ed.), *Contemporary British Philosophy*. London: Allen & Unwin. Reprinted in Sen and Williams 1982b:23–38.

Harsanyi, John C. (1955/1969/1973). "Cardinal Welfare, Individualistic Ethics and Interpersonal Comparisons of Utility." *Journal of Political Economy* 63:309–21. Reprinted in Arrow and Scitovsky 1969:46–60. Reprinted in Phelps 1973:266–85.

Harvey, J. (1969/1974). *Modern Economics: An Introduction for Business and Professional Students*. 2nd ed. London: Macmillan.

Hayek, Friedrich A. von (1960–1/1975). "The Non Sequitur of the 'Dependence Effect.'" *Southern Economic Journal* 27:346–48. Reprinted in E. Mansfield (ed.), *Microeconomics: Selected Readings*, pp. 7–11. 2nd ed. New York: Norton.

Head, John G. (1966). "On Merit Goods." *Finanzarchiv* 25:1–29.

Heath, Anthony F. (1974). "The Rational Model of Man." *Archives européennes de sociologie* 15:184–205.

   (1976). *Rational Choice and Social Exchange: A Critique of Exchange Theory*. Cambridge: Cambridge University Press.

Heine, Patricke Johns (1971). *Personality and Social Theory*. London: Lane.

Hochman, H. M., and J. D. Rodgers (1969). "Pareto Optimal Redistribution." *American Economic Review* 59:542ff.

Homans, G. C. (1961). *Social Behaviour: Its Elementary Forms*. London: Routledge & Kegan Paul.

Horton, B. J., et al. (1948). *Dictionary of Modern Economics*. Washington, D.C.: Public Affairs Press.

Hudson, W. D. (1970). *Modern Moral Philosophy*. London: Macmillan.

Hutt, W. H. (1936). "Consumers' Sovereignty," ch. 16 of Hutt, *Economists and the Public: A Study of Competition and Opinion*. London: Cape.

Ineichen, Bernard (1979). *Mental Illness*. London: Longman.

Inkeles, Alex (1969). "Social Structure and Socialization." In Goslin 1969b:615–32.

Jahoda, Marie (1982). *Employment and Unemployment: A Social-Psychological Analysis*. Cambridge: Cambridge University Press.

Kapp, K. William (1961). *Toward a Science of Man in Society: A Positive Approach to the Integration of Social Knowledge.* The Hague: Nijhoff.

Kiev, Ari (1972). *Transcultural Psychiatry.* New York: Free Press.

Kirsh, Sharon (1983). *Unemployment: Its Impact on Body and Soul.* Toronto: Canadian Mental Health Association.

Knight, Frank H. (1933/1951/1968/1971). *The Economic Organization.* Harper & Row, 1933, 1951. Extracted as "Social-Economic Organization" in Breit and Hochman 1968/1971:3–19.

Kraut, Richard (1979). "Two Conceptions of Happiness." *Philosophical Review* 88:167–97.

Krupp, S. R. (ed., 1966). *The Structure of Economic Science: Essays on Methodology.* Englewood Cliffs, N.J.: Prentice-Hall.

Lancaster, Kelvin J. (1966). "Change and Innovation in the Technology of Consumption." *American Economic Review* 56:14–23.

Lane, Robert E. (1979). "Cognition, Consciousness and Depression: The Effects of the Market and the Democratic State." Paper presented at a conference in Moscow. (A revised version appeared as Lane 1981.)

(1981). "Cognition, Consciousness and Depression: Effects of the Market and the Democratic State." *Micropolitics* 1(1):1–43.

Lange, Oskar (1938). *On the Economic Theory of Socialism.* Ed. B. E. Lippincott. Minneapolis: University of Minnesota Press.

Lerner, Abba P. (1972). "The Economics and Politics of Consumer Sovereignty." *American Economic Review* 62:258–66.

Liedloff, Jean (1975). *The Continuum Concept.* London: Futura.

Lindbeck, A. (1971). "The Efficiency of Competition and Planning." In M. Kaser and R. S. Portes (eds.), *Planning and Market Relations,* pp. 83–107. London: Macmillan.

Little, I. M. D. (1950/1957). *A Critique of Welfare Economics.* 2nd ed. London: Oxford University Press.

Lukes, Steven (1973). *Individualism.* Oxford: Blackwell.

(1974). *Power: A Radical View.* London: Macmillan.

McCloskey, H. J. (1976). "Human Needs, Rights and Political Values." *American Philosophical Quarterly* 13:1–11.

McDonald, Michael F. (1978). "Autarchy and Interest." *Australasian Journal of Philosophy* 56:109–25.

MacIntyre, Alasdair (1967). "Egoism and Altruism." In Edwards 1967, II:462–6.

Mackenzie, W. J. M. (1967). "Parsonian Theory," sec. 8.B of Mackenzie, *Politics and Social Science.* Harmondsworth, Middlesex: Penguin.

Mackie, J. L. (1977). *Ethics: Inventing Right and Wrong.* Harmondsworth, Middlesex: Penguin.

McLure, Charles E., Jr. (1969). "Merit Wants: A Normatively Empty Box." *Finanzarchiv* 27:474–83.

Mannix, Daniel P., and M. Cowley (1962). Introduction to *Black Cargoes: A History of the Atlantic Slave Trade, 1518–1865.* New York: Viking.

232   **References**

Marcuse, Herbert (1965/1968). *One Dimensional Man.* London: Sphere. Abacus Edition.
Maslow, Abraham H. (1962). *Toward a Psychology of Being.* Princeton, N.J.: Van Nostrand.
Meade, James E. (1964). *Efficiency, Equality and the Ownership of Property.* London: Allen & Unwin.
Mill, John Stuart (1861/1969). "Utilitarianism." *Fraser's Magazine,* Oct.–Dec. Reprinted in J. M. Smith and E. Sosa (eds.), *Mill's Utilitarianism: Text and Criticism,* pp. 31–88. Belmont, Calif.: Wadsworth.
Miller, David (1976). *Social Justice.* Oxford: Oxford University Press (Clarendon Press).
Millward, Robert (1971). *Public Expenditure Economics: An Introductory Application of Welfare Economics.* London: McGraw-Hill.
Mishan, E. J. (1960/1969). "Survey of Welfare Economics – 1939–59." *Economic Journal* 70:197–256. Reprinted in Mishan, *Welfare Economics: Ten Introductory Essays.* 2nd ed., pp. 11–86. New York: Random House.
    (1967). *The Costs of Economic Growth.* Harmondsworth, Middlesex: Penguin.
Montague, Roger (1967). "Happiness." *Proceedings of the Aristotelian Society* 67:87–102.
Moore, Wilbert E. (1965). *The Impact of Industry.* Englewood Cliffs, N.J.: Prentice-Hall.
    (1969). "Occupational Socialization." In Goslin 1969b:861–83.
Musgrave, Richard A. (1959). "A Multiple Theory of the Public Household," ch. 1 of Musgrave, *The Theory of Public Finance: A Study of Public Economy.* Tokyo: McGraw-Hill Kogakusha.
Myint, Hla (1948). *Theories of Welfare Economics.* New York: Kelley.
Nath, S. K. (1969). *A Reappraisal of Welfare Economics.* London: Routledge & Kegan Paul.
Nielsen, Kai (1962). "On Taking Human Nature as the Basis for Morality – An Exercise in Linguistic Analysis." *Social Research* 29:157–76.
    (1973/1976). "Alienation and Self-Realization." *Philosophy* 48. Reprinted in Timms and Watson 1976:117–32.
Nordhaus, William D., and James Tobin (1972). "Is Growth Obsolete?" In National Bureau of Economic Research, *Economic Growth,* pp. 1–80. New York: Columbia University Press.
Olson, Mancur (1968). "Economics, Sociology and the Best of All Possible Worlds." *Public Interest* 12:96–118.
Oppenheim, Felix E. (1975). "Self-Interest and Public Interest." *Political Theory* 3:259–75.
Pattanaik, P. K. (1968/1973). "Risk, Impersonality and the Social Welfare Function." *Journal of Political Economy.* Reprinted in Phelps 1973:298–318.
Paykel, Eugene S. (1973). "Life Events and Acute Depression." In J. P. Scott and E. C. Senay (eds.), *Separation and Depression.* Washington, D.C.: American Association for the Advancement of Science.

Peacock, A. T., and C. K. Rowley (1972). "Pareto Optimality and the Political Economy of Liberalism." *Journal of Political Economy* 80(3):476–90.

Peters, R. S. (1966). "The Consideration of Interests," ch. 6 of Peters, *Ethics and Education*. London: Allen & Unwin.

Phelps, Edmund S. (ed., 1973). *Economic Justice: Selected Readings*. Harmondsworth, Middlesex: Penguin.

Pigou, A. C. (1920/1932). *The Economics of Welfare*. 4th ed. London: Macmillan.

Plamenatz, John (1954). "Interests." *Political Studies* 2:1–8.

Plant, Raymond (1974). *Community and Ideology: An Essay in Applied Social Philosophy*. London: Routledge & Kegan Paul.

Polanyi, Karl (1944). *The Great Transformation*. Boston: Beacon.

Porter, Burton F. (1980). *The Good Life: Alternatives in Ethics*. New York: Macmillan.

Rawls, John (1971). *A Theory of Justice*. London: Oxford University Press. (1975). "Fairness to Goodness." *Philosophical Review* 84(4):536–54.

Reith, Lord, et al. (1966). *Report of a Royal Commission of Inquiry into Advertising*. Labour Party, Britain.

Rescher, Nicholas (1972). *Welfare: The Social Issues in Philosophical Perspective*. Pittsburgh: University of Pittsburgh Press.

Richardson, G. B. (1971). "Planning versus Competition." *Soviet Studies* 21:433–47.

Riesman, David (1950/1961). "Adjustment or Autonomy?" ch. 12 of Riesman, *The Lonely Crowd: A Study of the Changing American Character*. Rev. and abridged ed. New Haven, Conn.: Yale University Press.

Robinson, Joan (1962). *Economic Philosophy*. Harmondsworth, Middlesex: Penguin.
(1964/1972). "Consumer's Sovereignty in a Planned Economy." In *On Political Economy and Econometrics: Essays in Honour of Oskar Lange*, pp. 513–521. Warsaw: P.W.N. Reprinted in A. Nove and D. M. Nuti (eds.), *Socialist Economics: Selected Readings*, pp. 263–74. Harmondsworth, Middlesex: Penguin.

Rothenberg, Jerome (1961). *The Measurement of Social Welfare*. Westport, Conn.: Greenwood.
(1966). "Values and Value Theory in Economics." In Krupp 1966:221–42.
(1968). "Consumer Sovereignty." In D. L. Sills (ed.), *International Encyclopedia of the Social Sciences*, III, 326–35. New York: Macmillan.

Runciman, W. G. (1966). *Relative Deprivation and Social Justice*. Harmondsworth, Middlesex: Penguin.

Rutter, M. L., and N. J. H. Madge (1976). *Cycles of Disadvantage*. London: Heinemann.

Sabine, George H. (1937/1963). "The Theory of the National State," pt. III of Sabine, *A History of Political Theory*. 3rd ed. London: Harrap.

Samuelson, Paul A. (1950/1969). "Evaluation of Real National Income." *Ox-*

ford Economic Papers n.s. 2:1–29. Reprinted in Arrow and Scitovsky 1969:402–33.

Scanlon, T. M. (1975). "Preference and Urgency." *Journal of Philosophy* 72(19):655–69.

——— (1982). "Contractualism and Utilitarianism." In Sen and Williams 1982b:103–28.

Schuyler, Dean (1974). *The Depressive Spectrum.* New York: Aronson.

Scitovsky, Tibor (1951/1971). *Welfare and Competition.* Rev. ed. London: Allen & Unwin.

——— (1960/1964). "A Critique of Present and Proposed Standards." Reprinted in Scitovsky 1964:232–40.

——— (1962/1964). "On the Principle of Consumers' Sovereignty." Reprinted in Scitovsky 1964:241–9.

——— (1964). *Papers on Welfare and Growth.* London: Allen & Unwin.

——— (1976). *The Joyless Economy: An Inquiry into Human Satisfaction and Consumer Dissatisfaction.* Oxford: Oxford University Press.

Seldon, A., and F. C. Pennance (1965/1976). "Consumers' Sovereignty." In *Everyman's Dictionary of Economics.* 1st ed. pp. 86–87. Rev. ed., p. 74. London: Dent.

Sen, Amartya K. (1967/1972). "Isolation, Assurance and the Social Rate of Discount." *Quarterly Journal of Economics* 81:112–24. Reprinted as "The Social Time Preference Rate in Relation to the Market Rate of Interest" in R. Layard (ed.), *Cost-Benefit Analysis,* pp. 270–83. Harmondsworth, Middlesex: Penguin.

——— (1970). *Collective Choice and Social Welfare.* San Francisco: Holden-Day.

——— (1973). "Behaviour and the Concept of Preference." *Economica* 40:241–59.

——— (1974/1974). "Rawls versus Bentham: An Axiomatic Examination of the Pure Distribution Problem." *Theory and Decision* 4 (1974). Reprinted in Daniels 1974:283–92.

Sen, Amartya K., and Bernard A. O. Williams (1982a). Introduction to Sen and Williams 1982b:1–21.

Sen, Amartya K., and Bernard A. O. Williams (eds., 1982b). *Utilitarianism and Beyond.* Cambridge: Cambridge University Press.

Simon, Herbert A. (1955). "A Behavioral Model of Rational Choice." *Quarterly Journal of Economics* 69(1):99–118.

——— (1957). *Models of Man: Social and Rational.* New York: Wiley.

Smart, J. J. C. (1973). "An Outline of a System of Utilitarian Ethics." In Smart and B. A. O. Williams (1973), *Utilitarianism For and Against,* pp. 1–74. Cambridge: Cambridge University Press.

Sorenson, Richard E. (1977). "Growing Up as a Fore Is to Be 'In Touch' and Free." *Smithsonian* (May):106–15.

Stilwell, Frank J. B. (1972). *Regional Economic Policy.* London: Macmillan.

Streeten, Paul P. (1953). "Recent Controversies." Appendix to Streeten's translation of Gunnar Myrdal, *The Political Element in the Development of Economic Theory.* London: Routledge & Kegan Paul.

Taylor, Philip A. S. (1966/1969). *A New Dictionary of Economics.* 2nd ed. London: Routledge & Kegan Paul.

Teitelman, Michael (1972). "The Limits of Individualism." *Journal of Philosophy* 69:545–56.

Thayer, Richard (1973/1977). "Measuring Need in the Social Services." *Social and Economic Administration* 7:91–105. Reprinted in N. Gilbert and H. Specht (eds.), *Planning for Social Welfare: Issues, Models and Tasks,* pp. 297–310. Englewood Cliffs, N.J.: Prentice-Hall.

Thompson, Arthur A. (1973/1977). *Economics of the Firm: Theory and Practice.* 2nd ed. Englewood Cliffs, N.J.: Prentice-Hall.

Timms, N., and D. Watson (eds., 1976). *Talking about Welfare: Readings in Philosophy and Social Policy.* London: Routledge & Kegan Paul.

Tisdell, C. A. (1972). *Microeconomics: The Theory of Economic Allocation.* Sydney: Wiley.

Townsend, Peter (1979). *Poverty in the United Kingdom: A Survey of Household Resources and Standards of Living.* Berkeley: University of California Press.

Wall, Grenville (1975). "The Concept of Interest in Politics." *Politics and Society* 5:487–510.

Weisskopf, Walter A. (1971). *Alienation and Economics.* New York: Dutton.

Weizsaecker, Carl Christian von (1971). "Notes on Endogenous Change of Tastes." *Journal of Economic Theory* 3:345–72.

Wessman, A. E., and D. F. Ricks (1966). *Mood and Personality.* New York: Holt, Rinehart & Winston.

Whittaker, Edmund (1956). *Economic Analysis.* New York: Wiley; London: Chapman & Hall.

Winch, D. M. (1971). *Analytical Welfare Economics.* Harmondsworth, Middlesex: Penguin.

Wolff, Robert Paul (1968). "Liberty," ch. 1 of Wolff, *The Poverty of Liberalism.* Boston: Beacon Press.

   (1977). *Understanding Rawls: A Reconstruction and Critique of "A Theory of Justice."* Princeton, N.J.: Princeton University Press.

Worland, Stephen T. (1967). *Scholasticism and Welfare Economics.* Notre Dame, Ind.: University of Notre Dame Press.

Wright, Georg H. von (1963/1976). "The Good of Man," ch. 5 of Wright, *The Varieties of Goodness.* London: Routledge & Kegan Paul; New York: Humanities Press. Reprinted in Timms and Watson 1976:88–116.

Zigler, E., and I. L. Child (1969). "Socialization." In G. Lindzey and E. Aronson (eds.), *The Handbook of Social Psychology.* 2nd ed., III:450–589. Reading, Mass.: Addison-Wesley.

Index

advertising, 92, 95–7, 112
altruism, 42, 45, 48–9
  collectivistic vs. individualistic, 202
  democracy and, 202, 207, 210, 219, 223
  "other-regarding" wants and, 52–5
  "self-referential," 52, 219
  socialization and, 110
  socioeconomic coordination and, 188–9
  surplus, 49
anarchism as coordination mechanism, 188–9
Andel, Norbert, 57n
Anscombe, G. E. M., 166
Aristotle, 145
Arrow, Kenneth J., 52n
Atkinson, Anthony B., 167, 195
autonomy, *see* self-determination

Baier, Kurt F. M., 146
Balbus, Isaac D., 9
Bannock, G., 12n
bargaining as coordination mechanism, 187–8
Barry, Brian M., 6, 9, 30, 51–2, 105n, 107, 117, 125, 148, 169–70, 172n, 184, 187–8, 200–1
Bator, Francis M., 35
Baumol, William J., 13, 35, 72, 214n
Baxter, R. E., 12n
Bay, Christian, 9, 166
Beck, A. T., 212
Becker, Joseph, 211–12, 215, 217–18
Benditt, Theodore M., 9
Benn, Stanley I., 9, 61, 105n, 107, 166
Bergson, Abram, 13–14, 20, 36, 40
Blinder, A. S., 13
Boulding, Kenneth E., 44, 90
Bowlby, John, 212
Bradburn, Norman M., 157–8
Brandt, Richard B., 7, 43, 67, 68n, 75n, 78–81, 85, 90, 141–3, 146–7, 151–4, 160, 164
Brennan, M. J., 14, 22

Brenner, M. Harvey, 161
Brock, Dan W., 148
Brown, George W., 212
Buchanan, J. M., 200
Burkhead, J., 35, 41n, 57n

calculus principles of optimization and evaluation
  basic needs and, 181–5
  constitutive conception of interests and, 42–50, 51–5
  consumer sovereignty and, 18–20, 35
  distributive justice and, 46–9
  happiness and, 149
  normative judgments in, 132–5
  relativity wants and, 46–8
  social surplus analysis in, 128–9
  use of prices in, 125–7, 130–2
  want satisfaction and, 123–5
  welfare criteria in, 123–4, 129–30
Campbell, Angus, 156
"central concerns," 171–2, 174–5, 180–1
central control (planning), 180
  consumer sovereignty and, 36–7
  as coordination mechanism, 189
  democratic vs. oligarchic, 189, 223
  general deprivation under, 223
  poverty under, 198–202
  psychological depression under, 213–17, 219–22
  social isolation under, 210
  working conditions under, 204–5, 205–6
Child, I. L., 44, 109
Christian, David, 171
collective goods, 27, 33–4, 41n, 108n, 126–7, 177, 191–2, 208, 210, 218, 221
comparability problem for
  basic needs, 168, 170–3
  happiness, 149, 156–7, 159–60
  poverty, 191
  self-determination, 146
  self-realization, 146